The Origins of the Bicycle

Kirkpatrick Macmillan, Gavin Dalzell, Alexandre Lefebvre

Documentation, memory, craft tradition and modern technology

Andrew Ritchie

January 2009

An Early Scotch Velocipedist

[A letter from the *North British Daily Mail,* 27 August 1884, see Sources - E]

Sir, - I see that several correspondents answer "N.F.'s" question about who an early Scottish velocipedist was. I knew him well, being brought up together. I have been in his father's smithy hundreds of times getting my clogs shod, as well as other things. He was born at Byreflat, on the estate of Waterside, parish of Keir, by Thornhill, Dumfriesshire. He made his first wooden horse when he was at Byreflat, and by and by he made another on an improved scale, and a very braw horse it was, with bridle and saddle and stirrups, with a brown mane and tail. His first run to Glasgow was about the years 1836 or 1837. He started from Thornhill with the mail coach, via Sanquhar, Cumnock, and Kilmarnock, and was in Glasgow before the coach. He met with a misfortune in Glasgow, having come against an old woman in the street and knocked down, and was fined 5s. He had many a run to Dumfries on his "wooden horse," when none of the farmers could beat him. I could tell a great number of incidents that I have seen and heard and know to be true, which if "N.F." wishes to know he could call on me and I would tell him, and he, if he chose, could give you for publication. His name was Kirkpatrick M'Millan, son of Robert M'Millan, a country blacksmith, parish of Keir. He was named Kirkpatrick for Sir Thomas Kirkpatrick, Capenoch, Keir, the then Sheriff of Dumfriesshire.

I am, etc., A Native of Keir.

The John Pinkerton Memorial Publishing Fund

Following the untimely death of John Pinkerton in 2002, a proposal was made to set up a fund in his memory.

The objective of the Fund is to continue the publishing activities initiated by John Pinkerton, that is to publish historical material on the development of the bicycle of all types and related activities. This will include reprints of significant cycling journal articles, manufacturers' technical information including catalogues, parts lists, drawings and other technical information.

Published by the John Pinkerton Memorial Publishing Fund, 2009

ISBN 978-0-9560430-1-6

Printed by Quorum Technical Services Ltd. Cheltenham. January 2009

Table of Contents

Table of Contents

The Origins of the Bicycle

Acknowledgements

Thanks are due to many people for help in locating the generally inaccessible source material discussed here. Archivists and librarians in Glasgow and Edinburgh were always helpful.

Alastair Dodds, curator of transportation at the National Museum of Scotland, provided material and pictures from his files, and the Veteran-Cycle Club Macmillan study file was equally indispensable. Nick Clayton and Nicholas Oddy were a sounding board in giving me feedback on this somewhat controversial research project.

Cyril Hancock, secretary of the John Pinkerton Memorial Publishing Fund, guided the project through the committee stage, and Brian Hayward laboured with me over three days, with great patience, on the design and layout of the text and the illustrations, as well as being a kind host at his house in Gloucestershire.

Any mistakes in the presentation of this material are mine alone, and I would be happy to discuss any aspects of the project. My email address is: jabritchie@hotmail.com.

Andrew Ritchie

January 2009

Preface

The debate about "the inventor" of the bicycle has continued for many years. That it was indeed Macmillan who built early machines has been questioned by some researchers. A recently discovered photograph of what looked like a Scotsman on a lever-driven tricycle was initially hailed as important new evidence, only to be later found to have no connection with Macmillan.

Alastair Dodds, after having researched the subject in various Scottish archives and libraries, published his findings in 1991 in *The Boneshaker 127*, and concluded that the case for Macmillan as "inventor" of the bicycle was "not proven". Eighteen International Cycling History Conferences have been held since then, including much more debate on the subject, but without decisive conclusions being formulated.

Until now all the relevant original documentation (mostly from the 19th century) concerning the various claims for "priority", including that concerning Macmillan and Dalzell and the research undertaken and published by James Johnston, has been hard to locate and has not been collected together - hence the justification for assembling the source documents included in the second part of this book, and analysed in the first part.

Andrew Ritchie's suggestion here is that having all the available source documents easily accessible allows a fresh historical perspective on this now well-worn subject. In the first part, Andrew Ritchie has provided his own personal interpretation of them. But others may come to their own - perhaps different - conclusions.

The John Pinkerton Memorial Publishing Fund Committee therefore thought that this information should be made available to those interested in the subject, so that they might be able to reach their own opinions and conclusions.

Cyril Hancock

Chairman,
John Pinkerton Memorial Publishing Fund

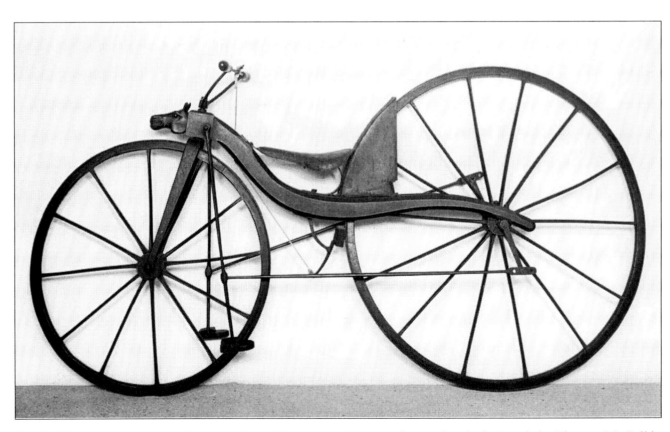

Fig. 1 This velocipede now in the collection of the Science Museum in London, in fact made by Thomas McCall in the 1890s and arguably based on an original by Macmillan, is now frequently presented as a Macmillan bicycle. [Source: Science Museum, London]

Introduction

A difficult aspect of dealing with this material has been how best to present it to the reader. How many people really care about the early history of the bicycle? How much does it really matter? Am I just talking to a handful of specialists in the history of the bicycle – most of whom I know personally – or are these historical issues, important issues in the history of technology, which I should try to make accessible to a wider audience.

The question of the "invention" of the bicycle, it might be argued, is not an insignificant thing. And the fact that I have to put those words in quotation marks needs some explanation. Briefly, we have to define "invention" before we can discuss who is an "inventor", or what the process of "invention" consists of. Hundreds of millions of bicycles have been manufactured and used over nearly 140 years, and millions of them are still in use on a daily basis for sport, recreation and utility. With the computer, the radio, the automobile, the camera, the washing machine, the bicycle is one of those useful tools of everyday life whose origins and history should be discoverable and well-known. Most of the bicycle's history is known. And yet, as far as its "invention" is concerned, we have a strange indecision where we feel that there should be certainty. And although one "inventor" is systematically pushed to the fore, and his name is found in every discussion of the history of the bicycle, we know little enough about what he actually did or made. On the important question of who was actually the first person (or who were the first people?) to create a bicycle, there is a lot of disagreement and uncertainty. What is my definition of a bicycle? Answer: a bicycle is a machine with two wheels in-line which can be balanced, steered and driven continuously forward using human muscle-power without the feet touching the ground.

I decided to divide the book into two halves, but the reader may decide to tackle either part first. The first part (The Origins of the Bicycle) is my exposition and exploration of the source material, my suggestions about what seems most likely to have occurred - my interpretation of the earliest bicycle history, based on the evidence contained in the Sources published in the second half. Here, I allow myself to speculate about how historical knowledge, and in this case the memory of some historical events, gets transmitted and what the role of oral transmission in the memory of events might be. I try here to construct a plausible scenario in my interpretation of the documentation and the surviving machines, without necessarily pushing definite conclusions forward.

The second part of the book (The Sources) is a kind of large and somewhat unwieldy Appendix containing a lot of source material which is difficult to find. I aim to achieve a completeness here because I felt that every scrap of information mattered. It needs to be available to refer to here because its cumulative weight and particularly its detail seems to be crucial to the solidity and credibility of my arguments. If I am to present a plausible argument to readers here, they need to be able to go to the source material, to digest it thoroughly, to help them decide whether or not to accept my arguments.

Frankly. I am more interested in exploring the idea of the "invention" of the bicycle, of presenting neglected documentation and asking lots of questions, than I am in asserting that I have found "proof". The stories of Macmillan, Dalzell, Lefebvre and others are fascinating. My aim is to bring them to life, to rescue them from the confusion of inaccuracy and semi-anonymity. Cumulatively, these stories from the pre-history of the bicycle add up to a persuasive, if still partially contested, narrative of early bicycle history. They cannot simply be dismissed. There is something going on here!

My extended grappling with this material may be where these explorations end. Or, in these times of Google and digital searching of historical source material, perhaps other pieces of the puzzle of the "invention" of the bicycle may still be found. Time will tell.

Andrew Ritchie, January 2009

Part One: The Origins of the Bicycle

Fig. 2 This portrait of Macmillan was first reproduced in 1899, captioned "the Inventor of the Bicycle". The whereabouts of the original of this photograph remains unknown. [Source: *CTC Gazette* Sept. 1899]

Prologue: Documentary versus Hearsay evidence – The "invention" of the bicycle and the nature of historical evidence

"I have for some considerable time been engaged in collecting information to prove that M'Millan was undoubtedly the first in the field to put driving gear - levels and cranks - on the old hobby horse or dandy horse......I will be glad if Ben-Jubal or any other gentleman can furnish any further news on the point - documentary evidence against hearsay being preferable."

(James Johnston writing to the *Glasgow Evening Times,* 2 Feb. 1892).

"Sir, - I read with interest, in Thursday's issue, Mr. Johnston's letter anent (about – AR) the invention of the bicycle. In further confirmation of our common opinion, he naturally desiderates documentary evidence in preference to hearsay, if such could be obtained. No doubt such evidence, if it exists at all, would be very satisfactory, especially in establishing the year in which a particular event was said to have happened. Nevertheless, your correspondent must not under-estimate the high value of so-called hearsay in a matter of this kind, especially when the report is so general as it is."

('Ben-Jubal', responding to the above, the *Glasgow Evening Times,* 6 Feb.1892).

"Unquestionably, documentary or tangible evidence, when it does exist, is most satisfactory in establishing the year in which a particular event was said to have occured, and Dalzell's friends, although they produce certain documents, cannot fix on any particular date. About 1846 is the nearest they can name. In the absence of documentary evidence - newspapers and letters in those days were not so common - we must not under-estimate the high value of oral or hearsay evidence in this matter from people still living in the district who have seen M'Millan on his machine hundreds of times."

(James Johnston writing to *The Scottish Cyclist,* 10 Feb. 1892).

A great deal of questionable nonsense has been written about Kirkpatrick Macmillan and the "invention" of the bicycle, and widely disseminated as the truth. The need for an "inventor" of the bicycle seems to have prevailed over the proven historical facts. In fact, the moment of "invention" is hard to define and hard to find. I hope this collection of documents and my comment on them will expand and solidify the discussion, even if it does not propose a definitive solution.

You do not have to search on the Internet long before you will be told, in no uncertain terms, that Scotsman Kirkpatrick Macmillan "invented" the bicycle. A recent search on Google produced some 1,500 'hits' mentioning him. Scrolling through page after page of these website entries, nearly the same information is repeated hundreds of times in many different languages, and with a varied amount of fictionalization. Briefly, Macmillan "invented" the bicycle sometime around 1840 (often cited as either 1839 or 1842). He is presented as a traditional blacksmith in rural Scotland who put cranks and levers onto the hobby-horse, thus "inventing" the first bicycle. It is usually not specified exactly what he "invented", or what his machine (or machines?) looked like, or what became of it (them?), although most frequently a still-existing "Macmillan-style" bicycle, probably made in about 1869 by Thomas McCall and now owned by the Science Museum in London, is illustrated, often captioned as "Macmillan's bicycle". Around Macmillan's home in Courthill, near Dumfries, the heritage industry has enshrined the "inventor" of the bicycle.

The Internet entry on Macmillan posted by the British Broadcasting Corporation (B.B.C.) will serve as an illustration of the mixture of fact and fiction which is currently available online. Noteworthy here is that no original sources are cited:

Kirkpatrick Macmillan (1812 - 1878). Born to a blacksmith, Macmillan held a variety of positions as a young man, before settling into the trade himself in 1824 and eventually returning to work with his father. At around that time he saw a hobby horse being ridden along a nearby road, and decided to make one for himself. Upon completion, he realised what a radical improvement it would be if he could propel it without putting his feet on the ground. Working at his smithy, he completed his new machine in or around 1839.

This first pedal bicycle was propelled by a horizontal reciprocating movement of the rider's feet on the pedals. This movement was transmitted to cranks on the rear wheel by connecting rods; the machine weighed almost exactly half a hundredweight and the physical effort required to ride it must have been considerable. Nevertheless, he quickly mastered the art of riding it on the rough country roads, and was soon accustomed to making the fourteen-mile journey to Dumfries in less than an hour. His next exploit was to ride the sixty-eight miles into Glasgow in June 1842. The trip took him two days and he was fined five shillings for causing a slight injury to a small girl who ran across his path.

He never thought of patenting his invention or trying to make any money out of it, but others who saw it were not slow to realize its potential, and soon copies began to appear and be sold for six or seven pounds. Gavin Dalzell of Lesmahagow copied his machine in 1846 and passed on the details to so many people that for more than fifty years he was generally regarded as the inventor of the bicycle. However, Macmillan was quite unconcerned with the fuss his invention had prompted, preferring to enjoy the quiet country life he was used to.[1]

Conspicuously absent from these many website accounts is a serious examination of any evidence for these claims for Macmillan as the "inventor". The essential facts, or what are assumed to be the essential facts, of this story are repeated uncritically – reliable source material is lost sight of completely. The story is embroidered with fictional facts, indeed, it has become mythical.

Several historical articles examining the Macmillan case, published in academically-oriented contexts, make a fuller and more satisfying presentation of the facts, questions and speculations surrounding Macmillan, and of the contradictions and difficulties of the historical evidence. But they are still disappointingly inconclusive because they leave much of the available documentary evidence and original source material unexamined.[2] They are particularly weak in minimizing and misunderstanding the significance of oral evidence collected in the 1890s and in putting too much emphasis on questioning the motives of James Johnston, who researched the issue in the 1890s.

On the one hand enshrined in popular histories as "the inventor" of the bicycle, and, on the other hand, dismissed by serious researchers as of marginal and questionable significance because of what has been seen as unreliable historical evidence, the blacksmith Kirkpatrick Macmillan (1812-78) thus presents the historian of the bicycle with a fascinating but problematic case-study.[3] And Macmillan cannot be considered in isolation. Other claimants to "priority" in the matter of the "invention"of the bicycle include Gavin Dalzell in Scotland and Alexandre Lefebvre in France, both of whom will also be considered here. This study thus sets out to examine Macmillan's historical role in the light of this wider context of other claims.

The bicycle has now become a universal fact of life, yet its "inventor" has not been definitively identified or agreed upon. Indeed, the progressive and evolutionary nature of the historical emergence of the bicycle, and its constantly changing design over the approximately 190 years of its existence, suggests that to define its early history primarily in terms of the search for "priority" and an "inventor" is by its very nature to pose an unjustified and unanswerable question. As with the invention of photography, or electricity, or the computer, it can be argued, many different people contributed different aspects and details, so that to name one single "inventor" is elusive and problematic. Yet over the years a legitimate question has constantly been posed: who was the first person, or who were the first people, to balance and steer a two-wheeled machine and drive it continuously forward using the legs applied to

some kind of a drive mechanism without them touching the ground, as with the hobby-horse? As early as 1883, an anonymous newspaper editor asked, "Who was the inventor of the bicycle?", and commented that, "The honour is really worth fighting for. As a means of conveyance it is truly revolutionizing the world".[4]

The question has been repeated frequently since then, and the answer has in general depended on who was asking the question. The search for the "inventor" of the bicycle has often been closely linked with chauvinistic national aspirations. French historians cite a French inventor (Pierre and Ernest Michaux or Pierre Lallement in the 1860s), the Germans can claim a German (Baron Drais in 1818), even the Russians put forward a candidate (Artomonov). Most recently Pierre Lallement, who worked in the United States in the late 1860s, has been proposed as an American claimant. It is not surprising, it is remarked by sceptics of the Macmillan scenario, that the Scots should have nominated Macmillan as their own Scottish candidate!

Macmillan's presence in Dumfriesshire is well documented, the essential biographical facts of his life and career indisputable. Yet there remains a significant problem that there is no concretely reliable documentation to connect him with certainty to a specific design of machine, that is to a particular "invention". Macmillan took out no patents, left no sketches, designs or personal correspondence linking him to his velocipedes, and made no attempt to put whatever bicycle-like machines he made into commercial production. So the normal historical evidence of artifacts, of patent registration or factory records, is non-existent. Copies of original machines do exist, however, as do many journalistic reports, and perhaps most significantly, evidence collected later from family and friends of Macmillan and Dalzell.

Fragile and difficult to store, subject to the destruction of hard use and decay, very early two-wheeled velocipedes have tended to disappear.[5] No machine exists today which we can suggest might actually have been made by Macmillan's own hands. Several machines that are arguably of the "Macmillan pattern" do survive, but are difficult to evaluate because they have been heavily restored or are next-generation copies of previous designs. Museum conservation and documentation over the years has been sloppy. In the case of several important machines, one of which is the Dalzell machine now in the Glasgow Museum, hardly a significant piece of documention relating to them has been safeguarded by curators. The three contemporary newspaper references (all from 1842) most closely associated with Macmillan's velocipede are frustratingly unspecific on several crucial details.

This book, then, sets out to examine the historical evidence relating to several alleged early makers, the actual surviving machines and the printed source material relating to Macmillan and others. It has a straightforward purpose, to answer the question: What do we know about Macmillan, and what else can we add to our knowledge with a further critical examination of the large amount of documentation which exists relating to him and others and to the "invention" of the bicycle in the 19th century? Can we arrive at a more accurate definition of the moment of "invention"?

The answer, I believe, is that we can. A clearer account of Macmillan's contribution can be gleaned from a more careful interpretation of the surviving documentation. In fact, Macmillan is not the only velocipede maker who may be assigned a role as "inventor", because as well as Macmillan's contemporary Dalzell, there is persuasive evidence in Paris of a French lock-maker, Alexandre Lefebvre, experimenting at the same time as Macmillan on a sophisticated machine. But my argument will drift decidely towards proposing the existence of a 'school' of velocipede/bicycle makers in south-west Scotland, and I will suggest that there is enough evidence to indicate that they copied each other's designs and that the design was widely circulated.

Because the evidence and source material is scattered among many newspapers and periodicals which are difficult to access, it became apparent to me that to be plausibly examined this material needs to be made accessible. Without it, the reader cannot form his or her own opinions, or properly understand the sequence of events and arguments. I quote from the source material in my analysis, but I cannot quote everything. Thus, the two-part structure of the book seemed to be the most logical and satisfactory way to present both the original source material and my own analysis of it.

Briefly, my account adopts a chronological emphasis as the best way to unravel the story. I begin with a news item concerning a velocipede rider published in 1842 in Glasgow and Dumfries newspapers and consider it in the context of the activities of the many "amateur mechanics" who published details of their work with human-powered vehicles in the period from about 1820 to 1860. In the late 1880s, following the rapid ascendency of the rear-driven "safety" bicycle (which quickly outmoded the high-wheel, or "ordinary" bicycle in the mid- to late-1880s), energetic enquiries began to be made about the origins of the bicycle, and Scotsman Gavin Dalzell was proposed for a short time as the "inventor". The evidence was a surviving machine and some receipts for blacksmith work dated 1847, which it was argued proved that the machine existed "several years before 1846". Dalzell's "priority", however, was soon challenged by claims made by various witnesses for Kirkpatrick Macmillan, a blacksmith from Courthill, near Dumfries. Macmillan's name was proposed as significant as early as 1883/84 in the *Scottish American Journal* and in the *North British Daily Mail*, the second newspaper concluding that it was "not prepared to say that he was the actual inventor of the bicycle, but that the machine must have been a novelty at the time."[6]

In the late 1880s and early 1890s, a Glasgow cyclist and journalist, James Johnston, became an ardent and active spokesman on behalf of Macmillan and published a series of articles in various outlets. His motives for this interest have been questioned. Was he more interested in a Scottish "inventor" than in the historical truth? Over a period of about four years, from 1888 to about 1892, Johnston conducted an extensive investigation and published his results. He interviewed people who had known and worked alongside Macmillan, he corresponded with other witnesses and he collected paper documentation where it was available. His interest in Macmillan was maintained well beyond this most active period, for he published several articles in 1899 and in 1911 corresponded with the Science Museum in London about Macmillan.[7] Unfortunately - a major oversight - Johnston did not examine or identify recognized early machines carefully or search diligently for other significant surviving early machines, which might then still have been traceable. Nor does he appear to have taken elementary steps to safeguard his research material. Johnston, an amateur historian, relied heavily on talking to witnesses and corresponding with them.

But although all of Johnston's original notes and other material is now lost, the results of his research were published in 1892 in four principal locations: *Bicycling News*, *The Scottish Cyclist*, the *Glasgow Evening Times* and the *Dumfries and Galloway Standard and Advertiser*. Johnston sent detailed summaries of his research to the editors of these publications, and in some cases he also generated a dialogue with readers who wrote in with their own memories and recollections. Johnston was thus responsible for having created a substantial body of historical data which has until now hardly been examined. In my examination, the legitimacy of Johnston's methods and intentions becomes an important interpretational question. Further discussions about the origins of the bicycle were published in Scottish newspapers in 1895, 1897 and 1904.

Johnston's period of research activity was validated, in a sense, when J. R. Nisbet, the editor of *The Scottish Cyclist*, presided over and adjudicated what was in effect a public resolution of the discussion as to whether Gavin Dalzell or Macmillan had been the first to "apply driving-gear to the hobby-horse". Nisbet announced in *The Scottish Cyclist* that, as a result of Johnston's research, "a satisfactory conclusion" had been arrived at, and that he recognized "Macmillan's claim to priority". Dalzell's son, J.B. Dalzell, even gave Johnston a letter which recognized Macmillan's "priority".[8] **[see Fig. 3]** Johnston publicly thanked Dalzell's son for the "gentlemanly and honourable way he has acted all through this matter", and pronounced

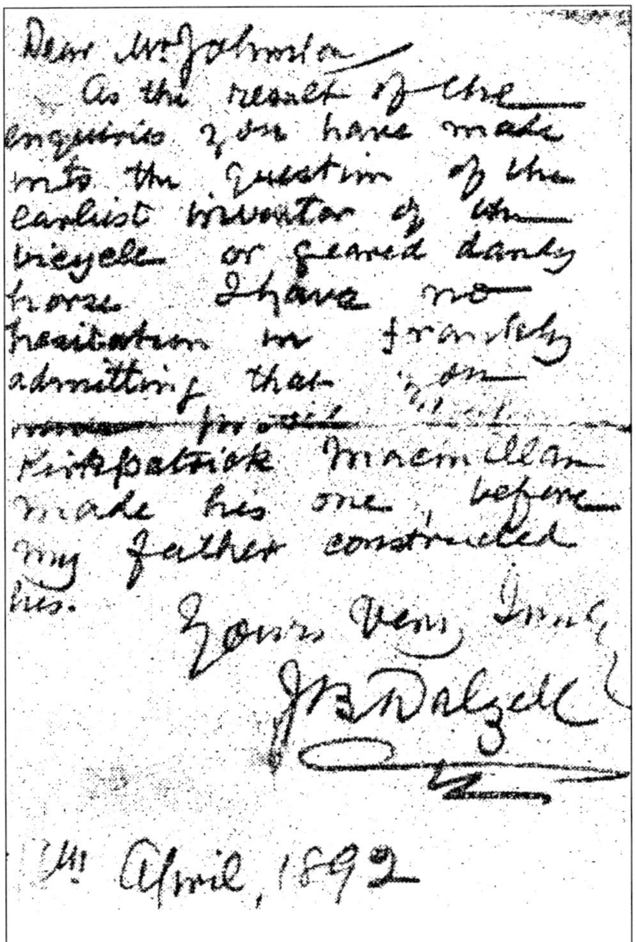

Dear Mr Johnston

As the result of the enquiries you have made into the question of the earliest inventor of the bicycle or geared dandy horse I have no hesitation in frankly admitting that you ~~[illegible]~~ Kirkpatrick Macmillan made his one before my father constructed his.

Yours very truly,

J B Dalzell

4th April, 1892

A reproduction of the letter written by Gavin Dalzell's son, in which he acknowledges that Kirkpatrick Macmillan was the first in the field with his lever-driven bicycle.

Fig. 3 J. B. Dalzell's recognition of Macmillan's "claim to priority" published in *Bicycling News*, 23 April 1892.

that "the verdict of the jury now reads – *first* Macmillan, and Dalzell a good *second*".[9]

From that date onwards, Macmillan was successfully enthroned in popular history as the "inventor" of the bicycle, without much further attention being paid to the actual data which Johnson and others had collected and published, or whether that data confirms or contradicts information available from other sources unconnected with Johnston. This version of the story of "the invention" of the bicycle was given more credibility when it was included by George Lacy Hillier in the 1896 edition of his widely circulated and influential Badminton *Cycling*:

> Gavin Dalzell, a cooper of Lesmahagow, Lanarkshire, was for a long time given the credit of being the first user of a crank-driven bicycle; but after an exhaustive investigation Mr. James Johnston of Glasgow has been able to establish that Kirkpatrick Macmillan, of Courthill, Keir near Penpont, Dumfriesshire, rode such a machine between 1830 and 1840. The cranks were fitted to the rear wheel, and long bars were attached to them and joined to swinging levers in front.[10]

Nevertheless, Hillier conducted no research of his own into these early machines.

Negative criticism has been directed at Johnston and *The Scottish Cyclist*'s Nisbet by some bicycle historians on the grounds that these were researchers determined to establish a Scottish "inventor", though it should be pointed out that, in the 1890s, in a conspicuously public forum, no other British candidates – English, Welsh or Irish – were put forward. In effect, it has been suggested, Johnston intentionally perpetrated a jingoistic, Scottish-biased, version of the "invention" of the bicycle in order to satisfy Scottish aspirations in the 1890s, in the face of active French claims for priority. And it is true that these aspirations were expressed and arguably encouraged by *The Scottish Cyclist*, one of the papers which published Johnston's research. An editorial of January 1889, in which the exhibition of Gavin Dalzell's velocipede at the Glasgow Exhibition was discussed, commented: "We believe…that Scotland's claim to the earliest honours in cycle construction will be demonstrated forthwith".[11] In February 1889, the editor again commented concerning the Dalzell machine that "the fact is indisputively (sic) proved that to Scotland – through Mr. Gavin Dalzell – must henceforth be given the honour of being the birth-place of the modern cycle".[12]

By 1892, when Johnston's research had been instrumental in satisfying the same editor that Macmillan predated Dalzell in the "invention" stakes, he once again expressed these aspirations: "To the happy conclusion arrived at, we have but to add the hope that no further claims will arise which seek to rob Scotland of the honour bestowed on her by such worthy sons".[13] Such comments cannot, of course, be ignored in the exploration of this complex material. But the idea that Johnston was involved in perpetrating an intentional fraud in his investigations also has to be seriously questioned in the light of the evidence.

It is further suggested by sceptics of Johnston's research that the evidence of his witnesses is unreliable. It is evidence, it is alleged, which is "hearsay" and therefore inadmissible. It is suggested that we cannot and should not trust what witnesses recollected in discussion or correspondence with Johnston in about 1890, that Johnston may have fed them what he wanted to hear, or coached them, in order to prove his point. My readers will have to decide, after they have read my exposition, about the extent to which Johnston is a trustworthy source, and also ask themselves, as I have tried to do, "Is there basic credibility in the details as reported by Johnston? What reason might these witness have had <u>not</u> to tell the truth about these far off events? Why would they bother to

The Origins of the Bicycle

lie about their memories of something as comparatively insignificant as an early bicycle?"

Integral to my discussion, then, is a recognition and consideration of this suspicion of Johnston's motivation and activities. But there is a further crucial factor. *We do not have to rely on Johnston alone for information and evidence.* As a test of Johnston's trustworthiness as researcher and a source of evidence, it is possible and essential to compare what he found and published with other material which was recorded and published about Macmillan, Dalzell, McCall and other principal participants both *inside* and *outside* Johnson's period of research and independent of it. My interpretation of the evidence concludes that the essential similarity of the stories about Macmillan, firstly, as they were uncovered by James Johnston, and secondly, as they were recorded by those <u>unconnected</u> with Johnston, suggests a historical continuity and agreement of salient details of the case which tends to over-ride suspicions of Johnston's Scottish 'agenda'. My analysis here suggests that oral transmission of memories cannot and should not be discounted as a significant source of historical evidence, particularly when they agree in specific details at different times and places, and from person to person. People's memories of distant, unusual events can indeed be vivid and accurate in the essentials. That Kirkpatrick Macmillan appears to have made an impact on people's memories in the 1840s is clear from the eye-witness accounts. I have included in my "Conclusions" a section which lists and compares these eye-witness testimonies.

James Johnston's status and trustworthiness as a researcher, and how much credit we are prepared to grant orally transmitted memories as evidence, are not the only issues I grapple with in trying to understand this source material. Just as important is the question - what do we actually mean and understand by the word "invent"?[14] Johnston and Nisbet both talked in terms of "priority" for Macmillan over Dalzell, and themselves did not make much use of the words "invent" or "invention". *The Scottish Cyclist*'s accounts were headlined either, "The Origin of the Rear-Driven Bicycle" or, "The First Rear-Driven Bicycle". Neither Macmillan or Dalzell, assuming that we have understood the machines which constituted their "inventions" accurately, could really be said to have "invented" the bicycle anyway (in terms of a totally original conception), because the hobby-horse (which had two wheels, a frame, and was able to be balanced and steered) already existed, and many other different human-powered machines with three and four wheels and various designs of transmission had been built and tested.

The "invention" with which we are concerned here was not, therefore, a totally new conception, but the important application of a drive system to an already existing machine, the hobby-horse, which made it *able to be driven continuously, steered and balanced without* *putting the feet to the ground.* So the question at issue resolves itself into the following proposition: what exactly, if anything, did Macmillan, Dalzell and Lefebvre "invent"? And were there other makers who may have been doing something essentially similar at the same time?

. . . .

Thus, a series of propositions is advanced here, to try to better understand the "invention" of the bicycle. A speculative theory of the evolution of technological artifacts in the early 19th century may also be usefully proposed. Artisan skills and traditions in the pre-mass-production world were passed from hand to hand in a way similar to that in which memories were passed from mouth to mouth. Artisan skill in the production of artifacts and tools was in fact the result of shared and accumulated memory. Individual memories exist in parallel with the written culture and are part of the larger cultural memory. As memories are passed on orally, they may be embellished by repetition and exaggeration, fancy and doubt. Memories may be weak in specificity and the accuracy of their details, but they can be very strong in shared essentials. The role of memory in written history is complex. Systematic memory (for example, memoirs or diaries) becomes incorporated into the written record. Isolated memories, recollections recorded in a haphazard way, may be given less credence, but can be just as revealing.

The design of technological artefacts is changed or improved as a new need or the need for change is demonstrated. The improvement is tried and remembered and thus design evolves. At a certain critical point in the design history of an everyday object and an increasing demand for it, it passed over in the 19th century from a hand-made to a mass-produced item, and was then manufactured and marketed. In the competitive market-place, the idea had then to be patented and protected, giving rise to the necessity for a claim to "invention" to be established. But an object which existed in unpatented ownership, and which was freely shared, copied and developed locally, cannot be said to have been "invented" in the usual definition of the word, where "invention" means that the object comes into being fully formed, with a precise perception of its origin and function. The search for its originator will prove difficult because much of the evidence will exist in the memories of those involved, as much as in whatever written records, if any, survive. A written record of those memories, even if collected well after the event, will then have particular value, especially if there is little other documentation, and *even if they have been embellished by folk-memory.*

My argument here, then, suggests that the fabrication of the earliest "bicycles" took place in a curious technological limbo, with an ambivalent purpose. They were neither tools in the traditional sense

Part One: The Origins of the Bicycle

(agricultural, or household), nor machines for performing a familiar transportational role (carriages or carts). As potentially useful transportation, they had the economic and practical promise of becoming a substitute for the horse and achieving independent man-powered movement. And they also defined new tasks and new possibilities, both functional and recreational. But in the period under discussion, these velocipedes were the preoccupation of a very small number of blacksmiths and "mechanics", pursuing what might almost be defined for them as an expensive hobby.

The history of the early development of the bicycle emerges from this complex interface between oral and written history, and the machine can be seen as a vaguely and hesitantly realized artifact, being grasped at only with uncertainty and difficulty. The pages of journals such as the *Mechanic's Magazine* and the *English Mechanic*, published in the period from the 1830s to the 1860s, reveal a plethora of velocipede designs and design ideas, with many solutions and partial solutions being proposed. If we persist in clinging to the idea of a lone, heroic individual "inventor", we under-estimate the role of craft skill and the transmission of shared memory, curiosity and traditional technological expertise in the early evolution of the bicycle. This study attempts to place the activity and achievements of Macmillan, Dalzell, McCall, Lefebvre and others in the context of artisan skills and traditions, and of an oral culture which had deep and lasting memories of their somewhat eccentric activities.

In the history of the velocipedes discussed here, those of Macmillan and others, securely documented historical facts rub shoulders with the less secure area of memory and oral tradition. But the research carried out between about 1881 and 1899, a period of the most intense activity in bicycle manufacture, creates a window of evidence and opportunity through which we are able to grasp at a more distant past, fifty years earlier. Reaching back into the 1840s via the documentation and memories of the 1880s and 1890s, we still have the possibility of creating a detailed, accurate and persuasive profile of Macmillan's work and that of his contemporary makers. Especially neglected is an evaluation of the eye-witness testimonies, both those collected by James Johnston and those published in various newspapers. The failure of bicycle historians to treat them as relevant source material has been surprising. If I have decided to give the oral testimonies more credibility, it is because the details contained in them tend to be corroborated by other evidence. I have listened to the "folk memory" preserved in these accounts, and, I hope, allowed it to speak to us judiciously.

Of course, this collection of documents and my analysis of them cannot be seen as the final word on the subject. Far from it. It is nevertheless a contribution. Other documentation may well come to light, particularly with the expanding technique of searching archival newspapers digitally using "optical character recognition" (OCR).[15] In view of the difficulty of obtaining the source material concerning Macmillan which has been collected and presented here for the first time, it is hoped that having the documentation accessible will stimulate further interest in this early history of the bicycle.

2. Kirkpatrick Macmillan in the early history of cycling

Fig. 4 The controversial nature of Macmillan's velocipede design remains central to a discussion of the early evolution of the bicycle. [Source: *The Boneshaker* 145, Winter 1997]

a. A brief outline of early bicycle history

In order to situate Kirkpatrick Macmillan in the context of the early history of the bicycle, a short general outline of the period from about 1820 to 1870 should be given.

The first large-scale mass-production of bicycles (known at first almost universally as "velocipedes") began in 1866-69, first in France, then in the United States and Britain. These were front-wheel-driven machines, the front wheel larger than the rear. They became a craze, thousands were manufactured, and were used for entertainment, sport and practical transportation. From these first "velocipede" bicycles, in a well documented evolution, the high or "ordinary" bicycle developed from about 1870 to about 1885 and the "safety" bicycle began to emerge in the late 1880s. The essential facts of this post-1866/67 development are not in dispute.

We are concerned here, however, with the forty-five year period prior to 1866/67, during which there were no bicycles as such, but there was a considerable amount of what might be described as experimental activity in human-powered vehicles (but activity within which certain patterns or trends can be perceived) and a well documented evolution of ideas and practice.

The history of the bicycle really begins with the hobby-horse, or Draisine. In Germany and England between about 1817 and 1820, the hobby-horse provided the germ of the idea of balancing and travelling on two wheels. It was commercially produced and created a brief craze, featuring prominently in the media of the period. The hobby-horse was a two-wheeled vehicle which could be driven forward by pushing the feet alternately against the ground and could also be steered. It could not, however, be driven forward continuously. On the flat and downhill it was practical; uphill it was not. Restricted in general to the young and athletic, its afficionados were seen as something of a joke by outsiders, and widely satirized.

Fig. 4.—DANDY-HORSE.

Fig. 5 The jaunty hobby-horse rider of about 1820 depicted in an 1869 publication was active and athletic. [Source: "Velox", *Velocipedes, Bicycles and Tricycles*, 1869]

Part One: The Origins of the Bicycle

After a brief craze, the hobby-horse faded from prominence, but was still used by a few athletic enthusiasts. It is important in the Macmillan story in that it was alleged to have been the inspiration for his crank-driven velocipede experiments. Indeed, there is a close similarity in general design between the hobby-horse and Macmillan-type machines, except for the addition of a drive-mechanism. In asking the crucial question, "What kind of machine was Macmillan's?" it should be borne in mind that some eye witnesses were in fact reporting a hobby-horse rider, although others spoke specifically about the "driving gear", distinguished between a driven and an un-driven machine, and in fact reported Macmillan's progress from one to the other.

In general, the period 1820-65 was characterized by intermittent but widespread experimentation in three- and four-wheeled velocipedes powered by one or more riders. There was a recognition of the interest and value of the idea of pursuing velocipede-making, but no agreement about the best solution. Many designs made use of practical offset rear crankshaft driven by treadles similar to the principle applied on Macmillan-style machines, although fantastic original designs were commonplace. These were discussed and illustrated in several mechanics' magazines of the period, and admired in terms of the advantages and economy to be derived from self-propelled transportation, seen as a potential boon particularly to the working man. These machines are discussed at length in a chapter entitled "Amateur Mechanics" in my book *King of the Road*.

Willard Sawyer of Dover was one of the most sophisticated and productive of these makers, a coachmaker who invested in the commercial manufacture of velocipedes before the 'bicycle' came into existence. Sawyer's machines, on four wheels, driven by long horizontal treadles to a rear-axle crankshaft (much like a typical child's toy car), were beautifully crafted and sold in a variety of different types. Early photographs show them in routine domestic use, and testimonials sent to Sawyer, and published in his catalogue, attest to their practicality.[16]

This environment of active experimentation is the wider context for an exploration of Macmillan's possible contribution. The crucial claim of many accounts is that Macmillan added "driving-gear" to the hobby-horse, and thus became the first person to "invent" and ride a "bicycle". On the basis of having made probably at the most a few experimental machines, which were never patented or commercially produced, and which we do not have a reliable and accurate contemporary technical description of, Macmillan might easily have faded into total anonymity. But surviving evidence indicates that the machines attributed to him and Gavin Dalzell (who claimed that he was inspired by and copied Macmillan) were the only British velocipedes to emerge out of this early period which were, a) on two wheels, b) able to be balanced and steered and, c) were able to be propelled continuously forward by a drive to the back wheel, the three characteristics which qualify them to be considered the direct predecessors of the modern bicycle.

In the course of this examination, I strongly question the idea that accounts of Macmillan were of three- or four-wheeled velocipedes.

The task of this inquiry, then, is to examine how well such a claim holds up to the demands of a rigorous historical analysis.

b. Macmillan's place in popular accounts

As outlined in Chapter 1 above, as a result of the research undertaken and oral testimonies collected by James Johnston and others in the late 1880s and early 1890s, Kirkpatrick Macmillan was elevated to the status of "inventor" of the bicycle. These accounts, together with a problematic newspaper story from 1842, were used in the 19th century to create the popular, mythical figure - Macmillan, "the inventor of the bicycle".

Questionable historical evidence was accepted as proven fact, and the probable outline of historical truth freely filled out and embellished with fictional detail. The main points of contention can be said to be the exact definition of a bicycle, and lack of agreement about exactly what Macmillan may have actually "invented".

Thus we read in *Bartleet's Bicycle Book* that "the first man to fit pedals to a bicycle was Kirkpatrick Macmillan", and in a Science Museum publication of 1972 that Macmillan "frequently rode this machine the 14 miles from Courthill to Dumfries".[17] In 1939, the Centenary Road Club, whose members were mostly bicycle manufacturers, was formed specifically to celebrate the centenary of Macmillan's "invention". This organization lobbied for official recognition of the neglected Scot. In 1946 they made a pilgrimage to Courthill, where the "invention" supposedly took place in 1839, and to remove any historical doubt or ambiguity they attached a plaque to the wall of Macmillan's smithy there to mark the exact spot of "invention". Macmillan was thus officially canonized for the benefit of the heritage industry.[18]

A number of accounts by the Scottish writer J. Gordon Irving further disseminated and popularized the mythical Macmillan, creating a "great Scottish inventor" who would become the focus of commemorative activities. The gist of Irving's generally unhelpful approach can be judged by the headline of an article of his - "The forgotten man among Scotland's great inventors" - which appeared in *The Scotsman*, and the article's conclusion, that Macmillan was "a typical Scots country blacksmith of the last century, whose invention has brought health and happiness to millions in every country in the world."[19] On what purported to be the centenary of Macmillan's invention, the *Gallovidian Annual* for 1940 published Irving's "He Builded Better than He Knew", a mixture of fact and fiction ("...the bicycle has become almost a national institution, and after 100 years we must come back to our faith and trust in simple things."). And in 1946, the same writer published, from Dumfries, Scotland, *The Devil on Wheels, The Story of the World's First Pedal Cyclist,* a heavily fictionalized account, replete with imaginary characters and dialogue from the 1840s.[20] This publication contains an interesting co-opting of history by the bicycle industry - a series of advertisements linking contemporary manufacturing companies to Macmillan, creating a highly speculative "tradition". By the 1940s, Macmillan had become the public property of the bicycle industry, a mythical presence who represented prestige, tradition and historical continuity. [**see Fig 6**]

At the time of writing, popular myth has triumphed to the extent that Macmillan's gravestone is freshly painted and engraved with the words "inventor of the bicycle", and the smithy where he "invented" the

bicycle can still be visited! Tradition has been fabricated to overlay the complexity of probable historical facts. The local authority, Nithsdale District Council, has issued a brochure, "Follow the KM Trail", which guides visitors through "Macmillan country", and an annual commemorative Macmillan ride takes place! Replicas of Macmillan's original "bicycle" (actually copied from McCall's probable copy of Macmillan) have been made and put on display in museums across the world and identified (often without documentation) as the precursor of today's bicycle. The need for a concrete "invention" to answer an awkward historical question has triumphed over the more complex truth.

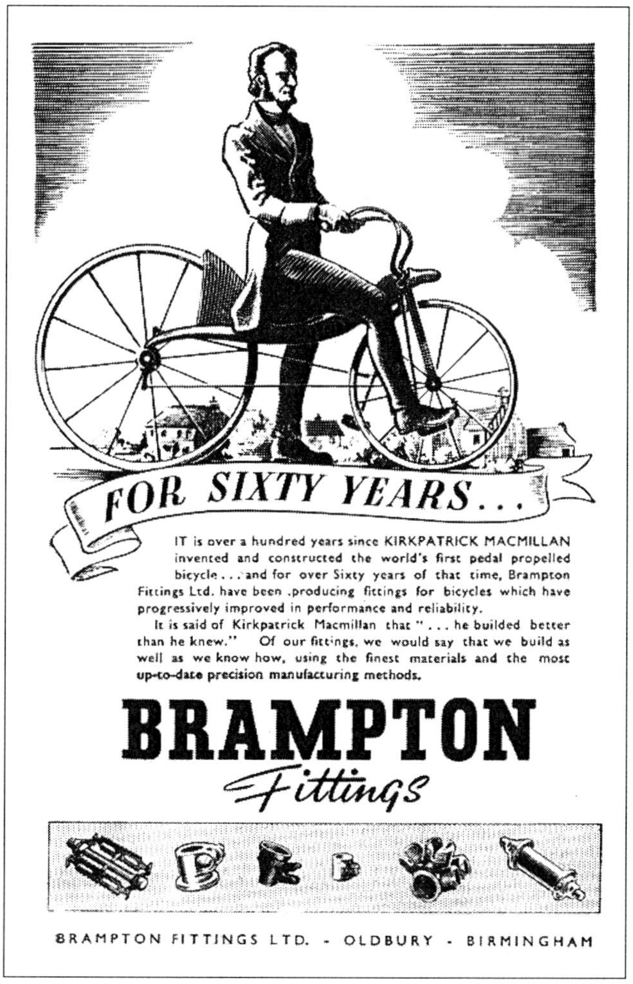

Knowing that I was researching and writing about Macmillan, a bicycle historian colleague of mine has attempted to discourage me from doing so. He thinks that the documentation is not capable of yielding any fresh information. He tells me that "it will simply encourage the making of more replicas!" Even those who have studied the source material fairly closely remain perplexed by the figure of Macmillan. They admit with a shrug that the documentation is sketchy and that they don't know exactly what Macmillan did "invent".

This account attempts to organize and clarify the source material relating to Macmillan, and by subjecting it to a fine examination to tease out a new evaluation of Macmillan in the history of cycling.

Fig. 6 The authenticity of the Macmillan "invention" was firmly incorporated into the official history of the British bicycle industry. [Source: Gordon Irving, *The Devil on Wheels*, 1946]

3. Kirkpatrick Macmillan (1812 -78): the documented facts

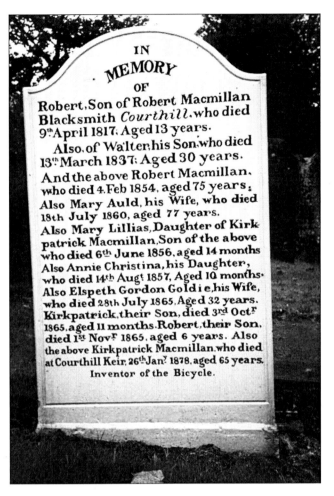

Fig. 7 The restored Macmillan family tombstone in Keir churchyard.

The essential biographical facts of Macmillan's life are secure and well-defined. The basic outlines of his family background are typically well-documented for the period.[21]

Kirkpatrick Macmillan was born 2nd September 1812 in Byreflat, Parish of Keir, about 10 miles from Dumfries and about 50 miles from Glasgow. He was the sixth of ten children born to Robert Macmillan and Mary Auld, who had been married on the 18th October 1800. Robert Macmillan ran a blacksmith's shop there, on the Waterside estates of James Hoggan. Kirkpatrick was named after one of the parish heritors, Sir Thomas Kirkpatrick. Later, Robert Macmillan ran the blacksmith's shop at Courthill.

Kirkpatrick's many siblings were John (b.1802), Robert (b.1804), James (b. 1806), Walter (b.1808), Hoggan (b.1810), (Kirkpatrick, b. 1812), Jean (b.1814), Mary (b.1819), Isobella (b.1820) and Anne (b.1822). Kirkpatrick's father, the blacksmith Robert Macmillan, died in February 1854. Macmillan was married on the

24th April 1854, when he was forty-two, to Elspeth Goldie, who was then only twenty-one. A first daughter, Mary-Lilias, was born 15th March 1855 and died on 6th June 1856. A second daughter, Anne-Christina, was born 22nd September 1856 and also soon died, on 14th August 1857. A third daughter, Mary, was born 22nd May 1858, followed closely by the birth of a first son, Robert on 22nd September 1859, a second son, John, on 17th February 1862 and a third son, also Kirkpatrick, on 14th October 1864.

In one terrible year, 1865, Kirkpatrick Macmillan lost his thirty-two year-old wife, Elspeth, on 28th July, his one year-old son and namesake Kirkpatrick on 3 October, and his six year-old son, Robert, on 1st November. Following this, of six children born, Macmillan had only two survivors, Mary and John.

Keir Parish Registers record that Kirkpatrick Macmillan died on the 26th January 1878, of "phthisis pulmonatis", at the age of 65, with his son John present at his bedside. Of his immmediate successors, his daughter Mary died in about 1928 and John, who was only fifteen when his father died, lived until 1946.[22] John was interviewed late in his life, in Liverpool, by J. Gordon Irving.[23]

The 1841 Census shows Robert Macmillan (60), blacksmith, living at Courthill with Mary his wife (55), Mary his daughter (20), three younger children and John Brown (15), an apprentice blacksmith. Kirkpatrick, then 29 years old, is not listed as a resident, indeed, all the other older male children, John, Robert, James, Walter and Hoggan had left Courthill. Kirkpatrick's name was absent from the 1841 Courthill Census because Glasgow census records show that he was then living in the city, with his older brother John.

Having formerly held a post as Rector of Dumfries Grammar School, John had moved to Glasgow in 1837 to become the Classical Master at Glasgow High School. Census Records for Barony Parish (Blythswood) show: "John McMillan, 35, Classical Master, High School", living at Gaysfield House, Shamrock St, with Cathrine (35), his wife, four children, Agnes Sinclair (30), governess Marion Brown (20), a female servant, and "Kirkpatrick McMillan, 25, artisan".

Glasgow street directories confirm John Macmillan's residence and career in the city. He is first listed in 1838-9 as: "John McMillan, M.A., High School, 5 Vincent Place". In 1839-40 he had moved to "Gayfield, City Road", where he stayed until 1842. By 1842-3, John is listed as: "Classical teacher, High

Fig. 8 The smithy in Courthill, where it is alleged that Macmillan produced his velocipedes. [Source: *CTC Gazette*, Sept. 1899]

School", living at 43 Cambridge Street. His brother George Hoggan was also in Glasgow, a teacher at Hutcheson's School, living on Upper Crown Street from 1841-2 to 1846-7.

From Isobella Marchbank, Macmillan's sister, we learn that while he was in Glasgow, Kirkpatrick worked at the Vulcan Foundry, located not far from his brother's house, on Washington Street.[24] We do not know for how long this employment lasted. And it may very well have been during this period that he attended some of Glasgow's well-known Mechanic's Institute classes, for according to son John: "It was his boast that he received most of his education by attending a night school when he was thirty years of age."[25]

Alastair Dodds' account confirms this possibility:

> The Vulcan Foundry was part of Robert Napier's shipbuilding and engineering empire. Napier was well-known for encouraging his apprentices to attend night school, many of whom went on to become engineers. At age 30, Kirkpatrick would not have been too old to have been one of these artisan apprentices working in the foundry by day and studying at night.[26]

Far from being a humble rural blacksmith, toiling in anonymity in a rural backwater, Macmillan as a young man worked, at least for a short time, in the expanding world of industrial manufacturing, an experience which would have given his existing mechanical skills an enlarged perspective. But the testimony of his son John, published in 1940 by J.Gordon Irving, describes the rustic living typical of Macmillan's early and later life rather than industrial labour in a Glasgow factory:

> My father began life as a farm labourer at the farm of Morton Holm, across Scaur Water, then became a coachman and later a blacksmith. He could also make wooden pumps, play the harmonium, pull out teeth, and was well known at parties in the district for his grand whistling and fiddling. When he gave up his work as a farm-worker, my father went as a coachman to a gentleman's house near the village of Holywood. One of his jobs here was to break in the horses, both on the flat and in jumps, as well as in the gig or carriage.[27]

The 1841 Census Record entry, when Kirkpatrick was living and working in Glasgow, may perhaps locate him close to the period of his involvement with velocipedes. By the early 1840s, according to the witnesses whose accounts are given in later chapters, Macmillan was employed as a blacksmith on the Drumlanrig Castle Estate of the Duke of Buccleuch, employment which may well have decided his return to his home area. Hence he had access to tools and a forge at three locations, his father's smithy at home in

Part One: The Origins of the Bicycle

Courthill, on the Drumlanrig Estate, and at the works in Glasgow.

According to James Johnston, Macmillan "before commencing business on his own account, appears to have spent some years at the smithy on Drumlanrig Estate, belonging to the present Duke of Buccleuch's father."[28] One of the other blacksmiths there, John Findlater, said that he had been Macmillan's neighbour at Mallowford smithy on the estate, and later at another new one at Drumlanrig Mains. He thought that Macmillan first came to Mallowford about 1835 or 1836.[29] According to one of James Johnston's informants, a Mrs. Elizabeth Bailey, Macmillan later lodged with her parents on the estate: "That was in the years 1842-43. How I remember the dates so exact is that my father got a situation near to Dumfries in May, 1843. We left Drumlanrig then, and Macmillan was with us till the day we left."[30]

If the 1842 account in the Glasgow newspapers of the velocipede accident in the Gorbals did indeed describe Kirkpatrick Macmillan's velocipede (see the next chapter: "Two crucial sources"), then it makes sense that he travelled backwards and forwards between Thornhill and Glasgow on it. He was young and strong, and had every economic reason to save money on the cost of a coach or horse. Perhaps he travelled that road on many occasions. If his brother, John, had also tried to ride the velocipede in Glasgow, and he was the one who had become involved in the minor accident, that could easily explain the "gentleman" of the newspaper story, since John was an M.A. and was teaching Classics at the High School in 1842, and would easily qualify as "a gentleman". But this is speculation, and I am jumping ahead of the evidence.

An example of the upward social mobility possible for an intelligent and ambitious man from a humble rural background, John Macmillan moved on once more in 1844 to teach at Edinburgh High School, where he remained. A street directory for 1871 lists him as "Emeritus Master and Examiner of the High School", living at 16, Buccleuch Place. He died in 1872.[31]

In 1892, during the period of media inquiry into the origins of the bicycle, a reporter from the *Dumfries and Galloway Standard and Advertiser* interviewed Mrs Marchbank (née Isobella Macmillan), one of Kirkpatrick's younger sisters, in Dumfries. Then seventy-two, Mrs Marchbank appeared to be "a woman of marked intelligence" and willingly gave the reporter information about the Macmillan family. Her father, Robert, she said, "though not much enamoured with what he regarded as the less useful, if not as the useless, branches, gave his children an excellent education, and had the satisfaction in after-life (sic) of seeing the male members make excellent use of the instruction received at the parish school." John, the oldest, "attended the university with a view of qualifying for the ministry. He abandoned that idea, however, and became successively

the rector of Dumfries Academy, Glasgow High School, and Edinburgh High School. At one time he officiated as tutor to John Bright."

According to Mrs. Marchbank, Kirkpatrick's brother, George, "rose to the position of second master of Hutchison's Hospital, Glasgow", and another brother, Robert, "became a clerk in that city". It was also from Mrs. Marchbank that the information came that "before taking over the management of the business at Thornhill, Kirkpatrick for a short period served in the 'Vulcan' Foundry, Glasgow", and that "he was a man of indomitable pluck; once he set himself to any complicated piece of work, he persevered until he had successfully mastered it."[32]

Family obligations were evidently stronger than the economic lure and risks of Glasgow, for in the early 1840s, Kirkpatrick returned to Thornhill to help his aging father with his blacksmith's shop and to take a job on the Drumlanrig Estate. 1851 Census Records for Courthill show: "Robert McMillan, Head, 72, Blacksmith (ret)", living with Mary Macmillan (67), "Kirkpatrick McMillan, 36, Blacksmith", two grandchildren, a housekeeper and two young apprentice blacksmiths.

Robert Macmillan died on the 4th February 1854, and thereafter Kirkpatrick remained at Courthill. He married on 23rd April 1854, only a few weeks after the death of his father, and had a family which was tragically affected by early childhood death and the death of his wife in 1865. 1861 Census Records for Courthill show: "Kirkpatrick McMillan, Head, 48, Blacksmith", living with Elspeth Goldie (28), two young children and a young apprentice, while the 1871 Census shows: "Kirkpatrick McMillan, Head, 58, Blacksmith" still employing two apprentices.

A rare further glimpse of Macmillan's working life outside the peremptory, routine entries of official records can be found in a newspaper account from 1862. In October, the Dumfries Union Agricultural Society's Show was held in "a spacious field at Nunholm", where "visitors amounted to several thousands in number, and included not a few of the neighbouring nobility and gentry. Mr Kirk, the enterprising landlord of the White Hart Hotel, had a tent 125' long, which barely sufficed to afford accomodation for his customers." Prizes were awarded for all categories of agricultural activity, and the report is especially interesting on "The Implements". It comments that, "Nowadays, when horse power and manual labour are being superseded in almost every department of agricultural work, anxiety to gain information and see the mode of working of the newest machines is felt by all interested in farmwork..... The number and variety of the articles entered made this department particularly interesting."

The Origins of the Bicycle

In the list of implements exhibited can be found a small item: "Mr Kirkpatrick M'Millan, Courthill, Keir - malleable iron swingle-trees, made by exhibitor".[33] Swingle-trees are a part of the mechanism which connects a plough, or other farm equipment, to the horses. It is, in a sense, reassuring to see Macmillan there, securely documented at work, exhibiting his handiwork. John Macmillan also remembered that his father "made several improvements to the plough" and exhibited "at the Dumfries Highland Show".[34]

These are the essential securely documented facts of Kirkpatrick Macmillan's life and career. It is not really very much information. The historian hungers for more specific and secure documentation of Macmillan's velocipede-building activities, a bundle of receipts or a photograph of him with a machine, but must remain content with less precise information. Macmillan's life's work as an artisan and blacksmith was contained within these narrow geographical and social limits. He does not seem to have been a typical artisan because his brothers became teachers. It appears that he made a positive choice to remain an artisan, perhaps because he loved the science of mechanics. It was from his manual and metal-working experience and his curiosity about velocipedes that any progressive experiments he made with them appears to have grown. And it is ironical that the one thing for which this man is now known, his probable contribution to the early evolution of the bicycle, still cannot be credited to him with certainty.

James Johnston, having researched Kirkpatrick Macmillan's life assiduously, published several summary biographies in various places. The following was published in *Bicycling News*, 19 March 1892:

I may conclude by saying Kirkpatrick Macmillan was a splendid trademan; anything he put his hand to was well done, and as a proof of his ability, his son informs me, he made several ploughs without even a screw in them – two of these were to the order of Mr. Gladstone, of Capenoch, near Penpont, a brother of the ex-Premier. Macmillan was of undoubtable pluck – once he set himself to any piece of complicated work, he persevered until success crowned his efforts. He belonged to a clever family. His brother John was at one time tutor to the late Mr. John Bright, M.P., and afterwards successively Rector of Dumfries Academy, Glasgow High School and Edinburgh High School. Another brother, George, was second master of Hutchinson's Schools, Glasgow, whilst a third was a clerk in that city. He was of a kindly disposition – one of the hail-fellow-well-met sort – a lively companion, and a man devoid of any pride. This is shown by his willingness to exhibit his bicycle, and to assist anybody to make one for themselves. He stood over six feet, a fine specimen of an athlete, and was admittedly a powerful and fearless rider, in fact, one of our earliest trick riders. On market days, when he frequently rode from Courthill to Dumfries – 14 miles – he appeared to have had no difficulty in keeping up with the farmers in their gigs. He died on 26 June, 1878, in his 65th year.

Fig. 9 Macmillan's sister, in centre, and two of his nieces, with Anne Marchbank on the left. [Source: *CTC Gazette*, Nov. 1938]

Fig. 10 Mary Marchbank, Macmillan's niece. [Source: *CTC Gazette,* Nov. 1938]

4. Two crucial sources, 1842 and 1869

a. A Glasgow velocipede incident documented in 1842

The hobby-horse, as we have seen in Chapter 2, was reported in the newspapers and popular press in 1819-20, when it enjoyed a brief fad. The hobby-horse achieved a partial definition of a "bicycle": it carried its rider on two wheels, it could be balanced and steered, but it could not be driven continuously forward without the feet touching the ground. The existence of Gompertz's velocipede, with its hand/arm assisted drive, indicates that a method of continuous driving was being sought. Most of the discussion about other three- and four-wheeled velocipedes in the first half of the 19th century were in "mechanic's", or specialized, technical publications, rather than in the daily press.[35] They were indicative of a widespread interest in the idea of human-powered transportation, and most were attempting to devise or explain a particular, individual solution to the problem of designing a human-powered vehicle.

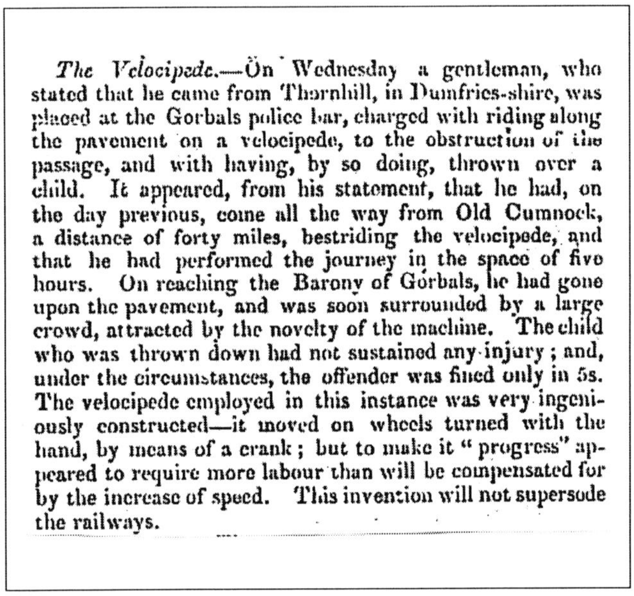

The Velocipede.—On Wednesday a gentleman, who stated that he came from Thornhill, in Dumfries-shire, was placed at the Gorbals police bar, charged with riding along the pavement on a velocipede, to the obstruction of the passage, and with having, by so doing, thrown over a child. It appeared, from his statement, that he had, on the day previous, come all the way from Old Cumnock, a distance of forty miles, bestriding the velocipede, and that he had performed the journey in the space of five hours. On reaching the Barony of Gorbals, he had gone upon the pavement, and was soon surrounded by a large crowd, attracted by the novelty of the machine. The child who was thrown down had not sustained any injury; and, under the circumstances, the offender was fined only in 5s. The velocipede employed in this instance was very ingeniously constructed—it moved on wheels turned with the hand, by means of a crank; but to make it "progress" appeared to require more labour than will be compensated for by the increase of speed. This invention will not supersede the railways.

Fig. 11 Published in at least three different newspapers, this Glasgow news item is one of the most important pieces of historical evidence in the Macmillan story. But was it about Macmillan? [Source: *Glasgow Herald,* 11 June 1842]

An unusual event, however, occured in 1842, when a short news story was printed first in one Scottish daily newspaper, the *Glasgow Argus* (9 June), before it was picked up and used soon after in almost identical form in several other papers, including the *Glasgow Herald* (11 June 1842), the *Glasgow Courier* (11 June 1842) and the *Dumfries and Galloway Courier* (13 June 1842).(**see Fig. 11**.) This news story about the velocipede was published in the Glasgow newspapers, apparently, because a minor crime had been committed,

a street accident involving the velocipede rider and a child, the perpetrator of which had been prosecuted and lightly fined. The child had only been "thrown down", however, and not seriously injured. The most unusual aspect of this short report of a seemingly mundane event was that "a velocipede" had been involved and that the "gentleman" who owned it had come 40 miles from Old Cumnock into Glasgow the previous day in five hours "bestriding the velocipede", and had created a commotion. He had "gone upon the pavement, and was soon surrounded by a large crowd, attracted by the novelty of the machine".[36]

The full text of the news item is a fascinating and unusual account of an early velocipede incident, when an actual machine can be seen in use, its rider being observed by and interacting with people in the street who were attracted by its "novelty". Even without the possible connection to Macmillan, it is an unusual account at this date. Who was this "gentleman, who stated that he came from Thornhill, in Dumfries-shire", and what kind of "very ingeniously constructed" velocipede was he "bestriding" when he arrived in the crowded streets of Glasgow, to become involved in a minor accident and to encounter a large crowd "attracted by the novelty of the machine"? The crucial question for us here, of course, is whether we are justified on the basis of the evidence in linking this account with Kirkpatrick Macmillan.

The news story from the *Glasgow Herald* reads in full as follows (all punctuation has been included precisely as in the original):

> The Velocipede - On Wednesday, a gentleman, who stated that he came from Thornhill, in Dumfries-shire, was placed at the Gorbals police bar, charged with riding along the pavement on a velocipede, to the obstruction of the passage, and with having, by so doing, thrown over a child. It appeared, from his statement, that he had, on the day previous, come all the way from Old Cumnock, a distance of forty miles, bestriding the velocipede, and that he had performed the distance in the space of five hours. On reaching the Barony of Gorbals, he had gone upon the pavement, and was soon surrounded by a large crowd, attracted by the novelty of the machine. The child who was thrown down had not sustained any injury; and under the circumstances, the offender was fined only 5s. The velocipede employed in this instance was very ingeniously constructed - it moved on wheels turned with the hand, by means of a crank, but to make it 'progress' appeared to require more labour than will be compensated for by the increase of speed. This invention will not supersede the railways.[37]

On the face of it, it is a short and simple report, but when they are examined more closely these few sentences pose a series of difficult interpretational problems. The story has frequently been cited as

The Origins of the Bicycle

documentary evidence to prove that Macmillan had indeed designed and made a "bicycle" by 1842, and had thus embarked on the ride into Glasgow from Thornhill. The actual wording of the report, however, supports such a conclusion only ambiguously and partially. This velocipede rider was indeed, like Macmillan, from Thornhill, and that is certainly strong evidence in favour of Macmillan. How many other people from Thornhill were likely to have been riding a velocipede, other than Kirkpatrick or one of his brothers? But that is the only detail here which specifically suggests that it was Macmillan. There is no mention of a particular individual by name, only of "a gentleman, who stated that he came from Thornhill, in Dumfries-shire", and that he claimed to have ridden the previous day from Old Cumnock, about 40 miles, in five hours. It has been presumed, if it was indeed Macmillan, that he had also ridden from Thornhill to Old Cumnock, perhaps the day before he arrived in Glasgow, an assertion that is in fact confirmed by other evidence.

What kind of a velocipede was it? The report stated that this "gentleman" was "riding along the pavement on a velocipede", that he was "bestriding the velocipede". It is important to note that we are not told here whether it was a two-, three- or four-wheeled velocipede. In the then current level of experimentation, it was as likely to have been three or four-wheeled as two-wheeled. But the use of the words "riding" and "bestriding" is significant because they do not describe the actions necessary to drive most of the contemporary three- and four-wheeled machines. It is logical to suggest that "bestriding" strongly suggests the description of a rider on a two-wheeled machine.

But from the report, we also learn that this was certainly not an old-fashioned hobby-horse, because the velocipede was "very ingeniously constructed", and upon entering the crowded city, "was soon surrounded by a large crowd, attracted by the novelty of the machine". This "very ingeniously constructed" machine was further described: "it moved on wheels turned with the hand, by means of a crank" (the passage has been punctuated exactly as in the original). Should the story be treated as an accurate eye-witness account or, as seems more likely, a journalist's report written from information given in the court? The description is ambiguous and confusing, suggesting that it was *not* an accurately observed, eye-witness description, and it can be interpreted in two different ways. Firstly, it could be interpreted to mean that the velocipede "moved on wheels driven by a crank turned with the hand", in which case, as a hand-cranked machine, it would not be recognizable as the Macmillan/McCall model. But a second reading of the description of the velocipede is that "it moved on wheels steered by hand, and was driven by a crank", a description of the steered front wheel and the drive-mechanism which is certainly acceptable as an ineptly-worded description of a Macmillan-style velocipede. Let us not attach too much significance to this ambiguous description in isolation

from other pieces of evidence, but allow it to be inconclusive for the moment.

What else happened in the Gorbals in June 1842? We learn that the velocipede "had gone upon the pavement", which was apparently considered illegal (presumably because the velocipede was considered to be a carriage) and that it was sufficiently unusual in Glasgow for a large crowd to gather, "attracted by the novelty of the machine". We learn also that the reporter thought that it was a slow and laborious machine and that he was of the sarcastic opinion that "it appeared to require more labour than will be compensated for by the increase of speed", and that it would not "supersede" the railways. Such an editorial aside is not of much significance except to emphasize the marginality and unfamiliarity of the machine.

The use of the word "gentleman" to identify the velocipede rider should also be noted, and needs to be examined. What kind of a person would be described as a "gentleman"? It has been objected that Macmillan, as a blacksmith, would probably not have been identified as such. Does the use of such a term exclude Macmillan from consideration? Did the court reporter simply use the term in a generic sense? Could it perhaps have been one of Macmillan's better educated school-teacher brothers, who might more accurately have been described as "gentlemen", who was in fact involved in the incident (a real possibility based on evidence to be discussed below)?

The report raises as many questions as it answers, and is frustrating in this respect. It appears to stand alone in 1842, and it is tantalizingly lacking in specificity. We wish that the reporter could at least have given us a name and made sure that his description of the machine was fuller and more accurate. Vain wish! But amid the doubts and questions, the appearance in court in 1842 of a velocipede rider *from Thornhill*, riding a machine which was unusual enough to attract the attention of a "large crowd", still has to be noted as a significant event. Once again, the question has to be asked: how many other velocipede riders besides Macmillan (or one of his brothers) were living in Thornhill in 1842?

In fact, the 1842 Glasgow newspaper reports are not the only source of information about this incident. There is further, corroborating evidence in four later accounts: first in a letter sent by "A Native of Keir" to the *North British Daily Mail* in 1884; second, in accounts given by Macmillan's sister, Mrs. Isobella Marchbank and her daughter Mrs Watret, recorded in 1892 by a reporter from the *Dumfries and Galloway Standard*; third, in an account given by blacksmith John Findlater to James Johnston and published in *The Scottish Cyclist* in 1892 and, fourth, in an account by Thomas Haining, a farmer, also given to Johnston, and published at the same time. What does the evidence of these accounts add to the ambiguities of the original 1842 newspaper text?

Part One: The Origins of the Bicycle

1. In the letter sent to the *North British Daily Mail* by "A Native of Keir" in 1884 (see **Sources E**), Macmillan was identified by name and location by a neighbour who "knew him well, being brought up together", who had "been in his father's smithy hundreds of times", who spoke of Macmillan's "first wooden horse" and then of a second, "another on an improved scale". This witness agrees with McCall's 1892 account (see below, Chapter 4, section b.), that Macmillan's velocipede went through a process of development, possibly from hobby-horse to crank-driven machine. The witness thought that Macmillan's "first run to Glasgow was about the years 1836 or 1837", when "he started from Thornhill with the mail coach, via Sanquhar, Cumnock, and Kilmarnock, and was in Glasgow before the coach". Possibly the dates of various different trips were here confused, but "A Native of Keir" remembered that Macmillan "met with a misfortune in Glasgow, having come against an old woman in the street and knocked her down, and was fined 5s". The child is here transformed into "an old woman", and the date is perhaps mistakenly given as five or six years earlier than 1842, but the essentials of the story are the same, containing crucial repetitive elements of oral transmission: the trip from the blacksmith shop to the big city, the making of an improved "wooden horse", the racing of the mail coach and the accident in the Glasgow street. Most importantly, Macmillan is specifically linked by name to the Glasgow street accident: "His name was Kirkpatrick M'Millan, son of Robert M'Millan, a country blacksmith, parish of Keir".[38] It should also be emphasized that this account, written in 1884, is substantially earlier than, and unconnected with, the later James Johnston research.

2. In the second corroborating account, 72 year-old Mrs. Marchbank, Macmillan's sister, "a woman of marked intelligence" who lived in Dumfries, in 1892 told a reporter from the *Dumfries and Galloway Standard and Advertiser* (see **Source J**) that she remembered well her father "starting on his memorable trip to Glasgow" and that "the accounts he gave of his exploits are also even now quite fresh on her mind."[39] Mrs. Marchbank would have been 20 in 1842. Why would she have lied about her memories of these events, or consciously altered her memories? The journey took place, she remembered, "at the time one of her daughters, now 49 years of age, was still a child at the breast. And the occasion is further impressed upon her memory by the fact that it was about the time of the Disruption in 1843".[40] Lack of precision about the exact date does not, of course, invalidate the essentials of the remembered events.

But Mrs. Marchbank's memory gave a different slant to the velocipede incident in the Gorbals than the 1842 and 1884 newspaper accounts. "At Glasgow he was met by two if not three of his brothers," she told the reporter:

They were anxious to see him ride the machine on the pavement…One of the 'Baillies' asked that they should induce him to do so, and on condition that his name was not mentioned, he undertook the responsibility of defraying any expense to which M'Millan's conduct might expose him. A crowd was of course attracted, and two policemen interfered. One seized M'Millan and removed him to the Police Office, and the other endeavoured as best he could to push the machine along the street. Robert M'Millan, Kirkpatrick's brother, no doubt to the great relief of the officer, took charge of the offensive 'horse'. Kirkpatrick was liberated on bail; and on the following morning appeared before the magistrate. He was fined 2s 6d; but what the exact nature of the offence libelled remains doubtful. The 'Baillie' to whom we have referred refunded M'Millan the amount of the penalty. While he readily conversed upon other features of the journey, M'Millan was always very reticent in alluding to this incident.

Mrs. Watret, Mrs. Marchbank's eldest daughter (Macmillan's niece), of Dumfries, was also interviewed. "With reference to the Glasgow incident, Mrs. Watret says her uncle denied that he had knocked down a little girl, and was of opinion she must have fallen from fright. When at the police office, either on the night of the arrest or next morning, some of the authorities took him into a back court in order that he might demonstrate to them how the machine worked; and he 'formed the figure of eight with it'".

These two accounts confirm that one or more of Macmillan's brothers was involved in this brush with the law, which was not as straightforward as the 1842 report suggested. People were astonished with the velocipede, crowds formed, the police were as interested in the machine as the crowds, an accident occurred, Macmillan's brother became involved and was probably confused with Kirkpatrick in the newspaper report. The two interviews with Mrs. Marchbank and her daughter were conducted by a careful newspaper reporter without an obvious axe to grind, who recognized that he needed to cross-check the stories of mother and daughter. "The foregoing statements were given with wonderful precision", he wrote, "and although the mother and daughter were interviewed at different times and places, without, so far as our reporter is aware, any consultation on the subject during the interval, there is entire agreement on almost every essential detail".

3 and 4. Two further versions of the story corroborate the essential facts. John Findlater, blacksmith, wrote to Johnston that: "On coming to Glasgow he (Macmillan) was surrounded by a perfect multitude of old and young folks anxious to get a look at him and his horse. In the excitement he unfortunately knocked down a child and got himself into trouble with the authorities, but on explaining that it was a pure accident he was set at liberty." Thomas Haining, farmer, wrote to Johnson; "I think if you make inquiries in the Glasgow Police Court you will find that M'Millan and his horse were both fined and confined in the Glasgow prison prior to 1846, for causing an obstruction in the streets."[41]

The Origins of the Bicycle

From where, if not personal contact with the events, did these diverse individuals get their accounts or their memories of the incident? Was the "gentleman from Thornhill" who was unnamed in the 1842 newspaper accounts Macmillan? The trip from Thornhill to Glasgow apparently made a lasting impression both on Macmillan's family and on local folk. There was no doubt in their minds that the rider was Macmillan. The story was embellished and cherished in popular memory, and when they were asked about it fifty years later, they gave accounts which varied in the details. But in the essentials, their memories had a strong and consistent outline and agreed in principle with the 1842 newspaper account. There is surely little reason to suppose that these five witnesses ("A Native of Keir,", Mrs. Marchbank, Mrs. Watret, John Findlater and Thomas Haining) would have been able to remember the 1842 or the 1884 newspaper stories in detail, or that they had copies of these in their hands when they were interviewed! On the contrary, the essentials of the story – the identification of the machine as the "wooden horse", the ride from Thornhill to Glasgow, the race against the mail coach, the accident to the child or woman, the run-in with the law – were strong in their memories. Mrs Marchbank's and Mrs. Watret's versions of the story certainly suggest a more complex and complete memory of events, involving a request from officials to demonstrate the velocipede which appears to have had unexpected results.

We shall refer again to these 1842 and later accounts of the velocipede incident as our story unfolds.

b. Rear-driven velocipedes made by Thomas McCall in Kilmarnock in 1869

We jump twenty-seven years now, to 1869, to take note of two letters which were published in the *English Mechanic and Mirror of Science*, a journal that concerned itself with a wide variety of technical and engineering issues and gave more coverage to discussion of velocipedes than any other publication in the late 1860s (see **Sources B**). Velocipedes of many different types were discussed and illustrated in the *English Mechanic*, which is also an important source of information about the introduction of the new, two-wheeled bicycle in 1868-9. But these two letters give crucial evidence of a continued interest in **rear-driven,** two-wheeled velocipedes, reinforcing the suggestion that the design existed, to a certain extent, in the public domain. The letters included two accurate illustrations, engraved from photographs, which are the earliest published illustrations of a "Macmillan-style" machine. The new, two-wheeled, **front-wheel-driven** velocipede underwent energetic development from 1867-69, when most production was devoted to this, the first manufactured "bicycle". But other designs were not immediately pushed aside by its success, and amateur mechanics wrote frequently to the *English Mechanic* to discuss alternative designs and ways of solving the velocipede problem.

The two letters from 1869 document the activities of Thomas McCall, of Kilmarnock, and were sent to the *English Mechanic* by someone who signed himself "Mechanical Hawk". In the first, headlined "The Kilmarnock Velocipede" (**see Fig. 12**), "Mechanical Hawk" wrote:

> Sir - I enclose a photograph of a velocipede, which meets with great approval here (Kilmarnock). I have tried it, and find it very light and easy of motion. It is two-wheeled, the driving wheel 3ft 6in., and steering wheel 2ft 8in. The wheels are of wood, and are double disked. The maker (Mr.T. McCall, Langlands Street, Kilmarnock) has raced and beaten some of the ordinary two-wheeled velocipedes in Glasgow. If, Mr. Editor, you think this is worth engraving, I shall be glad to benefit some of my numerous brother readers. I may add that the price is £5 10s.
>
> Mechanical Hawk.[42]

Fig. 12 McCall's "Kilmarnock Velocipe" was illustrated in 1869. [Source: *The English Mechanic*, 14 May 1869]

The second letter, published less than a month later (**see Fig. 13**), also from "Mechanical Hawk", was headlined "The Improved Kilmarnock Velocipede", and contained information about various changes that had been made in the design of the McCall velocipede:

> Sir - Since I last wrote, various improvements have been effected in the Kilmarnock velocipede. I now send you a photograph of it in its present stage. It has, as my brother readers will perceive, a far better steering handle, being fitted with a brake and gun-metal bearings; the connecting rods are also made alterable to a long or short leg. It is a remarkably safe velocipede, being so low and

easily mounted. The speed is from 8 to 12 miles an hour, though I have gone downhill at what I should think a much greater speed. The price, through improved fittings, has risen to £7. The machine weighs about 58lb.

Mechanical Hawk.[43]

Fig. 13 A second letter described changes made in the design of the McCall machine. [Source: *The English Mechanic,* 11 June 1869]

Who was "Mechanical Hawk"? Could it have been, as seems most likely, McCall himself? If it wasn't, then he appears to have been an associate and observer who felt close enough to the mechanics who read the *English Mechanic* to refer to them as "brother readers". But it is important to note what "Mechanical Hawk" doesn't say here. There was no mention of Macmillan here, or of the possibility that the velocipedes illustrated were based on a design from an earlier period, only that McCall was the "maker" and that "improvements" had been made in making the second machine, which suggests a machine being made with one eye on the rapidly developing, currently fashionable front-wheel-driven velocipede.

The evidence of the two line engravings, which we are told have been copied from photographs, is highly significant in the unfolding story. The first (with the breast-plate support) shows a machine identical in design to the velocipede now in the Dumfries Museum (which is a copy of his 1869 design which McCall agreed to make for James Johnston in the 1890s, while the second is identical to the design of the velocipede now housed in the Science Museum (see **Fig. 1**). We thus have documentation from 1869 for the essential design of two of the most important early velocipedes surviving in public collections.

Further evidence about McCall's activities in Kilmarnock comes from the *Kilmarnock Standard* in 1869. An advertisement reads: "Velocipedes! Velocipedes! Thomas McCall, cartwright, West Langlands Street, having made velocipedes 13 years ago, is prepared to make them to order upon the very best principle, at moderate prices." An article in the same issue of the paper continues:

Velocipedes. From our advertising columns it will be seen that more than one local firm will be happy to receive orders for the construction of these novel machines, which seem likely soon to become 'all the rage' here as in other places. On Saturday afternoon last, Mr McCall, wheelwright, Langlands Street, drove his specimen velocipede along John Finnie Street and Dundonald Road for more than an hour in presence of a large number of spectators. The vehicle was driven at a considerable rate of speed with apparently but moderate exertion on the part of the rider....The experiment as a whole appeared to be highly satisfactory.[44]

"Mechanical Hawk", the writer of the two letters to the *English Mechanic*, did not acknowledge that the machines he described had a relationship with Macmillan, but Thomas McCall comes vividly to life in an account which he gave later of his earlier activities (see **Source H**). Obviously stimulated by the discussions concerning the origins of the bicycle then going on in the press, Thomas McCall wrote to *Bicycling News* in 1892 giving important information about his involvement with early velocipedes. He gave testimony which questioned the precedence of Gavin Dalzell. In place of Dalzell, he proposed "a blacksmith of the name of Peter McMillan, who wrought at Drumlanrig Castle for some time and later on his own account at Pierpont, Dumfries-shire" [the place was Penpont: this is probably a printer's mistake – AR] as the person who had first fitted the "driving gear" in "about 1845".

McCall, without prompting, reported what he had seen and experienced; he was a crucial eye-witness of Macmillan's activities. He prefaced his account by saying, "at the outset", that he "lay no claim to being the inventor of bicycles or velocipedes…but perhaps have had something to do in improving and introducing them". He described the hobby-horse, in which "there was no driving gear whatever", before describing "the next improvement in velocipedes, viz., driving gear", which "was done by a blacksmith of the name of Peter McMillan…." Then comes his eye-witness account. As a boy, he wrote, "coming out of school one day", he had seen Macmillan riding his velocipede. "I followed him as he led it up a long hill and made a thorough inspection of it. On gaining the top of the hill the man got on and rode away. I ran after him for over half-a-mile, but he outstripped me". Here we have evidence of the difficulty of riding the treadle-and lever-driven machine: McCall saw Macmillan as he "led it up a long hill" because it could not be ridden uphill, before he was able to jump on and ride away upon reaching the top of the hill. The report has the ring of truth. McCall made his own machines, the materials for which he initially scavenged from broken-down hobby-horses, "after this principle…years after".[45]

The making of velocipedes was a gradual process for McCall. In 1892, McCall sent a photograph and a sketch to *Bicycling News*, which published a total of four illustrations concerning Dalzell and McCall (see

Section 6). A portrait of Dalzell was first, followed by Dalzell's bicycle, the one which was exhibited at the 1889 Stanley Show. A McCall machine followed, similar to the one illustrated in the *English Mechanic* (14 May 1869) but without a "breast-plate". Lastly was a line engraving of a photo of McCall himself with his bicycle which McCall said had been taken "25 years ago" (i.e., in 1867, more or less contemporary with the *English Mechanic* articles) by Bruce and Howie, of Kilmarnock.

This 1892 account thus provides important evidence, both in McCall's eye-witness account of Macmillan and the illustrations showing the similarity of the designs of the machines illustrated in 1892 with the 1869 *English Mechanic* accounts. The machines mentioned and illustrated in 1869 and 1892 can therefore safely be called Macmillan-McCall machines, *inspired according to McCall's own testimony* by an original (or originals) made by Macmillan. Macmillan's original might have been very close in design to McCall's machines or possibly more primitive. It is logical to assume that, since there was change and development between the two McCall designs submitted to the *English Mechanic*, McCall had also subjected whatever ideas he had borrowed from Macmillan to consideration and redesign. Exactly what the relationship between the Macmillan and McCall machines was we cannot now say, but his account of his connection with Macmillan was evidently an unsolicited eye-witness account. This reinforces the fact that Macmillan was a velocipede maker. It is very much in the tradition within which they were working that essentially similar designs would have been copied and transmitted with minor changes and improvements. According to the evidence, McCall borrowed Macmillan's ideas to make his own machines, and later he submitted his improved design to the *English Mechanic* as well as offering some for sale in Kilmarnock.

Significant in McCall's 1869 account was the statement that "the maker has raced and beaten some of the ordinary two-wheeled velocipedes in Glasgow". McCall's 1892 account (see **Sources H**) confirms that this McCall rear-driven, treadle machine was considered in 1869 to be a machine capable of rivalling the new front-wheel-driven velocipede, and was evidently being put into commercial production on a limited scale and sold. "In 1871", he wrote, "I exhibited my machine against some boneshakers…and received an order from a house (in Glasgow) for half-a-dozen of my sort". If these races were a test of the viability of the Macmillan-McCall design, it was evidently quickly proved to be a failure. Treadle-driven velocipedes were difficult to get going and did not accelerate well once moving. The backwards and forwards swinging motion of the treadles was not an efficient way to harness the energy of human legs, and the hanging treadle interferred with the steering. The front-wheel-driven velocipede, on the contrary, was easy to get going and to accelerate. The pedalling action was a rotating motion of the legs, which has never been superseded in the bicycle.

It is fascinating to note that as late as 1869, the Macmillan/McCall design was still seen as having sufficient merit that attempts were made to put it into limited production. The late survival of the Macmillan-inspired McCall design tends to contradict the assertion (stated by several of my colleagues – AR) that Macmillan was working in an isolated geographical vacuum, and had no wider impact on bicycle design. On the contrary, the demonstrated deficiencies of the rear-wheel-driven velocipede of the Macmillan/McCall design was integral to the ascendancy of the front-wheel-driven boneshaker post-1869. The transmission of craft memory from Macmillan to McCall kept alive a design which McCall may have changed and improved considerably, but which he acknowledged had originated with Macmillan. We might view these 1869 McCall machines as the end of the line for this out-dated treadle-and-lever system of propulsion.

Further discussion in the pages of the *English Mechanic* in 1870/1 gives evidence which supports this argument. As late as 1871, bicycle experimenters were still assessing the relative merits of front-wheel versus rear-wheel driving bicycles, and the Macmillan/McCall idea was still in circulation. In October 1870, Frederick Shearing wrote:

> I have a back-wheel bicycle, which I prefer to the common one. It is made almost like the 'Kilmarnock' which appeared in the Mechanic some time back. The driving wheel is 3' in diameter….I can stop anywhere and keep seated, the feet touching the ground on either side….It runs easy on level ground, but like the common bicycle it is hard work up-hill.[46]

Another reader, 'Irish Mechanic', replied soon after:

> Another delusion still entertained is that the treadle principle (to the hind wheel) has advantages over the direct action on the front wheel. The advocates of this theory are, perhaps, not aware that there were bicycles on this principle 20 or 30 years ago, but long since discarded. I saw one in Scotland, made and ridden by a millwright in Strathaven, and if you have any readers in that place, they will be able to confirm my statement. I am not aware where the design was obtained, but it has been quite eclipsed by the modern French bicycle.[47]

Strathaven, it should be noted here, is located very close to Lesmahagow, where Gavin Dalzell is reported to have made his velocipede.

Thomas McCall, who died in 1904 at the age of seventy, saw Kirkpatrick Macmillan's velocipede, memorized the design and copied it. What motive would he have had to lie when he wrote this letter to *Bicycling News*? His obituary in the *Kilmarnock Standard* (9 April 1904) described McCall as "one of the earliest pioneers of bicycle manufacture" (see **Sources - P**). It once again confirmed the essential facts that McCall himself had laid out in his letter to *Bicycling News*, that "when a boy at school in his native village (Penpont), he had seen Mr. Kirkpatrick Macmillan, the inventor of the rear-driven bicycle, riding his machine and later when serving his apprenticeship he constructed one for himself." McCall was born in 1834, so that if he saw Macmillan "when a boy at school", that would have been, say, between about 1842 and 1850. McCall himself says it was "about 1845".

As a witness, McCall appears to be strong and reliable. We will come back to him at a later stage. It should be emphasized that very little that has been discussed so far has any connection with James Johnston's later research.

Our interest in Thomas McCall's role has led us to the 1892 *Bicycling News* article, but we are jumping ahead of our chronological inquiry, and there is documentation from the 1880s which should now be examined.

Fig. 14 A copy of McCall's 1869 machine, made in 1896 by McCall himself at James Johnston's request for the Stanley Show, is now in the Dumfries Museum, here inspected by curator Truckell. [Source: Dumfries Museum]

5. Research in the 1880s proposes Gavin Dalzell as the "inventor" of the bicycle, and Macmillan is also suggested as a rival candidate.

a. Thomas Brown's 1881 account of Gavin Dalzell in *Bicycling News*

By the 1880s, cycling as a sport and recreation was well established. Awareness of the quickly developing technology was sufficiently keen that there was a lively curiosity in the history of the sport and the origins of the bicycle. A short comment in 1879 mentioned the possibility that it was a Scot who "made the first bicycle", and identified "Gavin Dalzell, who ran about on a two-wheeler selling tea in Lanarkshire in 1836, beating His Majesty's mails, and outstripping everything and everybody".[48] One much-repeated fact, that the velocipede rider raced the mail coach, was here introduced for the first time. Where did this idea come from?

In December 1880, "C. W" wrote to *Bicycling News* and asked, "Does any one know where the first bicycle was made, and who the inventor was, and also the maker…?" In answer to his question, another correspondent wrote that he had read elsewhere (he does not name the source) that "the first bicycle ever made and run successfully was constructed by Gavin Dalzell". He quotes his source, which stated that "this vehicle was not a dandy horse, but a bicycle in the true sense of the word", which "was still in existence, or was 2 years ago, when the writer saw it". The smaller wheel was in front, and it was distinguished "in the roughness of its make". Dalzell "outran the King's Mail Coach" and "during the race he ran around it three times, much to the delight of the passengers, and the disgust of the guard and driver, who had bet on the race".[49] This is the first mention, often repeated, of this detail of the folk story – that velocipede riders raced against and beat the mail coach.

Only two weeks later, "C. Wheaton",[50] who gave his address as 35, Long Acre in Covent Garden, London, wrote to *Bicycling News*, saying that after hearing rumours of a "Wonderful Bicycle in the Wilds of Scotland", he had made enquiries and obtained "the following full and true particulars" from Thomas Brown, of Lesmahagow, concerning Dalzell, who had "a decided talent for the invention of contrivances of a mechanical and scientific character". Thomas Brown's remarkably detailed account, published in *Bicycling News* on 7 January 1881, reads in part as follows (see **Sources C** for the full text of Wheaton's letter):

It is a fact established incontrovertibly by written proof, that so far back as the summer of 1846 at the very latest, Dalzell had a bicycle of his own invention in almost daily use. And, according to the oral evidence of many people, and also to a statement made in a paragraph published in a newspaper widely circulated in the Upper Ward of Lanarkshire, and which was not contradicted, his bicycle had been constructed several years before 1846.

Prior to his invention of the bicycle he had invented and constructed a tricycle, the propulsion of which was effected by its rider in a way both ingenious and unique. This tricycle, however, no longer exists, portions of it having been utilized in the construction of this bicycle, now at least thirty-four years old, which is still preserved by one of his family, T.B.Dalzell, at Lesmahagow.

His bicycle went by the name of the 'Wooden Horse', and was so styled spontaneously by the people. John Leslie, the village blacksmith, who did the ironwork, called it the 'Horse', and the pedal movements the 'Stirrups' in the bill he rendered; and to this day no one, either old or young, seems to dream of giving it any other designation. It is constructed chiefly of wood, and is strong and substantial. The only material difference between it and the present ones is its having the steering wheel in front smaller than the other [N.B., there were only two wheels, one in front of the other – AR]. The saddle, too, is so low that the rider starts himself with both feet on the ground. The stirrups, of iron, hang from the forepart, or croup, of the saddle, and are moved backwards and forwards alternately. They are connected by means of iron rods with the cranked axle of the driving wheel. The reins (handles) are bent back, so that they may be conveniently grasped by the rider.

Another peculiarity which is very noticeable is that the upper part of the driving wheel is clad with wood from the saddle to rather beyond the highest part of the wheel. The rider is enabled by this contrivance to mount freight behind him, either living or the reverse.

Frequently one, two, or even three lads perched behind the rider at one time, their arms clasped firmly round each other's waists, and all working as energetically as their strength would permit, the speed then attained being remarkable, and was secured by the lads assisting the rider, by resting their feet upon and assisting him in working the connecting rods already referred to. It had been proposed, though it was never carried out, to fix foot-pieces to these rods, and so to diminish the danger of the foot being crushed between the rods and the framework.

The simultaneous balancing and propelling of a bicycle without the feet of the rider touching the ground are now so generally known that few think anything at all about them. Yet this was not always so.

Indeed it is a fact.....that when Mr. Dalzell intimated his intention of making a second velocipede, that should only have two wheels, in place of three, and one wheel running

Part One: The Origins of the Bicycle

before the other, and moreover that the velocipede would both be propelled and balanced without the rider's feet touching the ground, not one person could he find to believe such an incredible feat was possible till the thing was actually accomplished by him. [Further evidence of two wheels rather than three. AR]

As a natural consequence, therefore, the 'Wooden Horse' excited a marvellous interest wherever it made its appearance, and people travelled long distances to get a sight of it. To satisfy the larger curiosity of others, descriptions of it had to be sent. Measurements and a diagram were asked for occasionally, and were as frankly given as they were anxiously sought.....As a result of this courtesy on the part of the inventor, and of the advice and assistance he was always happy to give, numerous bicycles of a similar type, and tricycles with treadle action, came into existence in Scotland......

Though the 'Wooden Horse' differs from the modern bicycle in matters of detail, there is one grand principle that underlies all bicycles. And it consists in the invention of a two-wheeled velocipede, the rider of which should be able to propel and to balance without aid extraneous to the machine; or in other words, without his feet touching the ground, as in the case of the dandy-horse".[51]

Brown's account is remarkable. Who was he? We do not know. But evidently Brown was close to Dalzell in Lesmahagow, and appears to have been a credible witness. Wheaton, in the bicycle industry in London, could have proposed another claimant than Dalzell had he known of one. Dalzell had first worked on a three-wheeled velocipede before making his first two-wheeled one, the "Wooden Horse", which was conspicuous enough that it "excited a marvellous interest wherever it made its appearance, and people travelled long distances to get a sight of it". It was used for carrying "freight", and sometimes more horse-power was generated by "two or even three lads" pressing down on the connecting rods". This was dangerous because a foot might slip and a leg be crushed. Most importantly, this "Wooden Horse" was a genuine bicycle; though it "differs from the modern bicycle in matters of detail, there is one grand principle that underlies all bicycles. And it consists in the invention of a two-wheeled velocipede, the rider of which should be able to propel and balance without aid extraneous to the machine; or in other words, without the feet touching the ground, as in the case of the Celeripede or Dandy Horse".

Certain soon-to-be familiar themes, which were transmitted orally, appeared in his account. Brown was aware of the fact that there was both oral evidence and a newspaper account which associated this machine with a pre-1846 date, and concluded that it "had been constructed several years before 1846". He assumed that the newspaper account we know to be from Glasgow newspapers in 1842 was about Dalzell, but his memory of an article "published in a newspaper widely circulated in the Upper Ward of Lanarkshire" enabled him to locate the article accurately to "several years

before 1846". Brown also refers to the habit of calling the velocipede "the wooden horse", adding that it "was so styled spontaneously by the people", and that "to this day no one, either old or young, seems to dream of giving it any other designation". Even John Leslie, the village blacksmith who made the ironwork, he said, "called it 'the Horse', and the pedals the 'Stirrups' in the bill he rendered".

There is no suggestion in Brown's account that Dalzell may have copied the design of his machine from someone else, but he had no reservations about giving the design to others! "To satify the larger curiosity of others", we learn, Dalzell provided descriptions: "Measurements and a diagram were asked for occasionally, and were as frankly given as they were anxiously sought." In November 1848, Francis Forrest had written to Dalzell requesting information and measurements, which were freely given. "As a result of this courtesy on the part of the inventor, and of the advice and assistance he was always happy to give, numerous bicycles of a similar type, and tricycles with treadle action, came into existence in Scotland".

Dalzell, in other words, was part of a pre-patent culture where the borrowing and lending of ideas was normal and accepted. In fact, as we read the account of Dalzell's machine, we hear many of the same elements of the story that are encountered in later discussion of Macmillan. The strong suggestion is given that two velocipede makers were working on similar machines at the same time, perhaps sharing their ideas, and that in the memories of witnesses Dalzell and Macmillan were, perhaps, not clearly separated. If they both rode in nearby locations on similar machines, this confusion is understandable. Wheaton, the sender of this letter, ends by asking whether it might be possible to borrow "this wonder from the 'Wilds of Scotland', and place it in our Stanley Exhibition?", a loan which would not be achieved for another eight years.

Charles Spencer had been involved with the bicycle since the very earliest days. He was the owner of a gymnasium in the City of London to which some of the earliest two-wheeled velocipedes in England had been imported from France in 1869, and was a general dealer in sporting goods. He also took part in a much-publicized 1869 ride on velocipedes from London to Brighton. In 1883, he published *Bicycles and Tricycles - A complete history of the machines from their infancy to the present time*, the first book which attempted to give a coherent history of the bicycle.[52] In it, Spencer quoted at length from the letter written by Mr. Thomas Brown of Lesmahagow, Lanarkshire which Charles Wheaton had sent to *Bicycling News*. Spencer must certainly have known Wheaton, since they were almost neighbours in London. Brown's account, wrote Spencer, "professes to give full particulars of the first authentic machine of the kind on record, its inventor being the late Mr. Gavin Dalzell, Merchant, of Lesmahagow, Lanarkshire".

The Origins of the Bicycle

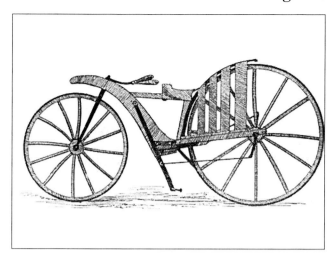

Fig. 15 Dalzell's machine was illustrated in *The Scottish Cyclist* in 1889 [Source: *The Scottish Cyclist*, 20 Feb., 1889]

Spencer's book contained the first published illustration of the Dalzell machine, very close in most details to the illustration which appeared in the 1889 *Scottish Cyclist* (**see Fig. 15**) and to the restored machine currently in the Glasgow Museum. This was the same machine exhibited at the Stanley Show and in Paris, possibly essentially the same machine which is still in Glasgow Museum. One noticeable difference between the Spencer illustration and the existing machine is the shorter nose of the main frame, which appears to have been lengthened during restoration. The biggest difference between the Dalzell machine and the McCall-built, Macmillan-inspired machine, a change which suggests the results of trial-and-error testing, was the moving back along the backbone of the fulchrum/pivot-point of the swinging arms, thus helping to free the drive mechanism from interfering with the steering rotation of the front wheel.

Brown's account of Dalzell thus began to oil the wheels of the historical search. In the 1880s, curiosity in the question had been formulated - Who was the first person to make and ride a bicycle? At first, in Brown's account, the answer was - Gavin Dalzell.

[The sources discussed in this section can be found in **Sources C**]

b. *Scottish American* and *North British Daily Mail* accounts, in 1883 and 1884, propose Macmillan

Suddenly, on the 27th September, 1883, as it were out of the blue, although there must have been an earlier source for the information, Kirkpatrick Macmillan's name appeared in a New York newspaper, the *Scottish American Journal*, in an article headlined - "The Inventor of the Bicycle".[53] This was the earliest mention of Macmillan published until then, in, at least accounts uncovered by this writer. The text in full reads as follows:

The Inventor of the Bicycle - Forty years ago a man named Kirkpatrick Macmillan, a blacksmith in the parish of Keir, Dumfriesshire, made a bicycle on which he soon became a clever rider. On this "dandy horse", as it was called in the district, from the fact that over the wheels was placed a small wooden horse, on which the rider sat, he made among other trips a run to Glasgow, distant from Keir some sixty miles, and managed to keep in front of the mail coach all the way, much to the amusement of the passengers. He accidentally knocked down a woman on entering Glasgow, for which he was fined at the police court. We are not prepared to say that he was the actual inventor of the bicycle, but the machine must have been a novelty at the time, as some of the Buccleuch family, then resident at Drumlanrig Castle, sent for the "smith", with the request that he would ride up on the machine, which he did, greatly to their astonishment. It was constructed of wood, and was worked on the same principle as the bicycle of the present day - the wheels, however, being more of a size with the smaller one in front.

The appearance of this story in 1883 is truly extraordinary! Where did it come from? Why was it published in a Scottish-American newspaper? None of the earlier accounts had mentioned Macmillan by name. What original Scottish source was the origin of this story (the newspaper was published in New York), for surely it must have a Scottish origin, probably another newspaper? Macmillan's name was correctly listed, his profession and geographical location were correctly identified, as was his relationship with the Buccleuch family. Most extraordinarily, the account again introduces some of the popular elements of the story which had already been included in Thomas Brown's account of Dalzell as published in *Bicycling News*:

- The bicycle was called a "dandy horse" and it had a little carved horse's head on it. It worked "on the same principle as the bicycle of the present day".

- Macmillan made a trip to Glasgow, during which he raced the mail coach, which amused the passengers.

- Macmillan had an accident in Glasgow, a "woman" was injured and he was fined

- Macmillan was asked to demonstrate the machine.

This first news item was followed two weeks later by an editorial in the same newspaper, again entitled "Inventor of the Bicycle": "Considerable discussion has taken place of late, both in the newspapers of this and of the Old Country, as to who was the inventor of the bicycle.[54] The honour is really worth fighting for. As a means of conveyance it is truly revolutionizing the world..... and the inventor of the bicycle will throughout time be looked upon as one of our greatest public benefactors."[55] But, oddly, the Editorial ignores Macmillan, and comes down in favour of Dalzell, quoting from Thomas Brown's account in the *Bicycling News* article from 1881 and concluding that:

Part One: The Origins of the Bicycle

"There can be little doubt that Mr. Gavin Dalzell was the inventor of the bicycle".

Where, then, did this earliest mention of Macmillan come from? There must be other English or Scottish original sources somewhere from which it was taken!

A Scottish newspaper provides further tantalizing information. *The North British Daily Mail*, 21 Aug.1884, printed a short request for information from someone called "N.F.", which I quote in full:

An Early Scotch Velocipedist.

Sir - A velocipede and its rider, said to have come from Dumfriesshire, passed Douglas, Lanarkshire, the rider halting at Douglas Mill for refreshments, and afterwards proceeding westward by way of Lesmagagow, in the month of August, 1846. Can any of your readers give the name and address of the rider of this velocipede, or the name of the place where the velocipede was made? - I am, etc., N.F.[56]

The request was answered by five letters published on

> AN EARLY SCOTCH VELOCIPEDIST.
> Sir,—A velocipede and its rider, said to have come from Dumfriesshire, passed Douglas, Lanarkshire, the rider halting at Douglas Mill for refreshments, and afterwards proceeding westward by way of Lesmahagow, in the month of October, 1846. Can any of your readers give the name and address of the rider of this velocipede, or the name of the place where the velocipede was made?—I am, &c., N. F.

Fig. 16 A letter in the *North British Daily Mail*, 21 August 1884.

22 August. The first writer had seen a velocipede rider in Old Cumnock "fly quickly past" him "in 1845 or 1846". He "could not conceive what it was till the following day, when I saw a man riding through the town with a large crowd after him." At about that same time, men employed by a local mill wright had "made several machines of the same pattern with some slight improvements." W. Blackstock wrote from Glasgow that "the name of the rider who passed through Lesmahagow in Oct. 1846 was Kilpatrick M'Millan, who made the velocipede at Courthill". He had "no hesitation in saying that the humble village blacksmith from Courthill is the great inventor and originator of the velocipede originally called the 'wooden horse'." Thomas Wright wrote that "the name of the man who came from Dumfriesshire to Glasgow via Douglas and Lesmahagow on a velocipede in the year 1846 was Kirkpatrick M'Millan, blacksmith…..he died several years ago." A fourth correspondent once again confirmed that the velocipedist was "M'Millan" but called him "Peter". The next day, 23 August 1884, another correspondent recollected that "about 35 years

ago" (i.e., 1850) he had frequently seen Gavin Weir, an engineer, "riding a bicycle made by himself, which was known as the 'wooden horse'.….He went from home considerable distances on business, and it has a very good speed."

Six days later, on 27 August 1884, "A Native of Keir" replied, testimony which deserves to be quoted in full:

> AN EARLY SCOTCH VELOCIPEDIST.
> Sir,—I see that several correspondents answer "N. F.'s" question about who an early Scottish velocipedist was. I knew him well, being brought up together. I have been in his father's smithy hundreds of times getting my clogs shod, as well as other things. He was born at Byreflat, on the estate of Waterside, parish of Keir, by Thornhill, Dumfriesshire. He made his first wooden horse when he was at Byreflat, and by and by he made another on an improved scale, and a very braw horse it was, with bridle and saddle and stirrups, with a brown mane and tail. His first run to Glasgow was about the years 1836 or 1837. He started from Thornhill with the mail coach, via Sanquhar, Cumnock, and Kilmarnock, and was in Glasgow before the coach. He met with a misfortune in Glasgow, having come against an old woman in the street and knocked her down, and was fined 5s. He had many a run to Dumfries on his "wooden horse," when none of the farmers could beat him. I could tell a great number of incidents that I have seen and heard and know to be true, which if "N. F." wishes to know he could call on me and I would tell him, and he, if he chose, could give you for publication. His name was Kirkpatrick M'Millan, son of Robert M'Millan, a country blacksmith, parish of Keir. He was named Kirkpatrick, for Sir Thomas Kirkpatrick, Capenoch, Keir, the then Sheriff of Dumfriesshire.—I am, &c., A NATIVE OF KEIR.

Fig. 17 "A Native of Keir" sent a letter replying to the earlier request for information about the Scottish velocipedist. [Source: *North British Daily Mail*, 27 August 1884]

I see that several correspondents answer "N.F."'s question about who an early Scottish velocipedist was. I knew him well, being brought up together. I have been in his father's smithy hundreds of times getting my clogs shod, as well as other things. He was born at Byreflat, on the estate of Waterside, parish of Keir, by Thornhill, Dumfriesshire. He made his first wooden horse when he was at Byreflat, and by and by he made another on an improved scale, and a very braw horse it was, with bridle and saddle and stirrups, with a brown mane and tail.

His first run to Glasgow was about 1836 or 1837. He started from Thornhill with the mail coach, via Sanquhar,

Cumnock, and Kilmarnock, and was in Glasgow before the coach. He met with a misfortune in Glasgow, having come against an old woman in the street and knocked her down, and was fined 5s. He had many a run to Dumfries on his "wooden horse", when none of the farmers could beat him. I could tell a great number of incidents that I have seen and heard and know to be true....His name was Kirkpatrick M'Millan, a country blacksmith. He was named Kirkpatrick for Sir Thomas Kirkpatrick, Capenoch, Keir, the then Sheriff of Dumfries-shire. I am etc., - A Native of Keir.

Once again, the familiar outlines of the story are repeated, but the documentation is more compelling for being a first-hand, eye-witness account. Here is someone who knew Kirkpatrick Macmillan and his father personally, who had been in their smithy "hundreds of times" and who could "tell a great number of incidents that I have seen and heard and know to be true." Macmillan's name is given correctly, the location was the writer's own neighbourhood. They were brought up together. The velocipede is again called a "wooden horse", and "a very braw (attractive) horse it was, with bridle and saddle and stirrups, with a brown mane and tail." The folk description, at first seemingly naive, should not easily be dismissed in the context of the other now familiar descriptions. Macmillan first made one horse - probably a simple hobby-horse, and then he made another "on an improved scale". He made his first run to Glasgow as early as 1836-7, and he also went to Dumfries many times. The accident in Glasgow in this account involved "an old woman". "A Native of Keir" sent his testimony unsolicited, seemingly without anything to prove. It is specific testimony that is hard to dismiss. The date of 1836-7, of course, must be questioned as speculative, but not rejected as totally implausible. If Macmillan had experimented with several machines, he might easily have taken one to Glasgow, even perhaps a simple hobby-horse, as early as that.

Yet another witness, James Smith, Jun, of Townhead, by Courthill, also wrote in the same issue of the paper that the velocipedist was called "Pate M'Millan", and, obviously thinking of the hobby-horse stage, remembered that the velocipede "was propelled forward by just touching the ground with the point of his boot." Also, "he used to ride from his blacksmith shop to Dumfries before the coach, which was counted a great feat in those days. There are some great stories told about him and his riding."[57]

The crucial thing about these accounts is that, as eye-witness testimonies, they predate all of the later 1889-92 inquiry and discussion, and again assert a series of key elements of the story, repeating many details of Thomas Brown's account of Dalzell. There is confusion between the two velocipede riders – Dalzell and Macmillan - but the story is essentially the same. These accounts predate James Johnston and his reports in *The Scottish Cyclist* and *Bicycling News*. Here are both Dalzell and Macmillan, seen and identified at

different times and places, springing in detail from the recesses of popular memory! How else can these accounts be explained? And they were not alone: other experimenters were also were making velocipedes of a similar kind. [The sources discussed in this section can be found in **Sources D and E**.]

c. Dalzell's machine exhibited in 1889 and *The Scottish Cyclist* enters the debate.

Gavin Dalzell died in 1863, but his son, J.B. Dalzell, was persuaded to loan the velocipede formerly owned by his father to the International Exhibition in Glasgow in 1888. There it formed part of the Historical and Archeological Collection brought together in the "Bishop's Palace", a reproduction of the ancient Castle of Glasgow. The catalogue of this exhibition called it "The First Bicycle, invented by Mr. Gavin Dalzell" and quoted various sources in support of this claim. An illustration of an obviously damaged velocipede, the main frame broken, was published in the exhibition catalogue (see Fig. 18.).[58] A writer in *The Irish Cyclist and Athlete* reported that a friend of his had written to him saying that she had seen the "the first bicycle ever made" there, and that it was "a rickety affair".[59]

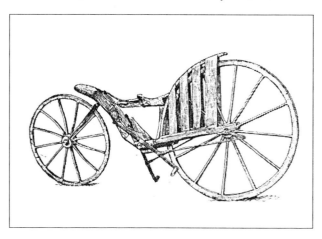

Fig. 18 Gavin Dalzell's bicycle, severly damaged was exhibited at the International Exhibition in Glasgow in 1888 [Source: James Paton, *Scottish National Memorials,* 1890]

The popular weekly journal *The Scottish Cyclist* entered the story. In January 1889, soon after the Glasgow Exhibition, the paper arranged for Dalzell's machine to be sent to Crystal Palace, London to the Stanley Show, the most important annual marketing venue for the bicycle industry, where "it attracted much attention from critical eyes, and was, undoubtedly, one of the curiosities of the Stanley Show for 1889".[60] *Bicycling News*, in reviewing the Stanley Show, mentioned that "in an out-of-the-way corner will be found the original bicycle by one Gavin Dalzell". The account confirmed that it was indeed in a poor state of repair on exhibition there:

......apparently being exhibited at shows does it very little good...possibly it has been knocked about in travelling. At any rate it is fast falling to pieces, and it would be well if some provision could be made for the preservation of so historical an antiquity....Its chief claim to notice lies in its antiquity, and the fact that it is driven by crank levers attached to the rear wheel".[61]

Some preservation apparently was done, for when the machine was sent to Paris for another exhibition later that same year, a surviving photograph, the earliest photograph of any of the very early bicycles, shows that repairs had indeed been made.[62]

As a result of this public display, the desire for a resolution to the thorny problem of identifying the "inventor" was once again expressed. "Who invented and made the first velocipede?" asked the editor of *The Scottish Cyclist*. The *Scottish Cyclist*'s editor (Nisbet) made big claims for Dalzell, although even the younger Dalzell was not totally confident of his father's claims.

Not only did he make the first velocipede, but his design must have been the actual prototype of the most popular machine of the day - the rear-driving safety. Mr. Dalzell is naturally desirous of putting the question of who was the inventor of the crude form of the earliest bicycle beyond doubt, and with the view of having the matter settled, we have done our best to induce him to exhibit his sample of the original machine. We believe.....that Scotland's claim to the earliest honours in cycle construction will be demonstrated forthwith.

The Scottish Cyclist admitted that this was "a big claim", but were confident that it could be substantiated. This would demonstrate "Scotland's claim to the earliest honours in cycle construction." As evidence of the early date of the machine, they promised that: "Mr. Dalzell has documentary evidence of a conclusive character in his possession, proving the date mentioned of his father's machine, which was "immediately prior to 1846."[63]

The demand for documentary evidence was, of course, a sound and sensible condition. This evidence, presented by J.B. Dalzell for *The Scottish Cyclist* to inspect in 1889, and reported in *The Scottish Cyclist* on 20 February 1889, consisted of dated receipts from January and February 1847 from blacksmith John Leslie "who made all the iron work used in its construction". These proved that "the gearing, which constitutes the chief wonder to the critical and historical reader, was actually on the machine while being ridden by Mr. Dalzell." There was also other unspecified "oral evidence of actual eye-witnesses of his father's progress on the machine along the roads of Lanarkshire", which, said the editor, "lies before us as we write."[64] This would presumably have been of a similar nature to the various eye-witness reports quoted so far. Unfortunately, none of this evidence survives.

The Scottish Cyclist also reported that Dalzell's documents "speak of the machine as 'the horse', the expression of simple country folk, to whom its construction was apparently suggestive of a hobby-horse." Not only that, but "it would seem that he was ever willing to give directions and instruction as to the building of his 'horse', and as a natural result of this courtesy, similar machines came into existence in other parts of Scotland. The fame of the 'wooden horse' became widely known." So once again, we have evidence of a verbal tradition both of the naming the unusual machine "the horse", and of the willing transmission of the design from maker to maker. J.B. Dalzell is reported to have produced a letter to his father dated September 1848 from Francis Forrest asking for information about his velocipede. Why would editor Nisbet have lied about these documents, which he said Dalzell had produced for him to inspect, and which "lie before us as we write"?

Bicycling News, which had been keeping track of the discussion in *The Scottish Cyclist*, voiced few doubts at this moment and put itself out on the limb in April, 1889 when it published a full-page speculative illustration by the well-known cycling artist, George Moore, of the Dalzell machine, captioning it without any hesitation: "The first rear-driving bicycle, invented by Gavin Dalzell", with a portrait of "Gavin Dalzell, the inventor of the original rear-driving bicycle" (**see Fig.19**).[65] Thus, briefly, Dalzell was prominently credited as "inventor". The first edition of Lacy Hillier's Badminton Cycling (1889) stated that "the most generally conceded claim is that of Gavin Dalzell, a cooper of Lesmahagow, Lanarkshire, who is said to have constructed and ridden a practical bicycle in 1836", getting his date wrong by 11 years. The dated receipts were from 1847.

But Dalzell's moment of "priority" would not last for long. As early as December 1888 *The Scottish Cyclist* had published a brief item hinting that Dalzell's claim was to be challenged: "An enthusiastic friend of ours is now prosecuting investigations, with the object of proving that Dalzell's machine is not the first bicycle. He believes it will be found that Dalzell copied one made by a blacksmith down Thornhill way".[66]

This was the first public hint of James Johnston's research and his subsequent campaign to displace Dalzell with Macmillan. Perhaps it was at this point that "A Native of Keir's" account of Macmillan came to the attention of these journalists. Even in this first burst of enthusiasm for Dalzell *The Scottish Cyclist* admitted that there was no certainty: "The honour has not been without its claimants in this country, the most credible of these claims being that of Kirkpatrick M'Millan, a native of Courthill, parish of Keir, Dumfriesshire, for whom it is asserted that he rode from Courthill to Glasgow, about the year 1836 or '37....no documentary evidence has as yet been forthcoming to support this shadowy claim". Was the

The Origins of the Bicycle

Scottish Cyclist picking up this information from "A Native of Keir" who had also noted the years 1836 and 1837 for Macmillan's "first run to Glasgow"? And was Johnston already letting his friends at *The Scottish Cyclist* know what he was in the process of discovering about Macmillan on his research visits to Courthill and Penpont?[67]

[The sources discussed in this section can be found in **Sources F**].

Fig. 19 With the publication of George Moore's illustration in *Bicycling News* in 1889, Gavin Dalzell was briefly enthroned as "the inventor" of the bicycle. [Source: *Bicycling News,* 6 April 1889]

FEB. 6TH, 1892. ··· BICYCLING NEWS. 87

THE ORIGIN OF THE REAR-DRIVEN BICYCLE.

GAVIN DALZELL'S CLAIM DISPUTED.

Although it is probable that the great question of the origin of the bicycle will never be satisfactorily settled, it has now been generally conceded for some years past that the first rear-driven bicycle was the invention of the late Gavin Dalzell, a blacksmith of Lesmahagow, Scotland. His machine was made in 1846, or the year previous, and the motive power was communicated to the rear wheel by means of roughly-made pedals attached to long swinging levers. This bicycle was exhibited at the Stanley Show at the Crystal Palace in 1889, and there attracted a great deal of attention. Within the last few weeks we have received an interesting letter from a Mr. Thomas McCall, of Kilmarnock, who, although he advances no claims on his own account, throws a new light on to those which have been made on behalf of Gavin Dalzell. The letter is of considerable interest, so we make no apology for printing it in full. It runs as follows:—

January 12th, 1892.

At the outset I may say that I lay no claim to being the inventor of bicycles or velocipedes as they were first named, but perhaps have had something to do in improving and introducing them.

The first idea in the way of a bicycle was simply a pair of wheels, a backbone to connect them, a seat between the wheels, so low that the rider's feet rested on the ground, and a cross-bar on which the rider rested his breast and arms.

There was no driving gear whatever, but the rider propelled himself and machine forward by leaning on the cross-bar and kicking behind with his feet on the ground.

GAVIN DALZELL'S BICYCLE.
(From sketch taken at the Stanley Show, 1889.)

On one occasion two men went away with a machine of this description; on reaching the top of a hill on the road they both got on to have a ride down the hill. This road lay at right angles to another road at the foot of a very steep decline. On coming down the hill, being without a brake of any description, they were totally unable to turn on to the other road, dashed across it, and stuck fast into a thorn hedge. Had it been a stone wall instead of a hedge the consequences would have been serious.

I now come to the next improvement in velocipedes, viz., driving gear.

This was done by a blacksmith of the name of Peter McMillan, who wrought at Drumlanrig Castle for some time, and latterly on his own account at Pierpont, Dumfriesshire. This would be about 1845.

I remember, when a boy, on coming out of school one day, seeing him with his velocipede. I followed him as he led it up a long hill and made a thorough inspection of it. On gaining the top of the hill the man got on and rode away. I ran for over half-a-mile, but he outstripped me.

It was after his principle that I made velocipedes years after, of which I will give account.

When I was an apprentice to the joiner and millwright trade I commenced to make one in my spare time. On hearing, however, that a smith eight miles off, had the remains of an old velocipede, without gearing (in all probability the one with which the two men had the escapade), I proceeded thither, bought it for 5s., and set out for home. On the way, however, the wheels broke down. I made new wheels, put cranks, connecting rods and pedals on, and for the first time owned a velocipede.

One day I rode 70 miles on this rude affair, from Sanquhar to two miles past Kilmarnock and back, but was well-nigh tired out. I disposed of that machine.

A few years after, at New Cumnock, I made an entirely new one without any drawings or reference, which was the one to which Mr. Galbraith refers, and which was in use over 20 years.

In 1871 I exhibited my machine against some boneshakers, which were in vogue at that time in Kilmarnock. I also rode into Glasgow, and received an order from a house for half-a-dozen of my sort. I made them along with some others. A clerk in connection with that firm in Glasgow (who was the best rider in Glasgow at that time), highly approved of my machine. I also made one for a surgeon in England.

I was advised to advertise it in an English journal, which

GAVIN DALZELL, OF LESMAHAGOW.

THOMAS McCALL'S BICYCLE.
(From rough sketch by the maker.)

I did, and sent a photograph of machine with rider, which was also inserted (English Mechanic).

Some years afterwards I received a letter from a man in England stating that a certain party was copying off my design, which he thought was not fair.

Of course I had no claim or letters patent, and as I was unwell at the time I took no notice of it.

The present safety bears a strong relationship to my design, to which many testify. The machines I made

Fig. 20 The publication of this illustrated article in *Bicycling News in* 1892, containing a crucial account from McCall, questioned Dalzell's role and elevated Macmillan's status as a bicycle pioneer. [Source: *Bicycling News*, 6 Feb 1892]

6. Debate in the press between 1888 and 1895: Thomas McCall and James Johnston propose Kirkpatrick Macmillan as originator of the bicycle

Inquiry into the origins of the bicycle increased in intensity during the boom of the "safety" bicycle in the late 1880s, as the bicycle became an everyday, household object. The national cycling press, and two Scottish daily newspapers, were drawn into the discussion. Between about 1888 and 1895, a lively forum was conducted, and research carried out. The people carrying out the search were not professional historians, but journalists. Research methods were discussed only to the extent of James Johnston's expressed preference for "documentary" rather than "hearsay" evidence.

Yet the eye-witness accounts, some summarized by Johnston, others sent in as letters to the editors of newspapers, have an elemental strength and credibility about them. Unfortunately for future historians, information, certainly including surviving machines, that was still available at the time was not systematically assembled, no museum curator was involved, no archival storage of documentation was carried out, and the result was what we have today, a history partially and unsatisfactorily told. The archives of all the participating researchers have been lost, and the only written evidence of that period of research which survives is what was published in a printed form, a puzzle which I am attempting to assemble and unravel here.

88   BICYCLING NEWS.   FEB. 6TH, 1892.

were safe and easily balanced, owing to the angle and formation of the shears of the front wheel, and which safety has. In this respect the velocipedes which I made were unique from all other boneshakers or high bicycles.

The only radical difference between my make and the safety is this: the power was conveyed to the rear wheel by means of swinging pedals, connecting rods and cranks, instead of, as in the safety, a chain.

This is a rough sketch of my machine. The wheels and backbone were all of wood.

On searching among my old papers I have come across one of the photographs which I got done 25 years ago, and which I enclose. There is a breast board on it, as you will see, but which I afterwards abandoned. You might please return the photograph when it has served your end.

THOS. McCALL.

1, High Street, Kilmarnock, N.B.

with his velocipede, he "followed him up a long hill, and made a thorough inspection of it"—an inspection which was so thorough that he remembered the details well enough a few years later to be able to construct a machine on the same plan. For the satisfaction of our readers we publish illustrations bearing on the subject. These include a sketch of Gavin Dalzell's bicycle which was made at the Stanley Show in 1889, and two drawings of the machine made by Mr. McCall — the one taken from his own rough drawing accompanying his letter, and the other from the photograph, which he also sends us—a faded print bearing the name of Bruce and Howie, photographers, John Finnie Street, Kilmarnock. The resemblance between the two machines, one made several years after the other, is distinctly striking. At the same time it lends us no aid in the solution of the problem. Who made the first rear-driven bicycle? On the evidence before us both Gavin Dalzell and Peter McMillan seem to have made machines of this description about the years 1845 or 1846. Perhaps some of our readers can throw some further light on the subject.

THOMAS McCALL AND HIS BICYCLE.
(From a Photograph by Bruce and Howie, of Kilmarnock.)

It will be seen that Mr. McCall gives the credit of first adding driving gear to machines, which has hitherto been awarded to Dalzell, to Peter McMillan, also a blacksmith, "who wrought at Drumlanarig Castle," and fixes the date of the latter's invention as "about 1845." It may also be noted that he knew the man, and that seeing him

Fig. 21 Continuation of *Bicycling News* article from 6 Feb. 1892.

Part One: The Origins of the Bicycle

Significantly, in all the discussion in Britain between 1888 and 1895, there appears to have been agreement that the origins of the bicycle were to be found in the pre-1867-69 developments, that is *before* the arrival of the mass-produced boneshaker. The search, it was agreed, was for the transitional machine, between the hobby-horse and the front-wheel driven boneshaker. Not once in this 19th century period of research was there a British researcher who seriously challenged the view that it was in the 1840s period that the answers were to be found. The evidence appeared to suggest that the original "bicycles" were to be found there.

We left the debate in the last chapter at the point where Gavin Dalzell's velocipede had been generally recognized as the ur-bicycle, probably made in the mid-1840s. The battered velocipede still survived (it is today in the Glasgow Transport Museum) and had been put on display in Glasgow, London and Paris. Its early date had been certified by blacksmith's receipts, and evidence from eye-witness Thomas Brown had been published. The editors of two reputable, well-circulated cycling papers, *The Scottish Cyclist* (editor - Nisbet) and *Bicycling News* (editor - Lacy Hillier) were prepared to accept evidence supplied by Dalzell's son, J.B. Dalzell, as sufficient to prove Dalzell's claim to being the earliest maker of what *The Scottish Cyclist* called "the crude form of the earliest bicycle." Dalzell, wrote editor Nisbet, "has documentary evidence of a conclusive character in his possession, proving the date of his father's inventions…... immediately prior to 1846."

In another article Nisbet showed that he was already aware that Dalzell's claim was being challenged by Johnston's research into Macmillan, calling it "the most credible of these claims", but he added that "no documentary evidence has as yet been forthcoming to support this shadowy claim."[68] Nisbet was evidently unaware of either the *North British Daily Mail* or the *Scottish American Journal* sources, in which Macmillan's name had already been advanced.

a. McCall's account in *Bicycling News*, 1892

We return now to the article from *Bicycling News* (6 Feb. 1892, see **Sources H**) containing the letter from Thomas McCall which has already been discussed in Chapter 4b.

The discussion in the two well-circulated papers, *Bicycling News* and *The Scottish Cyclist*, was sufficient to provoke an energetic response from Thomas McCall in a letter he sent to *Bicycling News* ("The Oldest Cycling Paper in the World", it claimed on its mast-head), which was published there on 6th February 1892, with editorial comment and four illustrations (**see Figs. 20 & 21.**) Entitled "The Origin of the Rear-driven Bicycle - Gavin Dalzell's claim disputed", it is one of the most important documents of this inquiry, and has in

my opinion been drastically under-estimated in evaluating Macmillan. We have previously encountered McCall in Chapter 4 as the subject of two letters written by "Mechanical Hawk" to the *English Mechanic* in 1869, "Mechanical Hawk" possibly having been McCall himself.

McCall's account, evidently sent unsolicited to the *Bicycling News* editor, G. Lacy Hilllier, is particularly significant for its lack of ambitious claims or attempt at self-aggrandisement, as well as for its spectaculat eye-witness account of Macmillan. "I lay no claim to being the inventor of bicycles or velocipedes as they were first named, but perhaps have had something to do in improving and introducing them." he wrote. The editorial comment accompanying the letter, probably written by Lacy Hillier, suggested that McCall, "although he advances no claims on his own account, throws a new light onto those which have been made on behalf of Gavin Dalzell."

The major impact of McCall's account was to throw Macmillan decisively into the ring against Dalzell as his leading rival, "to throw a new light" onto Dalzell's claims. McCall had known Macmillan and had seen him on his velocipede, he wrote, and had copied it in about 1845: "I followed him as he led it up a long hill and made a thorough inspection of it…...It was after his principle that I made velocipedes years after." The crucial passages in the account are as follows:

> The first idea in the way of a bicycle was simply a pair of wheels, a backbone to connect them, a seat between the wheels so low that the rider's feet rested on the ground.... There was no driving gear whatever. (i.e., it was a hobby-horse, AR)

> I now come to the next improvement in velocipedes, viz, driving gear. This was done by a blacksmith of the name of Peter McMillan, who wrought at Drumlanrig Castle for some time, and latterly on his own account at Pierpont, Dumfries-shire. This would be about 1845.[69]

> I remember, when a boy, on coming out of school one day, seeing him with his velocipede. I followed him as he led it up a long hill and made a thorough inspection of it. On gaining the top of the hill the man got on and rode away. I ran for over half a mile, but he outstripped me. It was after his principle that I made velocipedes years after, of which I will give account.….

> In 1871 I exhibited my machine against some boneshakers, which were in vogue at that time in Kilmarnock. I also rode into Glasgow, and received an order from a house for a half-a-dozen of my sort. I made them along with some others. A clerk in connection with that firm in Glasgow (who was the best rider in Glasgow at that time), highly approved of my machine. I also made one for a surgeon in England.

> I was advised to advertise it in an English journal, which I did, and sent a photograph of machine with rider, which

was also inserted......Of course I had no claim or letters patent.

The present safety bears a strong relationship to my design, to which many testify. The machines I made were safe and easily balanced, owing to the angle and formation of the shears (forks) of the front wheel, and which the safety has. In this respect, the velocipedes I made were unique from all other boneshakers or high bicycles.

The only radical difference between my make and the safety is this: the power was conveyed to the rear wheel by means of swinging pedals, connecting rods and cranks, instead of, as in the safety, a chain.....

On searching among my old papers I have come across one of the photographs which I got done 25 years ago, and which I enclose. There is a breast board on it, as you will see, but which I afterwards abandoned. You might please return the photograph when it has served your end."[70]

McCall does not say exactly when he made his first velocipede, but says that "when I was an apprentice to the joiner and millwright trade I commenced to make one in my spare time." He bought an old hobby-horse and "made new wheels, put cranks, connecting rods and pedals on, and for the first time owned a velocipede." McCall was born in 1834, so assuming the normal age of apprenticeship to have been between 15 and 20, this would indicate his making of this first machine to have been somewhere between 1849 and 1854. His obituary in the *Kilmarnock Standard* (1904) states that McCall

was notable as having been one of the earliest pioneers of the bicycle manufacture. When a boy at school in his native village (Penpont), he had seen Mr. Kirkpatrick Macmillan....riding his machine and later when serving his apprenticeship he constructed one for himself which is believed to have been the second ever made. After coming to Kilmarnock (when he was about 20, in about 1854) he manufactured for the Glasgow market, bicycles of the Macmillan type, with various improvements of his own.[71]

Bicycling News was impressed by the similarities between the Dalzell and McCall machines ("The resemblance between the two machines, one made several years after the other, is distinctly striking."), but understood and admitted that McCall's account still did not solve the problem of who had made this kind of rear-driven bicycle first. "On the evidence before us both Gavin Dalzell and Peter McMillan seem to have made machines of this description about the years 1845 or 1846. Perhaps some of our readers can throw some light on the subject." The question was thus thrown open to further public debate and research.

McCall's letter to *Bicycling News* predated a second round of *Scottish Cyclist* discussion, in which James Johnston became involved and appeared to act as a stimulus. It is interesting to observe that Johnston himself did not at any point interview or question McCall about his (McCall's) memories of Macmillan; surprising since McCall's eye-witness recollections had

been published in such a prominent location. It is not clear what interest McCall would have had in inventing or lying about the past. The photograph he encloses is important. The account has the ring of truth about it. McCall's claim that, as a schoolboy, he saw Macmillan with his velocipede is credible since McCall was born in 1834.

McCall's evidence here clearly suggests that Macmillan's idea for a rear-driven velocipede did not exist in a geographical and technological backwater, leading nowhere. On the contrary, it was later used by McCall as the model for his own commercial endeavours. His comments about how close his design was to the safety bicycle current in 1892 serve to demonstrate the closeness of the technological link between Macmillan and the safety bicycle. The boneshakers and high-wheel bicycle were the interlopers!

b. James Johnston enters the picture

James Johnston reacted quickly to McCall's 1892 *Bicycling News* revelations, sending an article to London for inclusion in the very next issue, 13 Feb. 1892.[72] In fact, Johnston had been researching Macmillan since 1889. He agreed with McCall in disputing the claims of Dalzell:

Mr. Jas. Johnston, of Glasgow, the discoverer of Macmillan.

Fig. 22 A portrait of Glaswegian James Johnston, called "the discover of Macmillan", was published in 1899. [Source: the *CTC Gazette*, Sept.1899]

Part One: The Origins of the Bicycle

For some considerable time past I have, when opportunity occurred in visiting Thornhill, Penpont and Dumfries districts, been engaged in collecting information to prove that Kirkpatrick McMillan (not Peter McMillan, although often called Pate McMillan by his friends) was the first and real inventor, and that Dalzell's is only a copy as regards the driving power....

After such a lapse of time it is exceedingly difficult to get hold of real tangible or documentary evidence. There were so few letters and newspapers in those days, and I am still busy collecting all I can bearing on the subject. To publish details of all the letters I have received from those who remember having seen and known McMillan personally would occupy many pages".

Johnston went on to give a list of acquaintances, neighbours and eyewitnesses of Macmillan, all of whom, he wrote, were "positive that McMillan had driving gear on his old dandy-horse for some years before 1846, the date agreed upon by Dalzell's friends when the latter made his bicycle."

Johnston had sought people out to interview, had personally spoken to some and received letters from others. They included John Findlater, Samuel Dalziel, John Brown, Thomas Haining, Robert Macmillan, James Black, etc. (see Feb 13 and 20th *Bicycling News*) These are the accounts which are dismissed as unreliable by several bicycle historians, as unfairly biased in favour of Macmillan, as proving that Johnston had a predetermined agenda to prove that the "inventor" of the bicycle was a Scotsman. And yet, it will be remarked, as we explore their contents, that they are strikingly similar in approach and detail to the other, earlier, reports which have already been noted.

Who was James Johnston? And what exactly was the nature of his interest in early velocipedes? Why was he interested in Macmillan?

Johnston was a tricycling enthusiast, "a true 'knight of the road' both in a commercial and a sporting sense, and if he is well known in the market towns of Southern Scotland, he is also a familiar figure on its roads." He was "a staunch advocate of rational tricycling as a health restorer", and as "a constant reader of cycling literature, our friend has dabbled to some extent in contributions to the press." Under the pen-name 'St. Mungo', he had contributed a series of articles to the *Scottish Athletic Journal* and *The Scottish Cyclist*, and was "a constant supplier of gossip, and little tit-bits of information" to those papers.[73]

Johnston's interest in the origins of the bicycle and the fact that he was, as he wrote, "related in a far-off way" to Macmillan, enthused him, and he probed deeply into Macmillan, interviewing descendants and local people, publishing articles and conducting a voluminous correspondence with witnesses and newspapers.

Unfortunately Johnston's correspondence, which would have been of great interest and importance, is lost. Today it is more common to suspect his motives, to castigate him for his sloppy methodology, and for his supposed partisanship, than to recognize that at least he left the documentation that he did!

The Scottish Cyclist, even in its first report of Dalzell's claims published on 12th December 1888, had already mentioned "an enthusiastic friend of ours who is now prosecuting investigations, with the object of proving that Dalzell's machine is not the first bicycle. He believes it will be found that Dalzell copied one made by a blacksmith down Thornhill way."[74] It seems probable, therefore, that it was the first series of *Scottish Cyclist* articles in 1889, and also the exhibition of Dalzell's machine the same year, that stimulated Johnston's own interest in the subject, and that most of his initial research was carried out in the period 1889-92. Since that time, he wrote, "I have been engaged in trying to solve the vexed question of the date and honour of the actual invention of the modern bicycle." The evidence of living witnesses of Macmillan's activities, he wrote, "is quite as strong and as good as that of Dalzell."[75]

Nevertheless, as we have seen, Johnston did not start his researches without already having strong evidence that Macmillan was a significant player in the "invention" stakes.

The first published accounts by Johnson himself came all in a rush, giving the impression that he was mounting something of a publicity campaign, which perhaps he was, both for himself and for a cause he believed in. *The Glasgow Evening Times* published a letter from Johnston on 4 Feb. 1892, *The Scottish Cyclist* another on 10 Feb. 1892 and *Bicycling News* another on 13 Feb. 1892. The text of all these articles was essentially the same. They asserted that Dalzell had copied from Macmillan, that witnesses could confirm this fact, that these witnesses agreed that Macmillan's velocipede had "an imitation horse's head on the front, and a breast-plate for the rider to lean on", and that Macmillan was "first in the field, before 1840, with his driving gear."

In these articles, Johnston showed that he was keenly aware of the pitfalls of collecting evidence in this difficult case. It is an awareness that it is important for us to bear in mind in assessing the value now of Johnston's researches:

Unquestionably, documentary or tangible evidence, when it does exist, is most satisfactory in establishing the year in which a particular event was said to have occured, and Dalzell's friends, although they produce certain documents, cannot fix on any particular date. About 1846 is the nearest they can name. In the absence of documentary evidence - we must not underestimate the high value of oral or hearsay evidence in this matter from people still living in the district who have seen M'Millan on his machine hundreds of times.[76]

We must agree with Johnston here that, as we have already seen, there were indeed many people who remembered Macmillan. We have already quoted from some of these eye-witness accounts.

Meanwhile, in this somewhat confusing and sudden profusion of correspondence, *Bicycling News* (which had published McCall's provocative letter on 6 Feb.) had sent its Glasgow reporter to interview McCall in Kilmarnock, where he was "entertained in a courteous manner", and learned that McCall himself had received correspondence from various witnesses. One of them reported that it "strikes me forcibly that Kirkpatrick McMillan made and used his gear-driven bicycle prior to the year 1845", and told the reporter that he had "bought his machine in 1851" when "the wheels were creaky, having been out of use for a long while." Another was John Findlater, who had been a blacksmith colleague of Macmillan's. McCall had forwarded the letters to *Bicycling News*, the contents of which led the reporter (or editor?) to conclude that "the very earliest date with which Dalzell seems to have been credited with riding his machine is 1845, and we here give proof of McMillan being in the field four or five years earlier than that."[77]

c. Eyewitnesses speak to James Johnston and the newspapers about Macmillan

The total documentation consists of an ongoing discussion between investigator Johnston, other writers responding to him, and editorial and reader input from *The Scottish Cyclist, Bicycling News*, the *Glasgow Evening Times* and *the Dumfries and Galloway Standard and Advertiser*. [The sources discussed in this section can be found in **Sources H, I, J and K**]

The Scottish Cyclist (10 Feb. 1892) talks of its "exhaustive inquiry" of "the ever-recurring topic" and headlines its article - "The First Rear-driven Bicycle. A Revival of the Question of Origin." Johnston was responding to the prevailing claims for Dalzell. Stimulated by these claims, he had "travelled many miles and conducted a deal of correspondence, in the pursuit of his object." *The Scottish Cyclist*'s editor, Nisbet, while still sceptical of his conclusions, which he thought "have generally fallen short of positive proof", spoke of "Mr. Johnston's assiduous and disinterested labours in the cause of truth", and was prepared to give credence to Johnston's claims, and began to print the results of his research. Johnston himself wrote that since reading the article concerning Dalzell, he had been "engaged in trying to solve the vexed question of the date and honour of the actual invention of the modern bicycle."[78]

Who did James Johnston actually talk to, or correspond with, and what did they say? The list of eye-witnesses includes an impressive number of people who were close physically and geographically to Kirkpatrick Macmillan. The following list has been assembled from all the four published sources:-

John Findlater [See Source I] – following a conversation with Johnston, Findlater made a written statement and sent it to him. Findlater was a blacksmith, a colleague of Macmillan's, and a neighbour of his in two different locations. He is an important witness. "Dalzell, you say, claims to have invented his gear about 1846," he wrote to Johnston, "but M'Millan had put it on many years before; I am positive, not later than 1839 or 1840.":

> What makes me so sure is that I have lived in this district all my days, working at my trade of blacksmith. I commenced my apprenticeship in 1826, and went to Mallowford smithy in 1833, on the Duke of Buccleuch's estate of Drumlanrig, and wrought there till 1840; then that smithy was abolished, and another new one erected by the Duke at Drumlanrig Mains, where I continued in his employment till 1848. I neighboured M'Millan at both these places, and think he came to Mallowford about 1835 or 1836.

Findlater stated that Macmillan either saw or got a copy of a hobby-horse from "Mr. Charters, a turner in wood by profession." Both Macmillan and Findlater made hobby horses on this model, but Macmillan "got tired of pushing it along by his feet on the road, and invented the driving gear, which consisted of two long rods fastened on the cranks of the axle of the rear wheel, the other end of the rods being fixed to stirrups which hung on each side of the fore part of the machine."

He was certain that Dalzell's velocipede was a copy of Macmillan's, and Dalzell may well have seen Macmillan's machine when he was passing through Lesmahagow on one of his Glasgow trips. He remembered Macmillan "riding his bicycle before the Dumfries and Glasgow coach all the way to Glasgow." He also remembered that "on coming to Glasgow he was surrounded by a perfect multitude of old and young folks anxious to get a look at him and his horse. In the excitement he unfortunately knocked down a child and got himself into trouble with the authorities, but on explaining that it was a pure accident he was set at liberty."

Macmillan was "a big, strong man, and a fearless rider." Findlater had "tried to mount his machine often, but could never get my feet into the stirrups in time to balance myself." He was sure that Dalzell "was not the first man to propel the velocipede by machinery." (*The Scottish Cyclist*, 17 Feb. 1892)

Findlater also sent a letter to *Bicycling News*, confirming that he had been a colleague of

Part One: The Origins of the Bicycle

Macmillan's at Mallyford and Drumlanrig. He had moved, he said, "from Burnhead to Alton on Whit-Sunday, 1844, and Mr. McMillan had cranks on his dandy-horse before that date." (*Bicycling News*, 20 Feb. 1892)

Thomas Haining [(See Source I] – had a conversation with Johnston in the train going from Dumfries to Thornhill, and then sent him a statement. Haining was a farmer near Thornhill, born in 1836, who remembered Macmillan's "wonderful wooden horse" from his school days. He confirmed that Macmillan was also known as "Pate", and that he "was a tall, strong, powerful man, and an expert rider." "To me it was a perfect wonder, but to the natives it was nothing new as 'Pate' and his dandy horse had pranced through the village long before I had gone to school….From memory his bicycle had a long wooden body, wheels of same material shod with iron, and he appeared to drive it with a pair of stirrups or pedals hanging from the fore part of the frame, which were connected by an iron rod to the cranks or axle of the hind wheel."

Haining further remembered "the imitation of a horse's head on the front of the velocipede", and "in my boyish wonder I was lost in admiration of the noble steed." He remembered Macmillan riding down the Main Street of Thornhill.

He also remembered that there was trouble in Glasgow: "I think if you make inquiries in the Glasgow Police Court you will find that McMillan and his horse were both fined and confined in the Glasgow Prison prior to 1846, for causing an obstruction on the streets." Haining was confident that Johnston "will have no difficulty in getting information from plenty of the old people in the neighbourhood of Thornhill, who will corroborate all that I have stated, and be able to give you earlier information than I can do". (*The Scottish Cyclist*, 17 Feb. 1892)

John Brown – responded to a letter from Johnston. He was a merchant in Penpont, very near Thornhill, and was about 60 in 1889 when he wrote. He had not the slightest hesitation in stating that Macmillan was " the first man to ride such a machine that I ever saw or heard tell of." As a boy, about 1839-40, "I remember of often running after Macmillan when on his machine in the company of a lot of my schoolmates, but found it impossible to outrun him, he got along so quickly." Brown was sure that Macmillan was long before Dalzell "as being the inventor of the first bicycle." Many old folks in his village would confirm what he was saying. (*The Scottish Cyclist*, 17 Feb. 1892)

Robert Hamilton – had a conversation with Johnston and then wrote him a letter. Hamilton was a miller from Dumfries, who from 1849 to 1859 was "intimate friends" with Macmillan while he was living at Keir Mill, near Penpont. Macmillan "made several dandy horses. I took a fancy to have one, too….and I got

M'Millan to put on the driving gear same as his machine. This was in the year 1849, but from what people said in the district when I went to it, he had had this gear for a number of years previously….I am positive M'Millan put on his driving-gear in or about 1840. The gear consisted of cranks attached to the axle of the rear wheel, fixed to levers which were fastened to stirrups or pedals dropped from the shoulders of the dandy horse. The front wheel was left free to steer with, and was the smallest of the two". (The Scottish Cyclist, 17 Feb. 1892)

Robert Macmillan - blacksmith, nephew of Kirkpatrick Macmillan, stated that his earliest memories of his uncle were "associated with the queer machine. It was made of wood, with the lesser wheel in front, over which was the figure of a horse's head….and was worked with cranks. His first production in that way may not have had cranks, but I never saw one without them." (*The Scottish Cyclist*, 17 Feb. 1892)

W. Thomson - of Blantyre, wrote Johnston several letters and confirmed that he saw Macmillan and his machine in Glasgow twice, in 1838 and in 1845, and "refers to the incident of M'Millan being interviewed by the police, and taken before one of the baillies for causing such a crowd on the streets….This is a traditional story in Penpont district, which is confirmed 47 years afterwards by this gentleman". "The beautiful carved head was the first thing that took my attention…I wish you to understand that the machine in 1845 was not new, neither was it his first trip to Glasgow on it." (*The Scottish Cyclist*, 10 Feb. and 17 Feb. 1892)

John Templeton - a native of Old Cumnock, wrote to the *Glasgow Evening Times*. "Previous to the year 1843", he remembered Macmillan arriving in Old Cumnock one evening, and calling "at the residence of his cousin, Mr. John M'Kinnell, the then parish school-master." In the morning, "M'Millan came out with his horse, and rode up and down the town to the great amusement of the crowds who ran after him. I saw him do what I have never seen another do since….standing on the saddle and guiding the front wheel with his hand, he came down what was then called M'Kinley's Brae at full speed." About that time, "several imitations of M'Millan's machine, with some improvements, were made in the engineering works of George M'Cartney, Cumnock, and for several years were in great vogue."[79]

Mrs. Elizabeth Bailey – after she had read Johnston's first letters in one of the Dumfries newspapers, Mrs. Bailey wrote to him that "when I was a little girl I sat many a time on Kirkpatrick Macmillan's shoulder holding on by his head while he drove his dandy-horse….. Macmillan was lodging with us at the time. That was in the years 1842-43." She also remembered the horse's head – "The head is correct – I can see it in my mind's eye as distinct as if it were before me." (*Bicycling News*, 5 March 1892)

William Fergusson – a nephew of Gavin Dalzell, wrote to Johnston that he had been staying with his uncle in 1846, and his uncle told him that he had seen a man the year before riding a velocipede down the Glasgow and Carlisle road. "He said this man was a blacksmith, from Thornhill, but he could not give me his name. Some years ago, when his son, J.B. Dalzell was writing about his father being the inventor of the velocipede, I wanted him to go to Thornhill and make search of the blacksmith his father told me of. I fear J.B.D. never took the trouble of going in search of the inventor, but wished it to be believed his father was the inventor of driving gear, viz., cranks and levers." After seeing Macmillan, Gavin Dalzell "had many a consultation with his friend John Leslie, the Lesmahagow blacksmith, with the result that they managed to make a copy of Macmillan's machine, with lever and crank driving." (*Bicycling News*, 19 March 1892)

A series of short mentions should also be noted:

Thomas Wright – stated that he was about 12 when he was Macmillan's nearest neighbour. "He had his first horse then; it had no driving gear…..It would be in 1838, or early in 1839, when he made his second horse….He made the gear himself. I was often at the smithy, and saw him working at it….I left the district at Martinmass, 1840….I think it probable his first trip to Glasgow would be in 1841…." (*Bicycling News*, 5 March 1892)

James Black, an oatmeal miller from Dumfries, who lived near Macmillan's Courthill smithy, confirmed that the "driving gear" was on Macmillan's velocipede "in 1843, and long before that".

Samuel Dalziel, another blacksmith at the Duke of Buccleuch's smithy, near Thornhill, wrote that Macmillan took the pattern of his dandy horse from one that belonged to Charteris. (*The Scottish Cyclist*, 17 Feb. 1892)

James Kennedy – who lived in New Cumnock, who was frightened by the sight of Macmillan riding into town late one night. He told the story to his shopmates, and they "made fun of him until they witnessed the unwonted spectacle of seeing Macmillan riding about the town next day. He (Macmillan) appears to have engaged in conversation with many of the residents from the fact that immediately after his visit a copy of his bicycle with levers and cranks was made at Macartney's Millwright and Engineering Works." (*Bicycling News*, 19 March 1892)

George Goldie – was the principle partner of Macartney's business referred to above. He remembered "distinctly Macmillan's visit to Old Cumnock prior to the Disruption in 1843, when he stayed with McKinnell, the schoolmaster, and then proceeded for Glasgow. Mr. Goldie is positive of the time, because McKinnell left the school when the Disruption took place." Mr. Goldie showed Johnston "a small copy of a horse's head, which belonged to the last bicycle made on Macmillan's principle at the shop. (*Bicycling News*, 19 March 1892)

Mr. D. Smith – Old Cumnock, an "Inspector of Poor (shoe-maker in his younger days)", "spoke confidently of seeing Macmillan and his horse before the Disruption of 1843. (*Bicycling News*, 19 March 1892)

Statements from relatives of Macmillan

To these many accounts should be added the testimonies of one of Macmillan's sisters, Mrs Isobella Marchbank (née Isobella Macmillan, in 1820) and her oldest daughter, Mrs Watret.

Their evidence is important not only because of who they were, but because the interviews with them were conducted in 1892 in Dumfries by a reporter from the *Dumfries and Galloway Standard and Advertiser* in response to the ongoing debate in the many newspapers, and were NOT generated by James Johnson.

Another of Macmillan's sisters, Mary Grierson Macmillan, spoke with 'Ben Jubal', who debated Johnston in the pages of the *Glasgow Evening Times*, but did not give evidence directly to Johnston.

Mrs Isobella Marchbank – Kirkpatrick's younger sister, by then Mrs Marchbank, had a vivid memory and appeared to be "a woman of marked intelligence and….readily complied with the request ….to state what she recollected of her brother's famous dandy-horse." He was, she told the reporter from the Dumfries and Galloway Standard and Advertiser, "a man of indomitable pluck; once he set himself to any complicated piece of work he persevered until he had successfully mastered it." Her first memory of the "dandy-horse" dated back 56 or 57 years (i.e., taken at face value, 1836 or 1837, a date mentioned by several other witnesses), but she was unable to say how this machine was propelled.

However, when she moved to Thornhill two or three years later after marrying George Marchbank, "she was frequently in the habit of seeing her brother ride through the town (Thornhill) on a 'dandy horse' of a more approved pattern....This machine she is quite positive was driven by means of gear attached to the back wheel with stirrups for the feet." She also remembered well his starting "on his memorable trip to Glasgow when he outdistanced the stage-coach, and the accounts he gave of his exploits are also even now quite fresh on her mind."

The report of what she told the reporter about the accident in the streets of Glasgow has been quoted in

Chapter 4a. This journey, Mrs Marchbank "distinctly remembers, was performed at the time one of her daughters, now 49 years of age, was still a child at the breast. And the occasion is further impressed upon her memory by the fact that it was about the time of the Disruption in 1843." But "though 1843 may be regarded as about the year in which the memorable trip was performed, the gear-driven machine and its rider had become quite familiar on the roads in the district for a considerable time previous." Also, a story repeated elsewhere, "the Duke of Buccleuch secured him to perform on the bicycle in the presence of a company of guests at Drumlanrig Castle," and "during the years he rode the bicycle he effected various improvements upon it."

Mrs Watret - The reporter from the Dumfries newspaper also spoke with Mrs Watret, Mrs Marchbank's oldest daughter, who "is able to corroborate her mother's statement on the most material points." She lived with her mother and uncle, Kirkpatrick. She had only a "faint recollection of "her uncle having another velocipede prior to the construction of the improved machine"….but, "regarding the gear-driven machine, however, she remembers quite clearly." She also gave a detailed account of the 1842 accident and arrest in Glasgow, which is also quoted in Chapter 4a.

The statements gleaned by the Dumfries reporter from Mrs Marchbank and Mrs Watret were "given with wonderful precision", and although they were interviewed "at different times and places, without, so far as our reporter is aware, any consultation on the subject during the interval, there is entire agreement on almost every essential detail. Their evidence, the newspaper concluded, "taken in conjunction with that of independent witnesses mentioned in Mr Johnston's correspondence, may, we think, be reasonably held to prove that three or four years prior to that in which there is any record of the existence of Dalzell of Lesmahagow's gear-driven velocipede (1846), Kirkpatrick M'Millan had not only applied driving gear to his 'dandy horse', but had become an expert rider."[80]

Mary Grierson Macmillan - Another of Macmillan's sisters, Mrs Mary Henderson (née Mary Grierson Macmillan, born 1819) informed "Ben Jubal", who engaged in an ongoing debate with James Johnston in the *Glasgow Evening Times* in February 1892, that "she remembers her brother making the dandy-horse in the smithy sometime about 1834. This was a bicycle without cranks. A few years later, he improved his machine by adding cranks." She remembers her brother making "his famous ride to Glasgow." She also told "Ben Jubal" that "her brother was certainly not long in adding cranks to his original dandy-horse, and that all was completed midway between 1830 and 1840. I saw the blacksmith myself frequently, and he always appeared to move about in an atmosphere of mechanical

thought and invention. He was only one member of a highly talented family."[81]

In addition, two letters published in *Bicycling News* give further eye-witness testimony:

James Geddes – wrote to Thomas McCall, and the letter was included in *Bicycling News*. He stated that it "strikes me forcibly that Kirkpatrick McMillan made and used his gear-driven bicycle prior to the year 1845. I bought his machine in 1851, and the wheels were creaky, having been out of use for a long while." He was "not aware if McMillan ever made another." Macmillan "went to Glasgow, and amused a crowd of students by cutting the 'figure eight' on the Green with his gear-driven bicycle, and came home before the coach." (*Bicycling News*, 20 Feb. 1892)

Andrew Macmillan Todd – wrote to *Bicycling News* that his uncle, William Nichol, of Drumlanrig Mains, "made the woodwork for Macmillan's machine, he (Macmillan) making the ironwork for my uncle necessary to convert his 'dandy-horse' into a rear-driver. My uncle's machine was still in good condition in 1880, when I used to ride it on Drumlanrig Castle Road…..My father used to frequently ride Macmillan's machine when a youngster, and he says that his shins are still marked by tumbles received from that refractory animal." (*Bicycling News*, 26 March 1892)

d. When were the 1842 newspaper accounts of the Glasgow accident first discovered?

It should be pointed out that several of these witnesses of Macmillan mention his accident in the crowded streets of Glasgow [Findlater, Haining, Thomson – "a traditional story", Mrs. Marchbank, Mrs. Watret], and one had suggested that Johnston "make inquiries in the Glasgow Police Court." But none had mentioned or quoted from the 1842 newspaper accounts discussed in Chapter 4a. Only the *Scottish American Journal* editorial article of Nov. 1883 had specifically mentioned "a statement made in a paragraph published in a newspaper widely circulated in the Upper Ward of Lanarkshire" (but not identified or dated) which had been assumed to be about Dalzell.

Why were the articles not used by Johnston's witnesses, and why was it unlikely that he could have used them to jog the memories of these people? Simply because, according to his own account of his research, Johnston had not yet found them.

So when were the 1842 newspaper accounts of the velocipede "accident" in the streets of Glasgow first discovered, and by whom? It was Johnston himself who found them later, although he does not say exactly how. In 1899, he wrote an article, published in *The Hub*, in which he again summarized his conclusions about Macmillan.[82] "I have written so much on the subject these last ten years (i.e., since 1889 – AR) that the subject matter is somewhat stale," he regrets. A Dumfresian living in Canada had written to him in 1892 saying that he had known Macmillan well and "remembered him performing a journey to Glasgow 'in the early forties' on a visit to three of his brothers resident there, and that a report of it appeared in a Glasgow paper, and was copied into a Dumfries one. I had heard this story often, and after eight years inquiry I was successful in tracing it, although at one time I had given up all hope of doing so".[83]

Johnston goes on to give the precise references in the *Glasgow Herald* and the *Dumfries Courier*, though oddly, he does not quote the full text of the 1842 articles here. Thus we do not know the exact year of discovery, but based on the fact that Johnston's interest in Macmillan appears to have begun in about 1889, we can conclude that Johnston discovered the 1842 reports in about 1897 ("after eight years inquiry" - AR).

If this is a correct interpretation of the "discovery" of the crucial 1842 documentation, then the memories of Johnston's informants could not have been "jogged" with it. What they told him, they pulled from the depths of their own memories, making it all the more remarkable that there was substantial agreement in so many of the details.

e. *The Scottish Cyclist* acknowledges "a satisfactory conclusion" and Dalzell's son capitulates to Johnston's Macmillan

A historical "conclusion" marked the end of this period of research in the 1890s which has defined perceptions of early bicycle history since then, and cemented in the public mind Macmillan's status as "inventor" of the bicycle.

In an article of 24 Feb. 1892, entitled "M'Millan's Claim Fully Established", the *Dumfries and Galloway Standard* was the first to summarize its conclusions. It decided that the evidence of Mrs Marchbank and Mrs Watret "taken in conjunction with that of independent witnesses mentioned in Mr. Johnston's correspondence, may, we think, be reasonably held to prove that 3 or 4 years prior to that in which there is any record of the existence of Dalzell of Lesmahagow's gear-driven velocipede (1846), Kirkpatrick M'Millan had not only applied driving gear to his "dandy horse," but had become an expert rider."

Bicycling News wrote on 19 March 1892 that Johnston "after an infinite amount of correspondence and research, has undoubtedly succeeded in proving that the first rear-driven, or gear-driven, bicycle was made by Kirkpatrick Macmillan some time between 1835 and 1840." The evidence of John Findlater, they thought, was especially convincing. And Nisbet, the editor of *The Scottish Cyclist*, also published with his own

evaluation of Johnston's research in March and April of 1892. On 23 March, *The Scottish Cyclist* published an editorial entitled "Macmillan v. Dalzell" and a summary article from Johnston, "The First Gear-driven Bicycle". Nisbet explained his reservations: Macmillan and his machine "were familiar to the several witnesses both before and after the gear was fitted", and "it will be admitted that to recall the exact date of transition from the ungeared to the geared condition is taxing the memory pretty severely." However, corroborative evidence although "hardly conclusive to the ultra-judicial mind," had "helped the witnesses to fix the dates."

A month later, on 27th April, *The Scottish Cyclist* printed another editorial, "Macmillan v. Dalzell - A Satisfactory Conclusion" and a further article by Johnston. "To Mr. Johnston chiefly belongs the great honour of having collected that evidence, and having demonstrated even to the satisfaction of the other side that Macmillan was before Dalzell….That he has been instrumental in fixing the honours upon Macmillan is his reward; but, added to that, the thanks of cycling historians and antiquarians are his proper due. His name will be forever associated with the elucidation of the evolution of the bicycle from the hobby-horse."

Johnston provided a trump card for his case when he succeeded in acquiring a written acknowledgement from J.B. Dalzell that indeed the documents he had collected proved that Macmillan had preceded Gavin Dalzell in fitting "driving-gear" to his velocipede. Johnston and J.B. Dalzell sat down together on 19th March and 16th April 1892 and compared notes "in the most friendly manner." They concluded that Johnston had pushed his research further, that "there are certainly points of similarity in the two machines, but the many points of dissimilarity confirm the theory of independent conception", with Macmillan preceding Dalzell.

Johnson's opinion was that "so far as we can ascertain, Mr. J.B. Dalzell, at the time he was engaged in establishing his father's claim to the first application of driving-gear to velocipedes, investigated all other known claims as thoroughly as seemed necessary, and no blame attaches to him that since then contrary evidence that finally assumed indisputable proprtions was gathered." He thought that the agreement "has been the means of reserving a certain modicum of honour to the memory of Gavin Dalzell." Finally, he wrote, "I cannot conclude without complimenting Mr. J.B. Dalzell on the gentlemanly and honourable way he has acted, his sole desire being, like myself, to get at the truth, and award honour to whom honour is due." [84]

Dalzell capitulated to Johnston in the following letter (**see Fig. 3**):

> Dear Mr. Johnston - As the result of the enquiries you have made into the question of the earlier inventor of the

Part One: The Origins of the Bicycle

bicycle or geared dandy horse, I have no hesitation in frankly admitting that you have proved that Kirkpatrick Macmillan constructed his one before my father constructed his. Yours very truly, J.B. Dalzell.[85]

About this 'resolution', the following points should be emphasized:

1. The failure of J.R. Nisbet, the editor of The Scottish Cyclist, to publish in full the documents that he, Johnson and J.B. Dalzell had in their possession, and to ensure that they were conserved for posterity, was a drastic mistake.

2. The criticism of Johnston's research - that he had a biased and chauvinistic agenda in proposing a Scottish "inventor" of the bicycle - should be countered by the understanding that Johnston's work on Macmillan was in fact directed at elevating one Scot, Macmillan, at the expense of another, Dalzell. Johnston was not proposing Macmillan in place of an English or a French candidate! I have also been at pains here to emphasize that Johnston did NOT instigate or collect much of the evidence, some of which was contributed unsolicited to the participating parties in the form of letters written to the newspapers involved, or independently conducted interviews.

3. Johnston's final comments show him as sitting on the fence in order to pacify the feuding parties who had been facing each other in Nisbet's office. Even though Macmillan was first, Johnston states, Dalzell did not copy from him, but their "conceptions were quite independent of each other" – an assertion not borne out by the evidence of the machines still in existence, or of the witnesses, who all testify to a climate of sharing and copying of ideas. It would have been more accurate for Johnston and Nisbet simply to have identified the historical reality - that the ideas about the earliest true bicycles were exchanged and shared, at a time when the concept of 'invention' was not given so much importance, and the makers were artisans applying their own individual craft skills and not thinking of the mass-production of their machines.

. . . .

Essential, crucial research into these early machines, documentation and individual memories of them did not subsequently progress much past 1892. Johnston's conclusions were allowed to stand. He had collected the information that was available to him, had interviewed many people, corresponded with others, sent voluminous reports to cycling and general newspapers. Many people had participated. There were no further challenges. If rival claimants in another part of Britain existed, there was no published documentation of them. If a French challenge to priority in this early period existed, it was not advanced. As Johnston himself wrote in 1899, "The French nation, some years ago, put up a statue to Michaux, as the inventor of the boneshaker of

the sixties, not knowing that such a man as Macmillan had ever lived."[86]

We are left, therefore with the extensive discussion in *Bicycling News, The Scottish Cyclist, the Dumfries and Galloway Standard and Advertiser* and the *Glasgow Evening Times* between 1888 and 1892 as a primary – even if not exclusive - source of information about Macmillan. William Brown's extended personal account in the *Dumfries and Galloway Standard* in 1895 (**see Sources L**) is a rare and tantalizing later witness account. James Johnston's 1899 accounts in *The Hub* (see Sources N) and *The Gallovidian* (**see Sources P**) do not add anything new to what he had already published by 1892. John Macmillan's memories, gleaned by J. Gordon Irving and published in 1940, add only a few new corroborative details.

Undoubtedly, the energy and curiosity of James Johnston and J.R.Nisbet was the driving force behind the publication of their research and their conclusions. "It may be asked what particular object or interest I have had in gathering information about Macmillan," wrote Johnston in 1899; "Simply for love of the sport, and as an old cyclist I was anxious to prove that to my native county of Dumfries belongs the honour of being the birthplace of the invention of the bicycle....If Kirkpatrick Macmillan did not invent the bicycle, then I wonder who did."[87] But this energy and curiosity do not explain the earlier information about Macmillan explored in Chapters 4 and 5 particularly the accounts published by the *Scottish American* (1883) and by 'A Native of Kier' in the *North British Daily Mail* (1884).

Johnson's historical perceptions, of the necessity for "first inventors", and that "invention" was possible to ascribe, were of course a product of his times. Our own, early 21st century, interpretation of the search for the origins of the bicycle can draw on wider historical perspectives.

Evidently the history of the "invention" of the bicycle in the 1830-1840s period is more appropriately understood as a process of the sharing of ideas between makers rather than the later concept of legal patents and lone-wolf innovators.

I have intentionally refrained from trying to pin precise dates to Macmillan's copying of the hobby-horse and his experiments with "driving-gear," preferring to let the ambiguities of the documentation remain unresolved. But the years between 1835 and 1845 define the parameters of my inquiry. Reading the accounts of eye-witnesses, some published by Johnston in *The Scottish Cyclist* and *Glasgow Evening Times*, and some offering their own evidence unsolicited, it is hard to see how this body of evidence could have been "cooked up" by Johnston feeding his informants information, or inviting them to agree with his pre-formed opinions of their activities. There is too thick a web of agreement about so much of the

The Origins of the Bicycle

Macmillan story. Even if the most sceptical stance towards Johnston's motivations and methods is proposed, then Thomas McCall and Mrs. Marchbank gave essentially the same information, and the 1842 newspaper account backs up any doubts that might be left in our minds by Johnston's witnesses.

In the end, it is, in my opinion, the sum total - the consistency - of all the documentation and the evidence, presented here as a chronological process, which is so persuasive and hard to reject, and necessitates a re-evaluation of the true role and historical significance of Kirkpatrick Macmillan.

Fig. 23 The Dalzell velocipede now in the collection of the Glasgow Museum of Transport, was photographed at the time of its acquisition. With it is either Dalzell's son, who presented it, or a museum curator. [Source: Glasgow Museum of Transport]

Fig. 24 The Dalzell machine (probably copied from Macmillan), as it now exists. [Source: Glasgow Museum of Transport]

7. The shadowy James Charteris (or Charters), early velocipede maker

In the oral testimony relating to Kirkpatrick Macmillan, the name of James Charteris (or Charters), a wood-turner from Dumfries, is mentioned several times. Not a leading player in the story, he nevertheless occupies a fascinating niche and helps to illuminate the elusive historical moment of transition from hobby-horse to crank-driven two-wheeled velocipede, arguably the moment of the "invention" of the bicycle.

Charteris was mentioned by John Findlater, of Carronbridge near Thornhill, and by Samuel Dalzell, who had both been blacksmiths at the Duke of Buccleuch's smithy near Thornhill, in letters they wrote to James Johnston which were published in *The Scottish Cyclist,* 17 Feb. 1892 and *Dumfries and Galloway Standard,* 24 Feb. 1892 (see **Sources E and J**). Findlater stated that he and Macmillan had been apprentices together on the estate at Drumlanrig. He remembered that it had been a hobby-horse, or "dandy horse," belonging to Charteris which had originally inspired Macmillan. According to Findlater, Macmillan had first seen the hobby-horse either in Thornhill, or in Dumfries. "It had no driving gear at all," he wrote, "he (Charteris) just propelled it by sitting legs astride and pushing it with his feet on the ground." Findlater claimed that Charteris' hobby-horse inspired Macmillan to make one for himself, and Findlater himself made another. But "McMillan got tired of pushing it along by his feet on the road, and invented the driving gear." Johnston also quoted Samuel Dalziel, blacksmith at the Duke of Buccleuch's smithy, at Drumlanrig Mains, as having written that Macmillan "took the pattern from one that belonged to Charters."[88]

Charteris' identity is more firmly sketched out in an article entitled "The Origin of the Cycle," published in the *Dumfries and Galloway Standard and Observer* in 1897, in which a Mr. David Johnston, a nephew of Charteris' (no relation of James Johnston), was interviewed.[89] Charteris, who had died in 1861 aged 75, had evidently by then acquired a reputation in Dumfries as connected with early bicycle history, because his name had "often been mentioned in connection with the first inception of the bicycle....It has been commonly stated and accepted that Mr Charteris was the maker of a bicycle of a very crude form." Charteris was a wood-turner, whose machinery was driven by water power. He also used water power to drive other kinds of machinery in his mill. He experimented with steam engines for himself and for other businesses in Dumfries, and he also experimented with electricity and was one of the founders of a Mechanics' Institute. He was, in short, an entrepreneur in power application.

According to this article, it had been " commonly stated and accepted that Charteris' machine was a simple hobby-horse or "dandy horse," which he bought in Glasgow or made himself. But, disagreeing with Findlater's account, David Johnston was sure that it included some kind of driving mechanism. Johnston could not remember "anything very tangible about the propelling power, but it was certainly not propelled by setting the feet on the ground. They were placed on pedals or stirrups just the same as in the modern bicycle....The bicycle had little light wooden wheels, built on the principle of a cart wheel, with a slight iron tire - just such a one as you would now hoop a cask with." Could Charters' machine thus have been an earlier version of the Macmillan-Dalzell design? From these reports, it seems possible.

More information on Charteris was uncovered by Bryce Craig in researching the life of John Gibson, an early 19th century Dumfries cabinetmaker.[90] Gibson made a "velocipede" in 1819, most likely, according to the fashion of the day, a typical hobby-horse, and an account book still in the possession of the Gibson business in the 1940s contained a complete accounting for this machine. Gibson received assistance from a "J. Charteris" in making the velocipede, and paid him 10s 6d, out of a total cost of £4 4s. So Charteris was definitely involved in velocipede making in 1819, when the hobby-horse was popular.

Bryce, the author of this article, gives further information about James Charteris: "In M'Dowall's Memorials of St.Michael's and in the obituary notices in the *Dumfries and Galloway Standard,* he is described as a turner and one of the founders of the Dumfries and Maxwelltown Mechanics' Institute. M'Dowell goes on: "Besides being an industrious and ingenious mechanic, Mr. Charteris devoted much time to scientific subjects, more especially electricity, in which he was an adept.'" Bryce quotes from a news item in the *Dumfries Weekly Journal* of 7 Sept. 1819, reporting in Dumfries "a most ingenious travelling machine which has lately been invented by Mr.James Stewart.... which for ease, safety and convenience far surpasses anything of the kind we have ever seen. It runs upon four iron wheels, the rider guiding it with a pole in the centre, and his feet being in stirrups, never touch the ground. The inventor has termed it The Waterloo Travelling Carriage."

These facts, of course, do not help us in any way in elucidating Macmillan's precise later role in early bicycle design. But they do reveal an important truth. Charteris was exactly the kind of progressive, skilled artisan-craftsman who experimented with velocipedes, as he experimented with other industrial processes, in this period. Like Macmillan, he had one foot in traditional crafts and the other in emerging industrial technologies. For an enterprising mechanic, the idea of the velocipede was part of the current of the times in Dumfries. As a velocipede builder, Macmillan's activities should not be seen as unique or as chronologically the earliest in the progression of velocipede experimentation, but rather as part of a design continuum. Others had worked and were working on the problem. Macmillan and Dalzell inherited from their predecessors the ideas with which they themselves would work in the 1830s and 1840s.

Charteris was an obscure wood-turner who springs to life from this documentation as an altogether plausible presence. He is a link in the chain of documented history. A lot of the evidence of bicycle pre-history has been destroyed – but, remarkably, a small detail like this about the probable source of Macmillan's inspiration can be plausibly documented and credibly recovered from history.

Fig. 25 A fanciful pre-bicycle, allegedly sketched in the 1830s was described as "rude and primitive in constuction" [Source: 'Velox', *Velocipedes, Bicycles and Tricycles* 1869]

Fig. 26 Two fanciful 'celeripedes' in action, illustrated in 1869, may have been actual one-off creations, variations on the theme of the hobby-horse. [Source: "J. F. B." *The Velocipede, Its past, Its Present and Its Future,* 1869]

8. Macmillan as mechanic and artisan; the progressive industrial and educational environment of south-west Scotland in the 1830s

In the period following the 1832 Reform Bill in Britain, a confident and idealistic idea was expressed that there was no form of employment and no working man who was incapable of making a contribution to science; all practical work had theoretical applications. In 1835, Henry Brougham, the founder of the Society for the Diffusion of Useful Knowledge (begun in 1826 in London) and the first Mechanics' Institutes, told the Manchester Mechanics' Institute members that "those men who are daily employed in handling tools, working amongst the very elements of mechanical science, or always using mixtures of chemicals drugs in a mechanical way, are amongst the very persons whose situation is the best adapted in the world for actually making discoveries and inventing improvements."[91] In other words, practical experience could bring its rewards.

In this exploration of Macmillan, the extraordinary development of industry, manufacturing and commerce in south-west Scotland in the early years of the 19th century cannot be over-exaggerated. Both heavy industry, coal, iron and steel and lighter manufacturing made the area one of Britain's industrial heartlands. The port of Glasgow was its import and export centre. Transportation improved as increased demand was made upon it. Roads were improved, the canals used to capacity, shipbuilding flourished. Most crucially, the first railways were opened in the mid-1820s.

Though there is no specific evidence connecting the Macmillan-style, treadle-and-crank-driven velocipede to other forms of machinery, its fundamental conception is extremely simple and in tune with an existing level of technology based on steam power, and machinery utilizing pistons, connecting rods and cranks. The Macmillan-style, two-wheel velocipede, if we agree to accept the approximate date of its appearance as about 1840, was certainly no extraordinary design breakthrough. On the contrary – it had an almost naïve folkishness in its design. That James Charteris, wood turner, was one of the founders of the Dumfries and Maxwelltown Mechanics' Institute in the 1820s, and that Kirkpatrick Macmillan, blacksmith, attended night school in Glasgow in about 1840, as well as working at the Vulcan Foundry, is evidence of the progressive educational and technological environment of south-west Scotland in the first part of the 19th century.

In 1796, Dr. John Anderson of Glasgow College had invited tradesmen and mechanics to a course in experimental physics. He was succeeded by Dr. George Birkbeck, who in 1800 gave a course of lectures on mechanical subjects "solely for persons engaged in the practical exercise of mechanical arts, men whose situation in early life had precluded the possibility of acquiring even the smallest proportion of scientific knowledge". These were the earliest institutes in Britain devoted specifically to the technical education of working-class people. The enthusiasm for Mechanics' Institutes which followed saw them spread quickly; Glasgow Institute was founded in 1823, Manchester, Aberdeen and Dundee in 1824 and Ayr, Carlisle, Dunbar, Dunfermline and Dumfries in 1825. Mr. Charteris, "a very ingenious mechanic, who started a series of lecturers on electricity", was the vice-president of the Dumfries institute.[92]

Timothy Claxton, a mechanic who in 1839 wrote a book called *Hints to Mechanics on Self Education and Mutual Instruction*, thought that every man "is the maker of his own fortune". When the distinguished academic Dr. Birkbeck began to lecture at Anderson College, Claxton wrote, he was "introduced to a direct intercourse with the artisans of Glasgow, many of whom exhibited a degree of eager curiosity which they had no means of gratifying, and a vigour of intellect for the cultivation of which no provision had been made". These intelligent mechanics were a kind of aristocracy of labour in Glasgow, who could hope to benefit from the profound technological and social changes which were taking place:

> Mechanics, it is well known, have a thousand opportunities of turning to good account, in the course of their every-day occupations, the knowledge they receive in these schools of science, either by suggesting new and improved methods of working, or devising and facilitating the execution of original and intricate designs....Their situation, in fact, is the best adapted in the world for actually making discoveries and inventing improvements".[93]

An editorial in the first issue of *The Glasgow Mechanics' Magazine and Annals of Philosophy* commented confidently that "the present age is no less remarkable for its wonderful improvements in the Arts and Sciences, than for the general diffusion of knowledge amongst all classes of the community". It was of the opinion that "no institutions have contributed more to the production of this heart-cheering spectacle than those which have been raised solely for the instruction of working mechanics. Glasgow, the second city of the Empire in wealth and population had the honour of giving birth to the first institution of this nature".[94] In 1836, the Glasgow Mechanics' Institution was still thriving. A newspaper reported at the beginning of November that it "was opened for the Session, and as usual on such an occasion, the Hall was completely crowded". During the summer "several hundreds of volumes have been added to the Library, and some extremely useful and valuable additions have been made to the apparatus".[95]

In England, there appears to have been general admiration of the comparatively high levels of education in Scotland. In 1831, a writer in The Spectator said that 1000 parochial schools "most miserably endowed, have rendered the two million of Scotch population the best-educated and best-behaved in the world", while in 1836, a committee of the General Assembly of the Church of Scotland referred to the fact that in rural parishes and lesser towns of the Lowlands all school-age children could read and most could write.[96]

Though there was poverty, unemployment and degradation among the urban industrial proletariat, there was also a hope of escape through education. A higher level of professional experience led to a better place on the social ladder. The industrial revolution was creating a larger middle class. And traditional craft activities, like wood-turning, blacksmithing or carriage-making, and the craftsmen who performed them, were being gradually transformed. A blacksmith, for instance, would of course shoe horses and make farm equipment, but he would increasingly repair mass-produced items, experiment with steam engines, electricity or water-power, or make velocipedes. Old distinctions were breaking down, and new kinds of occupations emerging.

Glasgow's manufacturing and commercial energy, and the presence of well-qualified, entrepreneurial mechanics, was typically demonstrated as the first wave of velocipede manufacturing hit the city in 1869. Though McCall evidently had hopes of succeeding speculatively with his Macmillan-style rear-driven velocipedes, realistically any serious interest in a rear-driven velocipede lost commercial credibility as the Paris, New York and London-proven front-wheel driven design swept it aside.

By the end of May 1869, a total of six velocipede makers and sellers were advertising their products in the *Glasgow Daily Herald*, and several velocipede riding halls were open for business where the public could rent a machine and learn to ride, and even watch the "French lady on a Velocipede". Anderson Bros, 93 Stockwell Street, were "Manufacturing Velocipedes of all Kinds and Sizes, on the Newest and most Improved Principles.... Gentlemen's Clubs and the Trade supplied".[97] Wylie and Lochhead, 45 Buchanan Street, were also in business, "having some time since procured from Paris some of the most approved of the velocipedes in use there, as Patterns, and having since, aided by the best mechanical skill, busied themselves in Improving upon those Patterns, they have now the pleasure of announcing that they are in a position to supply Velocipedes greatly Improved in Strength and Accuracy of Adjustment, and consequently of Solid, Smooth, and Steady Action".[98]

The language of commercial production and advertising was a striking contrast to the world of the rural blacksmith, with his hand-to-hand and mouth-to-mouth transference of ideas and skills.

The first front-wheel-driven bicycles were quickly recognized as having an athletic and sporting potential, which was not mentioned as an objective or an interest in the earlier Macmillan/Dalzell developments. The Lancet commented that the velocipede movement had:

> taken on a remarkable development and in France and America especially velocipedes have become an established institution....We have lately had an opportunity of examining velocipedes and seeing them in use. Our attention was especially directed to the character of the muscular exercise....the mode of locomotion promised a very agreeable method of taking useful and healthful exercise."[99]

By July, there were velocipede races at the Kirkintilloch Grand Athletic Games and a "Grand Tilting Tournament, Flat Races, Velocipede Races and National Games" at Balfron.[100]

The need to sell a manufactured product on the retail market and to publicize commercial entertainment created specific, detailed documentation such as newspaper advertisements and company catalogues upon which the historian can rely. Races are soon reported in the papers, and a new sport begun. At that moment, we have moved from a world of individual craft technology and "hearsay" memory of it into a very different world of small-scale industrial mass-production.

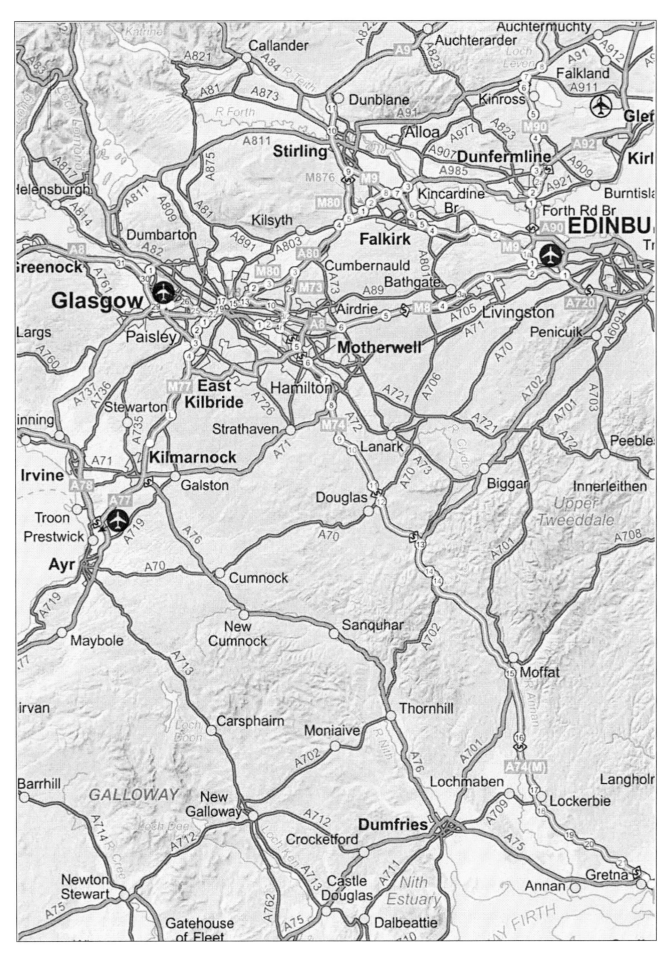

Fig. 27 Map of south-west Scotland, to show the geographical relationship between Thornhill, Glasgow and Dumfries.

9. Other claimants: the case of Alexandre Lefebvre

There is a machine in the collection of the San Jose Historical Museum, San Jose, California, which bears many striking resemblances to the Macmillan/Dalzell/McCall-style machines which are the object of this inquiry. It is a fascinating machine, which raises the question as to whether south-west Scotland was unique in pursuing the idea of a balanced, continuously-driven bicycle in the 1840s.

Fig. 28 The Lefebvre velocipede, now in the San Jose Museum, California. [Source: Andrew Ritchie]

a. Alexandre Lefebvre, 1808-1888: the documented facts

The essential, documented biographical facts are as follows. Alexandre Lefebvre was born in Paris on 10 April, 1808, the son of Louis Antoine Lefebvre and Marguerite Besançon.[101] He married Barbare (or Barbe) Daniels, and in Saint Denis they produced seven children, including Denise (b. 9 July 1832), Julie (b. 9 Nov. 1934, died 1841), Céline (b. 15 Nov. 1836), Antoine (b. 17 Jan. 1841), a second Julie (b. 14 Dec. 1842), Estelle (b. 2 Nov. 1845) and Emile (b. 4 Sept. 1850). On the birth certificates of his children, Alexandre Lefebvre is called either "ouvrier" (worker), "ouvrier serrurier" (worker and locksmith), "mécanicien" (mechanic) or "serrurier mécanicien" (locksmith and mechanic). During this time he lived successively at "rue de Saulges", "rue des Fontaines", and "rue de la Fromagerie". When he left France, Lefebvre left behind some of his adult children, and in 1861 and 1863, Céline gave birth to daughters, and in 1867 Antoine ("ouvrier mécanicien") married Constance Bainville.[102] Lefebvre, according to family accounts, like many other immigrants prior to the completion of the trans-continental railroad, came around the Horn to California with his wife and at least one daughter, Estelle, and may have had the intention of going to the California gold mines.

In San Francisco, Lefebvre appeared in city directories from 1864 until 1879, where his occupation was listed variously as "mechanic", "machinist", "locksmith" and in 1879 as "machinist, blacksmith and locksmith". He lived variously at 608, 720 and 722 Lombard St and afterwards in 1875 at Montgomery Avenue. The presence of "Estelle Lefevre (widow), California Laundry", on the same block of Lombard Street in 1863 may be significant in locating Alexandre there: could she have been his sister? Emile Cardinet is listed as a neighbor on the "north side Lombard" in 1862, with "fish" as his occupation, and subsequently married Estelle Lefebvre, Alexandre's daughter.

Of Lefebvre's velocipede-building activities in San Francisco, we have only the information apparently given by Estelle Cardinet to a reporter from the *Sacramento Evening Bee* in 1900, that "after his arrival in San Francisco, Lefebre (sic) made a number of velocipedes for residents of that city, whose names Mrs. Cardinet is unable to recall, excepting that one of them was a Mr. Huck, of the firm of Huck and Lamb".[103] In this instance, we again confront the problem of whether we should rely on this witness's memory and truthfulness. San Francisco went through a substantial boneshaker "craze" in 1869, but there is no more information available at present about the design, date or quantity of Lefebvre's San Francisco velocipedes. Whether his San Francisco machines were of the rear-wheel, treadle-driven design or the front-wheel driven design is not known.[104]

Lefebvre's death certificate shows that he died on 27 August 1888 at 2022, Central Avenue, in the city of Alameda, California, of "apoplexia". It gives his occupation as "locksmith" and notes that he had been in the United States "28 years" and had been resident in Alameda for 8 years. He was buried in St. Mary's Cemetery, Oakland on 30 August 1888.[105]

In 1896, Estelle requested proof of the authenticity of a velocipede which she still owned, and received a response from the Mayor of Saint-Denis and an affadavit from Ernest Lapierre, who claimed that he had worked for Lefebvre there, and had indeed been termed a "foreman mechanic" in a document of 1867.[106] Lapierre testified that a Lefebvre velocipede had existed as early as 1843. Probably, this interest in the Lefebvre machine was stimulated by the 1896 bicycle boom, then very much in the news.

Estelle Cardinet lived in Alameda (1880-88), then in Santa Rosa (1896), in Sacramento (1900) and lastly in Hayward, where she died. In 1900, she exhibited the velocipede in Sacramento at the Street Fair and Trades Carnival (see article below from *Sacramento Bee*),

Fig. 29 Estelle Cardinet photographed in 1933 with her father's velocipede. [Source: *Oakland Tribune*]

which suggests that she was still aware of the historical importance of her father's machine and interested in publicizing it. In 1933, the year before she died, she was again photographed with her father's velocipede, and the photograph was published in several newspapers. To one newspaper she declared "that the cycle is the original first wheel built by her father".[107] Estelle Cardinet (née Lefebvre) died in Hayward, California on 19 April 1934 at the age of 88, when it was noted that she had been in the United States "73 years", (that is, since 1860/61). She, too, was buried in St. Mary's Cemetery, Oakland.[108] Other than the four documents discussed below, no further primary documentation of Lefebvre's velocipede-building activities has been uncovered to date.

These are the facts of Lefebvre's life, as far as they can be documented at present.

b. The San Jose Museum and the Lefebvre velocipede

After Alexander Lefebvre's death in 1888, the San Jose Museum's velocipede became the property of Estelle Cardinet (née Lefebvre). On her death in 1934, it was passed on to her daughter Mathilde Anderson (née Cardinet), whose son Albert Anderson presented it to the San Jose Museum in 1958. There is thus a documented provenance for the velocipede, which stayed within the family until it passed to a public collection, and has therefore not been restored or otherwise altered, except for clumsy repairs to saddle, handlebars and perhaps to pedals.

The San Jose Museum has not, to date, been particularly interested in further research into the Lefebvre velocipede. Museum acquisition papers indicate the presence of what is described as a "French passport" when the machine was presented, but despite my repeated requests dating back to the late 1970s to search for this "passport", which could be very revealing, it has so far not been found or produced. As far as I know, no new documentation has been uncovered since I originally researched the velocipede in 1975 and published an article about it.[109]

Three documents in the possession of the San Jose Museum gives us the following information. In 1896, Estelle Cardinet wrote to France requesting evidence of the date and authenticity of the velocipede which she then had in her possession, evidently with some particular purpose in mind. The result was a letter from "J. Houdebert, Employee in the Secretary's Office of the Town Hall of St. Denis", enclosing an affadavit and a sketch of the velocipede drawn by Ernest Lapierre, apparently from his memory of it, with parts labelled and identified. That Lapierre was intimately acquainted with the Lefebvre family, and a person with considerable technical expertise, is indicated by his presence as a witness at the marriage of Antoine Lefebvre in 1867, where "Ernest Léopold Lapierre" was described as "Contre maître mécanicien" (foreman mechanic or overseer).[110] Although there are significant differences between the Lapierre sketch and the San Jose Museum's machine, particularly in the details of the drive mechanism, there would surely be little argument with the assertion that the similarities are such as to confirm that a very similar machine is involved.[111]

I am printing here my translation from French of these three documents. The originals are owned by Jim Cardoza, a family descebdant , in San Jose, California. The Museum's copies, from which my xerox copies were made, have a stamp on them saying that they were made by the "Electric Blue Print and Photo Co., 1214, Webster St, Oakland" (California).

b.-1. Text of letter from J. Houdebert to Estelle Cardinet[112]

Department of Seine
Town of Saint-Denis
Secretary's Office
4 October 1896

The Origins of the Bicycle

Madam,

I am enclosing here the certificate which you asked for in your letter of 7 October last, and a plan which has been prepared by Monsieur Lapierre. These two documents are intended to establish the authenticity of the Bicycle of the late M. Lefebvre, our fellow countryman, which is in your possession.

I hope, Madam, that these documents will fulfill adequately the purpose for which you require them, and would like to assure you of my very best wishes.

J. Houdebert – Employee in the Secretary's office of the Town Hall of St. Denis

N.B. It is upon the authority of the above-named person that the stamped Affadavit has been provided.

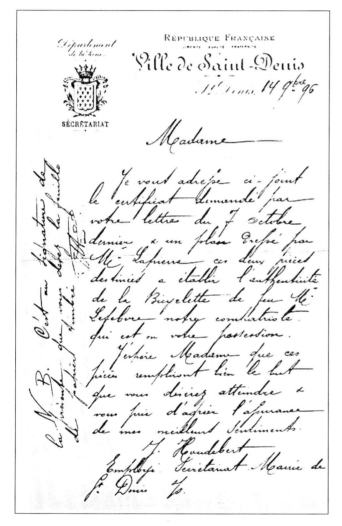

Fig. 30 Text of Houdebert's letter to Estelle Cardinet, 1896. [Source: San Jose Historical Museum]

b.-2. Text of the Lapierre Affadavit[113]

The Mayor of the Town of Saint-Denis hereby officially acknowledges the statement made by Monsieur Ernest Lapierre, 67 years of age, mechanic, living in Saint-Denis at 67, rue de la République, in response to a request from Madam Estelle Cardinet, née Lefebvre, living at the present time at 28, College Avenue, Santa Rosa,

California, which verifies that the bicycle which she has in her possession, and of which a design [or pattern – AR] is enclosed, was indeed made by her father Monsieur Alexandre Lefebvre.

Monsieur Lapierre certifies –

- Firstly, that in 1843, when he was apprenticed to Monsieur Lefebvre, who was in business as a mechanic [or engineer – AR] on the rue des Fontaines (today known as rue Marguerite Pinton,) the latter possessed the bicycle mentioned above, which was made with his own hands.

- Second, that he knows that Monsieur Lefebvre made many trips on the machine, one of which he remembers especially well was from Saint-Denis to Havre.

This document has been drawn up at the request of Madame Estelle Cardinet, née Lefebvre, in order to establish the authenticity of the said machine.

Signed in St. Denis, 9 November 1896

The Mayor

[Also signed by "The Declarant – E. Lapierre, designer and mechanic" ("Dessinateur Mécanicien") and stamped with official seals]

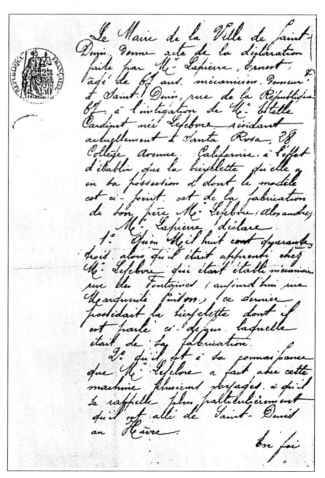

Fig. 31 Text of Lapierre affadavit, 1896. [Source: San Jose Historical Museum]

b.-3. Sketch by Lapierre of the Lefebvre velocipede.

The sketch by Lapierre, on a separate sheet of paper, is headed, "Sketch [or outline - AR] of a specimen of the Lefebre Velocipede, St. Denis, 1st Novembre 1896, E. Lapierre, 67, rue de la Republique, St. Denis, Seine, France" ("Lefebre" here is spelled with an acute accent!). The sketch is numbered and a "Legend" describes the various parts as follows:

A. Crank of the back wheel – right side

A'. Rod connecting the crank A to the joint B

B. Joint which connects the rod A' to the pedal E

C. Crank of the back wheel – left side

C' Rod connecting the crank C to arm D

D. Joint which connects the rod C' to the pedal F

E. Pedal mounted on the joint G, right side

F. Pedal mounted on the joint H, left side

G. Arm fixed to the axle N, right side

H. Arm fixed to the axle N, left side

J. The body of the velocipede in wood

K. Saddle with coiled spring

L. T-shaped handlebar in wood

M. Metal framework carrying the axle bearings of the back wheel which carry the cranks A and C, and covered with waxed cloth just like the part M'

M'. Framework supporting the joints B and D and pedals E and F

N. Axle for arms B - D

O. Forks for the front wheel and the handlebars

Explanation of the workings; sitting on the saddle K, with the two feet on the pedals E-F and the hands on the handlebars, movement is achieved by pressing down on one of the pedals, pedal E for example, which once arrived at the bottom of its stroke has turned crank A through half a circle, that is from point P to point Q, just as crank C has moved in the opposite direction, lifting the arm H up to point B again, and the pedal F up to its highest point. This pedal is pressed and the revolution is complete when it arrives at the bottom of its stroke, and thus the drive is achieved.

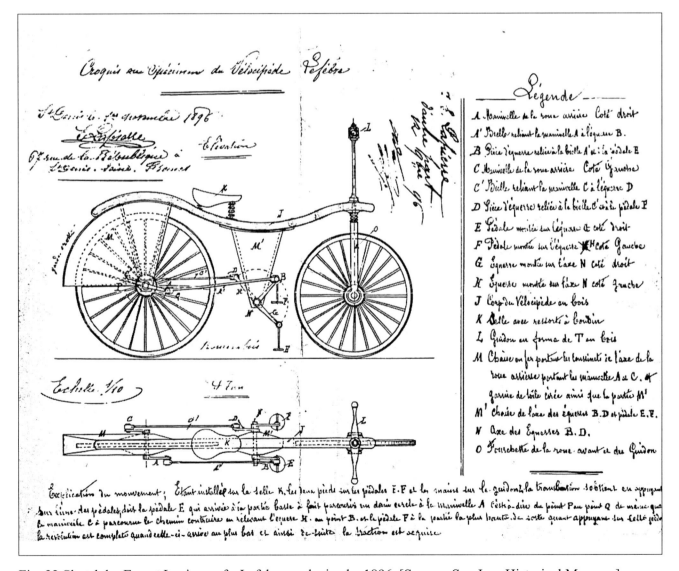

Fig. 32 Sketch by Ernest Lapierre of a Lefebvre velocipede, 1896. [Source: San Jose Historical Museum]

c. Article from *Sacramento Evening Bee,* 1900[114]

One further document is worth quoting in full. The *Sacramento Evening Bee*, 2 May 1900 printed an article headlined "The First Pedal Velocipede That Was Ever Made Is Now on Exhibition in the Street Fair". The article appeared four years after Estelle Cardinet's inquiry to Saint Denis and the responses to it from France, and it is suggested that Estelle Cardinet may have exhibited the machine more than once:

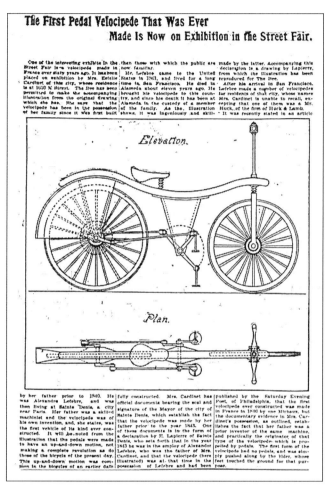

Fig. 33 News item concerning the Lefebvre velocipede. [Source: *Sacramento Evening Bee,* 2 May 1900]

One of the interesting exhibits in the Street Fair is a velocipede made in France over sixty years ago. It has been placed on exhibition by Mrs. Estelle Cardinet of this city, whose residence is at 1610 K Street. The Bee has been permitted to make the accompanying illustration from the original drawing which she has [i.e., the drawing by Lapierre just sent from France, interpreted as "an original drawing" – AR]. She says that the velocipede has been in the possession of her family since it was first built by her father prior to 1840. He was Alexandre Lefebre [sic], and was then living in Sainte Denis [sic], a city near Paris. Her father was a skilled machinist and the velocipede was of his own invention, and she states, was the first vehicle of its kind ever constructed. It will be noted from the illustration that the pedals were made to have an up-and-down motion, not making a complete revolution as

do those of a bicycle of the present day. This up-and-down motion was common in the bicycles of an earlier date than those with which the public are now familiar.

Mr. Lefebre came to the United States in 1861, and lived for a long time in San Francisco. He died in Alameda about eleven years ago. He brought his velocipede to this country, and since his death it has been at Alameda in the custody of a member of the family. As the illustration shows, it was ingeniously and skillfully constructed. Mrs. Cardinet has official documents bearing the seal and signature of the Mayor of the city of Sainte Denis, which establish the fact that the velocipede was made by her father prior to the year 1843. One of these documents is in the form of a declaration by E. Lapierre of Sainte Denis, who sets forth that in the year 1843 he was in the employ of Alexandre Lefebre, who was the father of Mrs. Cardinet, and that the velocipede (here illustrated) was at that time in the possession of Lefebre and had been made by the latter. Accompanying this declaration is a drawing by Lapierre, from which the illustration has been reproduced for The Bee.

After his arrival in San Francisco, Lefebre made a number of velocipedes for residents of that city, whose names Mrs. Cardinet is unable to recall, excepting that one of them was a Mr. Huck, of the firm of Huck and Lamb.

It was recently stated in an article published by the Saturday Evening Post, of Philadelphia, that the first velocipede ever constructed was made in France in 1846 by one Michaux, but the documentary evidence in Mrs. Cardinet's possession, as outlined, establishes the fact that her father was a prior inventor of the same machine, and practically the originator of that type of the velocipede which is propelled by pedals. The first form of the velocipede had no pedals, and was simply pushed along by the rider, whose feet touched the ground for that purpose.

It is interesting to see the earliest date claimed here in 1900 by Estelle Cardinet for her father's velocipede being pushed backwards to "prior to 1840", but the date is still very close to Lapierre's chosen date. This article, written by a literate journalist for an important California newspaper, contains Estelle Cardinet's persuasive oral testimony. She says "the velocipede has been in the possession of her family since it was first built by her father", it was "of his own invention" and "the first vehicle of its kind ever constructed". Interestingly, the Bee reporter appears to have accepted the suggestion of the Lapierre affadavit, that more than one machine probably existed, but one idea - "The documentary evidence in Mrs. Cardinet's possession, as outlined, establishes the fact that her father was a prior inventor of the same machine, and practically the originator of that type of the velocipede which is propelled by pedals".

d. The search for origins and "inventors" of the bicycle in the 1890s

In understanding the background to this 1896 documentation, Estelle Cardinet's request to Saint-Denis for authentication of her father's velocipede has to be seen in the context of the wider search for the origins of the bicycle during the bicycle "boom" of the 1890s.

In the early 1890s, Scottish researcher and journalist James Johnston conducted and published his inquiries into the Macmillan velocipede, concluding that the blacksmith was, in effect, the "inventor" of the bicycle.[115] In France, in 1893-94, an extended debate was conducted into the role of Pierre and Ernest Michaux as "inventors" of the front-wheel driven bicycle in the 1860s, and discussion in the press focused on the creation of a memorial to them in Bar-le-Duc, which was eventually opened with much fanfare in September 1894. To celebrate the occasion, a race from Paris to Bar-le-Duc was organized by the town and numerous other races held there. Another monument recognizing Michaux was erected in Paris in 1896, on the occasion of the first Automobile and Cycle Show.[116] It is evident from both these "campaigns" that the search for precedence was strongly linked to national pride and chauvinistic aspirations.

It appears likely that Estelle Cardinet would have been aware of this ongoing debate, and the erection of the Michaux memorial in Bar-le-Duc. Probably she had received some of the newspaper reports from relatives in France, which inspired her to pursue the possibility of including her own father among the pioneers of the bicycle when she wrote to Saint-Denis in 1896. This suggestion neither strengthens nor weakens the essential facts of the Lapierre affadavit, but serves to set it in the context of a wider late 19th century search for the origins of the bicycle. We do not know whether Estelle Cardinet had a wider agenda or not, or whether her research into her father's machine received any further publicity in France; perhaps the exhibition of her father's machine was one of her immediate objectives.

Questions and objections can of course be raised as to the conclusions which can be drawn from the Lapierre affadavit and sketch. We have only Lapierre's memory and his word for the date of 1843 for the existence of a Lefebvre velocipede, and we may legitimately raise the question as to whether Estelle Cardinet might have prompted him for an early date. But there is no inherent reason, either, to distrust him because he gives the velocipede an early date. As stated above, Lapierre was 67 in 1896 and therefore had been 14 in 1843, old enough to have an accurate memory of events, and in the 1867 description of him as "contre mâitre mécanicien" (foreman mechanic, or overseer), we have evidence, certainly, that he was a well-qualified professional. Why Lapierre would have had a good reason intentionally to lie or "reconstruct" his memory

is not immediately obvious. National chauvinism as a motivating factor can be advanced, but there is no hint in the Saint-Denis correspondence that Estelle Cardinet and Lapierre were seeking intentionally to edge out Michaux and prove precedence for Lefebvre.

e. Critical evaluation of the Lefebvre evidence

The contents of the Lapierre affadavit, as is often the way with historical documents, confirms essential facts as well as raising crucial questions. Lapierre's memory may not have been accurate, but the obvious differences between the existing Lefebvre machine and the Lapierre sketch also strongly suggest that we may be dealing here with more than one machine, and that the Museum's machine may have been made in California according to a previous, French prototype design. On the other hand, the striking similarities between the two differing versions demonstrate that in 1896 Lapierre still had an accurate enough memory of the essential characteristics of the machine that he had had contact with in France. Lapierre would have been 14 in 1843, old enough, certainly, to have had a clear memory of it. It is logical to assume that the latest date at which he would have had contact with a Lefebvre machine would have been at the moment of Lefebvre's departure for America in 1860-61. Yet 35 years later, he remembered it well, if not absolutely accurately.

The way forward to a more comprehensive understanding and dating of this important machine should consist of –

1) further research in the Saint-Denis archives, to see what more can be learned about Lefebvre before he left France for California,

2) further study of mid-19th century French carriage-building to ascertain how the details of the Lefebvre machine correspond or not stylistically with other light-wheeled vehicles of the period, and –

3) materials analysis of the metal, wood and paintwork of the velocipede to try to determine its place of manufacture.[117]

The stakes are significant historically. The machine has the stamp of age and authenticity about it, and a well-documented provenance. It may be that the account attested to by Ernest Lapierre in his affadavit is correct and the velocipede was indeed made in France by Lefebvre, or at least one of several that he made in France, possibly as early as 1843, before he left for the United States in 1860 or1861. Or it may be that Lefebvre made this particular machine in San Francisco after 1861, one of a group he made in California to the basic design of his earlier French models. If Lapierre's date of 1843 is correct, this would make the San Jose specimen the earliest reliably

The Origins of the Bicycle

documented surviving "bicycle." Even if one is not persuaded by Lapierre's 1843 date, and assumes an 1861 date or soon after, the machine is certainly on a par of importance with those of the Macmillan copies by Gavin Dalzell (Glasow Museum) and Thomas McCall (Science Museum), and can still be dated reliably to the pre-boneshaker period, with strong evidence of the existence of earlier models of a very similar design. Lapierre's date of 1843 can legitimately be questioned, but as documented, written evidence it cannot simply be dismissed. Even if Lapierre was mistaken in putting forward the 1843 date, or intentionally pushed it further back, he must certainly have known the machine when Lefebvre left for California in 1860/61, which still marks it as a very early, continuously-driven two-wheeled velocipede. This is the logic of the historical situation.

The design similarities between Lefebvre, Macmillan (via McCall's copies) and Dalzell strengthen the case for all of them to be put into the 1840s period, that is, firmly pre-boneshaker (late 1860s), and for the existence therefore of an early "school" of bicycle-like, crank-driven, balanced velocipedes, machines which answer the basic definition of a "bicycle," that it be a two-wheeled machine which is balanced and steered and driven continuously forward with the legs by means of a propulsion system.

Further, although I do not feel that the machine is in any immediate danger, alteration or "restoration" by unqualified persons is always a possibility which has to be guarded against. The history of very early surviving machines indicates that the people most likely to damage them as historical evidence are precisely those who have institutional care of them. Hopefully, the anti-restoration philosophy is firmly in place at the San Jose Museum, and the Lefebvre velocipede has not yet yielded all of its secrets. The machine is in substantially original condition, and a detailed metallurgical, chemical and stylistic analysis of it could still be carried out, and hopefully establish its date and its "nationality."

10. Conclusions

a. A review of the evidence

This untidy collection of historical evidence does not yield its true story very easily. Heavily restored surviving machines, correspondence published in various late-19th century newspapers, interviews conducted by a questionably objective researcher, line drawings and old photographs – all of these provide the historian with a fascinating exercise in historiography. But can they provide any definitive answers?

On the basis of this material, can we conclude that there is enough evidence to give Macmillan the title "inventor" of the bicycle, and confirm the truth of the popular myth of the lone inventor already in widespread circulation? Pretty obviously, we cannot. No documents attest to his having made a particular machine at a certain date. There are no patents or dated receipts for handiwork performed. But on the other hand, if we accept that the question about the first bicycles ought not to be phrased in terms of the search for a lone inventor, then does the evidence explored here at least provide an accurate and persuasive overview of the earliest makers of various "bicycles" (defined here as human-powered machines on two wheels, capable of being effectively balanced and steered while being driven forward continuously with the legs), who shared their ideas, one of whom was Macmillan? I think it does.

I began this research influenced by the scepticism of some of my colleagues who have also studied the evidence. They have emphasized the difficulties of the documentation of Macmillan, and have tended recently to discredit the story of the historical Macmillan. The alleged Macmillan-type design led nowhere, and is therefore irrelevant, they say. Lefebvre, too, has been minimized; his machine was built later, after he came to San Francisco, it is suggested. The first true bicycles were manufactured in the late 1860s, it is said. What happened before that is only of marginal significance. One bicycle historian told me: "the best cure for the Macmillan disease is to ignore it and hope that it will go away…it just encourages the building of replicas".[118]

Are my colleagues justified in thinking that further exploration of the topic is unproductive? I believe they are mistaken and that a re-reading of the evidence is badly needed, and has been necessary here.

As my own goal, I was determined to stay rigorously embedded in the source material, to try to make sense of it. I tried to carry out a systematic analysis of the documentation, and to be open to the complexity of the historical evidence and to incorporate the strength of the memories of participants and eye-witnesses. I paid particular attention to how evidence given to the newspapers was generated – was it asked for, or was it offered unsolicited? Where others have said, "These witnesses were probably forgetting, exaggerating, mis-remembering or lying, and are therefore not credible," I preferred to look for consistency in the scattered accounts and ask, "Why would these witnesses have lied about what they remembered? and "Does this witness corroborate what other witnesses say?" In particular, I tested the evidence collected by James Johnston against evidence from other sources. I decided that there are no blatant inconsistencies in the essential facts of the Macmillan story.

I hope this book will help to provide answers to the following questions: How should we evaluate the significance and credibility of the source material? How should we approach and evaluate detailed research conducted more than a century ago by an allegedly somewhat partial researcher? Ultimately, what criteria should we use in weighing the scarcity of conclusive documentation (dated documents, machines of certain provenance, etc) against a considerable weight of other historical evidence, particularly oral testimony?

Macmillan's popular status as "inventor of the bicycle" has been rightly questioned. The absence of conclusive proof has not been acknowledged in the many popular accounts. The perplexing 1842 news items can still not be proved to be a description of Kirkpatrick Macmillan, although I think there is a very strong probability that they do describe him or possibly one of his brothers. But other evidence, from the early 1880s, and that produced by the 1889-92 inquiry, has been under-utilized in research into Macmillan, and these accounts - more than 100 years closer to the events than we are today – must be taken seriously, and I hope have been sensibly analysed here.

A total of nearly thirty named people gave oral and written testimony of having known or seen Macmillan with his 'horse' (see Section B, "Witnesses" below). They included his immediate family, fellow blacksmiths, neighbours and others who knew him personally or knew of him in some way. Some of these reports were generated simply by geographical proximity – the people who made them lived in the towns through which Macmillan passed on his rides. These memories were published on many separate occasions in many different publications. And they are not invalidated by the alleged partisan intentions of Johnston – because the testimony elicited by Johnson overlaps with and is confirmed by testimony submitted voluntarily to newspapers. The testimony collected before Johnston came on the scene is consistent with what he collected. Also, considering that the main criticism of Johnston is of having pushed a pro-Scottish "invention" agenda, it is interesting that in

The Origins of the Bicycle

the oral testimonies themselves there is never a mention of Macmillan's velocipede as a Scottish invention, or any kind of chauvinistic claim in the interviews themselves. Their evidence is very clear and straightforward – they simply report what they knew, saw or remembered.

The sum total of the historical evidence shows that there was an energetic interest in velocipede design and manufacture in England and Scotland between the 1830s and 1869, when the bicycle industry really began. Unpatented designs circulated among "mechanics" and were shared and developed. They can be found in the pages of the *Mechanics' Magazine* and *The English Mechanic,* where mutual support and the practice of sharing technical information was much in evidence. One theme which appears prominently in the eye-witness accounts published here is the sharing and copying of Macmillan-style velocipedes from person to person. This, I believe, is what connects Charteris, Macmillan, Dalzell and Thomas McCall, each copying from and perhaps improving on the work of their predecesors.

I have suggested here that the activities of Macmillan, Dalzell and McCall were typical of this wider velocipeding trend, with the crucial difference that they were one group which had begun to understand and explore the possibilities of balancing and driving on two wheels, rather than driving unbalanced on three or four. I do not accept the suggestion that three- or four-wheeled machines were being talked about here. All of the evidence indicates that Macmillan added "driving gear" to hobby-horses, not to three or four-wheeled velocipedes.

This interest and expertise in velocipedes was based in craft technology, that of traditional blacksmithing and the carriage trades, with skills contributed by carpenters, wheelwrights and engineers. It was nourished and stimulated by the latest trends in industrial technology and manufacturing. The blacksmiths who made these earliest "bicycles" were not thinking in terms of mass-production or capital investment in their ideas, but were amateurs fascinated by the challenges. They were craft-educated, active participants in practical design and manufacture. Contrary to the popular image of a rustic, rural blacksmith, Macmillan was a man in touch with current trends, methods and materials in industrial technology. Although he lived in a country village, Courthill was no more than a few miles from Britain's second industrial city. Although there was rural poverty and periodic economic distress, there was also the opportunity for educational and commercial self-improvement and advancement. Macmillan came from a self-reliant rural background; his brothers were well educated and occupied prestigious teaching positions.

With the foundation of early Mechanics' Institutes, Glasgow and Dumfries were two progressive centres of adult education in Britain. "Mechanics" had the chance to climb the educational ladder and to become skilled workers and entrepreneurs. There was widespread availability of technical and educational books. Macmillan himself worked for a time in the Vulcan Iron Works. He was certainly not experienced only in shoeing horses and repairing farm equipment.

The lack of any commercial development of Macmillan's velocipede is not surprising. These "bicycles" never advanced past the experimental stage; they were prototypes. Production is expensive and demands investment. There needs to be a realization of a demand, of the marketability of a product, and evidently neither Macmillan nor Dalzell felt the need to profit from their ideas. Both, it appears, were willing to share their ideas with others, but interest in velocipeding remained restricted to the few. Contemporary accounts suggest that other people saw their activities as strange and eccentric, not likely to enjoy a wide appeal. Later, McCall did attempt to exploit the commercial potential of the idea, but by then (1869) he had unanswerable competition from the sudden success of the two-wheeled boneshaker.

That Macmillan, Dalzell and McCall were not alone in exploring the possibility of the rear-driven, two-wheeled velocipede is suggested by the arguably almost contemporary French velocipede of Alexandre Lefebvre, very similar in overall design to the Macmillan design. In all of these cases the evidence is strong that the makers were building on the idea of balancing on two wheels first demonstrated by the earlier Draisienne and hobby-horse.

The evidence of McCall's letter to *Bicycling News* in 6, Feb.1892 [see **Section 6.a**] is especially significant. Here was a man who might have pushed himself to the fore as an inventor of the bicycle, but who chose not to. He gave important eye-witness testimony, under-valued until now. He acknowledged having copied Macmillan in the 1840s, and twenty-five years later (1869) he was still putting the developed design into limited production in Scotland. He acknowledged having had "no claim or letters patent". Only later, in the light of the explosion of bicycle production of the 1880s and 1890s, did the idea of "invention" become critical and historical precedence sought and disputed.

It does appear from the historical evidence that Kirkpatrick Macmillan was, if not proveably the first, a critically important player in this period of experimentation, and that his design of velocipede was influential in south-west Scotland, and communicated through personal contact and local reputation. We do not know with certainty what Macmillan's velocipedes looked like, or exactly when he made and used them, but the evidence from Dalzell's and McCall's copies is overwhelmingly strong that his was a two-wheeled, rear-driven velocipede. Many witnesses testified that he owned one or more hobby-horses, and that he added "driving-gear" to them. Both Dalzell and McCall testified that they copied from Macmillan. These points of connection strengthen the case for Macmillan.

I believe we should tend to believe Johnston's witnesses in essence rather than to disbelieve them, especially when they agree with each other in so many important details, and are corroborated by other eye-witness evidence from the early 1880s. The presence of eye witnesses who agree on many of the essential points is a crucial source of historical evidence, and the weight of the oral evidence is, to me, persuasive and compelling.

When all is said and done, is the early history of the bicycle so important? Why would the family, friends and neighbours of Macmillan have lied? We cannot perhaps pin them down to precise dates or to precise machines. Their memories may slip and falter, but why would so many different people report seeing things that in fact they had not seen? In the end, what justification would they have had for doing so?

And then......who was "A Native of Keir", and on what grounds can we possibly dismiss his testimony? As a fabrication? As a lie? Or as Scottish chauvinism?

b. The Witnesses

The following is an attempt to identify briefly those who reported, in one way or another, having seen or had personal experience of Gavin Dalzell and Kirkpatrick Macmillan.

Dalzell

Thomas Brown, from Lesmahagow, was interviewed by C. Wheaton and the account was published in *Bicycling News*, 7 Jan. 1881 and in Charles Spencer's *Bicycles and Tricycles* {1883}. "...so far back as the summer of 1846 at the very latest, Dalzell had a bicycle of his own invention in almost daily use.....his bicycle had been constructed several years before 1846."

Macmillan

A. Witnesses interviewed by Johnston, or sending letters to him, or quoted by him

Samuel Dalziel, a blacksmith at Drumlanrig Mains, wrote a letter to Robert Macmillan, a nephew of Kirkpatrick Macmillan, saying that Macmillan took ideas from "Charters, a turner or joiner" in Dumfries. (*The Scottish Cyclist*, 17 Feb. 1892).

John Findlater, a blacksmith in Carronbridge, wrote to James Johnston in 1889. Findlater stated that "the first and real inventor of applying driving gear to the dandy horse was an old fellow-apprentice of mine, named Kirkpatrick M'Millan, blacksmith, Courthill....M'Millan put it on, I am positive, no met later than 1839 or 1840....What impresses the fact so well in mymory (is) that he had driving gear on his one when we

wrought together at Mallowford from 1835-6 to 1840." (*The Scottish Cyclist*, 17 Feb. 1892.)

Thomas Haining, a farmer in Laight Tynron, wrote to Johnston in 1889 that he "went to Penpont school in 1843....Pate and his dandy horse had pranced through the village long before I had gone to school...he appeared to drive it with a pair of stirrups or pedals hanging from the fore part of the frame, which were connected by an iron rod to the cranks or axle of hind wheel....You will have no difficulty in getting information from plenty of the old people in the neighbourhood of Thornhill..." (*The Scottish Cyclist*, 17 Feb. 1892).

John Brown, a merchant in Penpont who was appointed trustee for the family when Macmilllan died in 1878, told James Johnston in 1889 that he had "not the slightest hesitation in stating that M'Millan was the first man to ride such a machine....He had some sort of way of propelling it by machinery but I regret I cannot exactly say how at this distant date.....As a boy at school here about 1839-40, I remember of often running after M'Millan when on his machine in the company of a lot of my schoolmaates...." (*The Scottish Cyclist*, 17 Feb. 1892).

Robert Hamilton, a miller at Keir Mill, near Penpont, wrote to Johnston in 1889 that he was "confident M'Millan was the first man to put driving gear on the dandy horse.....I remember of Kirkpatrick M'Millan well, as he and I were intimate friends. He made several dandy horses. I took a fancy to have one too....I got M'Millan to put on the driving gear same as his machine. This was in the year 1849, but he had had this gear for a number of years previously...I am positive M'Millan put on his driving gear on or about 1840." (The Scottish Cyclist, 17 Feb. 1892).

Robert Macmillan, a blacksmith, nephew of Macmillan, wrote to Johnston in 1889 that "I can well remember seeing him riding on his dandy horse when I was at school more than fifty years ago....It was made of wood, with the lesser wheel in front, over which was the figure of a horse's head, and was worked with cranks. His first production in that way may not have had cranks, but I never saw one without them." (*The Scottish Cyclist*, 17 Feb. 1892).

Mrs Elizabeth Bailey, wrote to Johnston from Dumfries. She "sat many a time on Kirkpatrick Macmillan's shoulder...while he drove his dandy-horse...Macmillan was lodging with us at the time, and wrought in the smithy at Drumlanrig Mains. That was in the years 1842-43." She added: "certainly there was driving gear on it....There were places he put his feet on to move it along, and not on the ground." (*Bicycling News*, 5 March 1892).

Thomas Wright, wrote to Johnston that "he went to be 'Pate's' nearest neighbour. He had his first horse then;

it had no driving gear....It would be in 1838, or early 1839, when he made his second horse....He made the gear himself. I was often at the smithy and saw him working at it." (*Bicycling News*, 5 March 1892).

George Goldie, partner in Macartney's Millwright and Engineering Works, told Johnston in person that he "remembers distinctly Macmillan's visit to Old Cumnock prior to the Disruption in 1843." (*Bicycling News*, 19 March 1892).

Mr. D. Smith, Inspector of the Poor, Old Cumnock, "spoke confidently of seeing Macmillan and his horse before the Disruption of 1843." (*Bicycling News*, 19 March 1892).

William Fergusson, of Glasgow, a nephew of Gavin Dalzell of Lesmahagow, gave Johnston a statement that his uncle Gavin Dalzell had indeed seen "a blacksmith from Thornhill riding a velocipede down the Glasgow road." (*Bicycling News*, 19 March 1892).

W. Thomson, from Blantyre, wrote first to the *Glasgow Evening Times* (published in *The Scottish Cyclist*, 17 Feb. 1892) and also sent Johnston several letters. In 1845 he met Macmillan while he (Thompson) was staying with his brother. "The Dumfries or Thornhill blacksmith, who bestrode the 'queer thing'.....showed me the machine. It was neatly made and it was ornamented with a horse's head....He had made several of these machines." In 1845, "the machine was not new, neither was it his first trip to Glasgow on it." (*The Scottish Cyclist*, 10 Feb. and 17 Feb. 1892).

B. Witnesses interviewed by others

James Geddes, sent a letter to Thomas McCall which McCall sent on to *Bicycling News*. Geddes stated that "....it strikes me forcibly that Kirkpatrick McMillan made and used his gear-driven bicycle prior to the year 1845. I bought his machine in 1851, and the wheels were creaky, having been out of use for a long while." (*Bicycling News*, 20 Feb. 1892).

Mrs Marchbank (sister of Macmillan) and Mrs Watret (her daughter, niece of Macmillan) were interviewed by a reporter from the *Dumfries and Galloway Standard and Advertiser*, 24 Feb. 1892 (see **Chapter 6.c**).

Mary Grierson Macmillan, who was Mrs Henderson, the sister of Macmillan, was cited as a contact by "Ben Jubal". "She remembers her brother making the dandy-horse in the smithy some time about 1834. This machine was a bicycle without the cranks. A few years later he improved his machine by adding cranks. On this improved machine he made his famous ride to Glasgow." (*Glasgow Evening Times*, 6 Feb. 1892).

William Brown, a blacksmith, visited Macmillan twice in 1844 "which was some time after the invention". On the first occasion, all they saw was an old-style hobby-horse, but "seeing the necessity for some mechanical means of driving.....his second bicycle was much superior to his first attempt." On the second visit, Brown "took precise measurements of Macmillan's second machine, with a view to constructing one similar." (*Dumfries and Galloway Saturday Standard*, 15 June 1895).

C. Witnesses offering accounts from other sources, e.g., writing letters to newspapers

"J. T." saw a velocipede rider in Old Cumnock "in 1845 or 1846". (*North British Daily Mail*, 22 Aug. 1884).

W. Blackstock, identified a rider passing through Lesmahagow as "Kilpatrick M'Millan, who made the velocipede at Courthill." (*North British Daily Mail*, 22 Aug. 1884).

Thomas Wright, identified a velocipede rider who "came from Dumfriesshire to Glasgow via Douglas and Lesmahagow" as "Kirkpatrick M'Millan, blacksmith, Parish of Keir." (*North British Daily Mail*, 22 Aug. 1884).

"A Dumfriesian", identified the velocipede rider as "Peter M'Millan, blacksmith, Keir Mill, Thornhill." (*North British Daily Mail*, 22 Aug. 1884).

"A Native of Keir", identified Kirkpatrick M'Millan as the early velocipede rider, and gave details of the Glasgow accident. (*North British Daily Mail*, 22 Aug. 1884).

Ben Jubal (correspondent with newspaper), wrote to *Glasgow Evening Times* (13 Feb. 1892) saying, "I saw the blacksmith myself frequently".

Thomas McCall, velocipede maker in Kilmarnock, sent an extensive account of his relationship with "Peter McMillan, who wrought at Drumlanrig Castle for some time, and latterly on his own account at Pierpont, Dumfriesshire." (*Bicycling News*, 6 Feb. 1892).

John Findlater, also wrote to *Bicycling News* that he "wrought along with Mr. McMillan for some years both at Mallyford and Drumlanrig Mains" and that "Mr. McMillan had cranks on his dandy-horse before 1844." (*Bicycling News*, 20 Feb. 1892).

John Templeton, wrote to the *Glasgow Evening Times* that "Previous to the year 1843....Kirkpatrick M'Millan rode into Old Cumnock late one summer's night. In the morning, he came out with his horse, and rode up and down the town to the great amusement of the crowds who ran after him." Templeton added that "several imitations of M'Millan's machine, with some improvements, were made....and for several years were in great vogue." (*Glasgow Evening Times*, 22

Part One: The Origins of the Bicycle

Feb. 1892, also quoted by Johnston in *The Scottish Cyclist*, 5 March 1892).

<u>Andrew Todd</u>, wrote to *Bicycling News* (26 March 1892) from England stating that his uncle, William Nicol, of Drumlanrig Mains, "made the woodwork for Macmillan's machine, he (Macmillan) making the ironwork for my uncle necessary to convert his 'dandy horse' into a rear-driver. My uncle's machine was still in good condition in 1880, when I used to ride it on Drumlanrig Castle Road….My uncle used to frequently ride Macmillan's machine when a youngster….". (*Bicycling News*, 26 March 1892).

c. Witnesses and the Evidence of Oral Testimony:

Chronological date. The date at which Macmillan did this or that ("invented" this or that) would necessarily be affected by the varied technical expertise and perceptions of those being interviewed, and therefore a range of dates would be expected. But on many occasions dates are recollected by reference to other events, e.g., "at the time of the Disruption", or "when the baby was at the breast". In other cases, several repeated events may easily be telescoped into one inaccurately dated event – e.g., Macmillan's various rides to Glasgow. But in spite of the apparent lack of specificity, there is a compelling agreement in dating Macmillan's velocipede building activity within the period 1835 to 1845.

Idea of improvement from hobby-horse to driving-gear. Although there is lack of specificity as to when this happened, there is consistent testimony that some kind of development occurred in Macmillan's work. He made more than one machine – he may even have made several. Chart these stories. He began with the hobby-horse, which Charters may have inspired in him, and he added a drive mechanism, he may even have experimented with several models with drive mechanism. He was a tinkerer, he did not arrive at a finished product – it was always in process!

His ideas were always shared. Just as he took his ideas from others, Macmillan's ideas were not secret or protected, but shared. They were not seen as his patentable, private property. Others, McCall and Dalzell for example, saw his machine and copied it.

His machine and his behaviour elicited interest, surprise and astonishment wherever he went. In Glasgow, his presence attracted a crowd which caused an accident, other people reported (memory embellished in the telling!) being frightened out of their wits as he sped past! This would be understandable for a novel machine.

The machine was known as and universally referred to as "the horse", "the wooden horse". This was reinforced by the fact that he put a horse's head on the front of the frame – still seen in McCall's 1890 copy.

Macmillan raced the coach, or mail coach, on his journeys.

He was strong and athletic.

The Glasgow incident. On one of his journeys into Glasgow, he was involved in an incident where a crowd gathered, and in which either a child or an old woman was hurt. He was taken to the police station and later fined, but there was more interest than desire to punish in his treatment.

Machine later broken up. Macmillan appears to have gone through a period of interest in velocipedes, and then to have lost interest. His machine(s) fell into disuse and was later broken up.

d. Summary of conclusions

1. The evidence points decisively to the presence of "bicycle-type" velocipedes in the Dumfries area of south-west Scotland, near to the industrial centre of Glasgow. There is convincing evidence that the idea of a hobby-horse driven with a crank mechanism enjoyed currency in this area between 1835 and 1845, that it was a craft-based original idea which was shared, improved upon, recognized as novel and interesting and greeted with astonishment:

- These machines were remembered with precision and concern for detail by many separate identified individuals.

- The accounts were laced with information and have strong connecting threads, which agree in summary although they vary in specific detail. These differences answer the definition of historical or oral folklore, defined as providing variety or variation of testimony within similarity.

- These deeply ingrained and consistent patterns of folk memory revealed in the oral testimony, some collected by James Johnston, some submitted to various newspapers in the 1880s and 1890s, allow us to understand better the historical record of Macmillan. This layer of evidence, which consists of interviews with and correspondence from family, business associates and neighbours of Kirkpatrick Macmillan, is a strong, rich source which has been unjustifiably neglected until now.

- Scottish accounts of Macmillan began well before James Johnston began his research in about 1889, and these earlier accounts were not connected with his allegedly chauvinistic ambitions.

- The existence in San Jose, California of the Lefebvre machine probably made in Paris in the 1840s, suggests that south-west Scotland was not alone in

The Origins of the Bicycle

experimenting with a drive mechanism for the existing "draisienne" or "hobby-horse".

2. Criticism has been voiced that it is 3- or 4-wheeled velocipedes described in the testimonies, but there is abundant evidence that it is two-wheeled machines being talked about. This view is strengthened by the frequent references to "improvements" of the basic hobby-horse and the addition of "driving-gear" to hobby-horses. The characteristics of the story and the machine as described in the evidence:

- The novel idea was shared, copied and improvements were made.

- The rider is between two wheels, sitting on a seat.

- Some kind of a drive mechanism has been added to the hobby-horse.

- The machine is called "the horse", or "the wooden horse", and is described as having had a wooden horse's head mounted on the front.

- The rider raced the mail coach and made certain specific long trips, from Thornhill to Dumfries, for example, or from Thornhill to Glasgow, which were greeted with surprise.

- In Glasgow, the rider had an accident, appeared before a magistrate and was lightly fined.

- The rider was asked to demonstrate the machine in various locations, including before the Magistrates in Glasgow, and for the Duke of Buccleuch at Drumlanrig Castle.

- People were unaccustomed to seeing such a machine and were so surprised to see it under certain circumstances (when it was dark, or the "horse" was going fast downhill), that they thought it was something spooky, and a legend grew up around it.

3. But who was this rider, or riders? Can a specific individual be assigned the role of "inventor"?

- A consistent pattern of evidence links Macmillan to the geographical area where he lived, and supports the fact that he made many journeys on his "horse".

- Witnesses identify him as "Kirkpatrick M'Millan", "Kilpatrick M'Millan", "Peter McMillan" or "Pate M'Millan". They are all the same person. Other witnesses identify Gavin Dalzell as associated with the machine. The evidence provides an explanation of this apparent discrepancy in a pattern of borrowing, copying, and "improvements", from Charteris, through Macmillan, Dalzell and McCall. Other unnamed amateur makers are also mentioned, for instance in Old Cumnock and Strathaven.

4. Why was there no production or patent? Not an easy question to answer (when did widespread patenting of new ideas and artifacts in fact begin?):

- The chronological and geographical context in the 1840s was one of traditional craft technologies, where the idea of "ownership" of a new idea was not yet embedded in commerce and production.

- There was as yet no need for the protection of a profitable entertainment or sport within which "ownership" of the velocipede, or the need for a patent, had emerged.

- Neither was there yet a proven and consistent practice of travelling on velocipedes – even though the hobby-horse was widely known about and the idea for such vehicles was regularly discussed in the mechanics' press. As long as the very few makers were willing to share their ideas, production was limited to a few experimental models.

- The Macmillan-style vehicle did not reach a critical mass of interest which made a patent necessary, and was never mass-produced. The commercial success of the boneshaker overlaid the clumsy, less than ideal treadle-and-rod construction, and with one exception (Peyton and Peyton, Bourne's Patent, (**see Fig. 34**) rendered further experimentation with levers and rods on a two-wheeler undesirable. Front wheel pedalling was better, smoother, more direct, more efficient. McCall's efforts to sell the Macmillan-style bicycle in Glasgow were evidently not very successful.

PEYTON & PEYTON,

BORDESLEY WORKS, BIRMINGHAM,

MANUFACTURERS OF THE

IMPROVED BICYCLE.

BOURNE'S

PATENT.

Advantages as compared with the ordinary Bicycle—

1. Increased power. The rider can mount hills, and go along rough roads.
2. On account of the hind wheel being the driving wheel, there is no strain on the arms and shoulders.
3. There is an easy seat instead of a saddle, by means of which a serious objection, raised by the medical profession, is removed.
4. The action of the legs is easier and much more natural, resembling walking, and the legs are not dirtied, nor are they liable to be injured by the action of the guide wheel.
5. It is easier to mount *at any time*. It can be started *up-hill, even* without assistance. It has not to be started before mounting, but in the act of mounting, as the rider takes his seat.
6. It is easier to learn, because it is easier to mount, to start, and to work.

PRICES.

	£	s.	d.
With Double-dished Wheels (driving-wheel 3 feet diameter), Stained or Painted, and the Ironwork Painted	8	8	0
With Double-dished Wheels (driving-wheel 3 feet diameter), Stained or Painted, and the Ironwork bright, with Lamp	12	12	0
With Double-dished Wheels, Stained, and the Ironwork bright, Vulcanized India-rubber Tires to Wheels, with Lamp and Plated Mountings	16	16	0

P. and P. are also manufacturers of the Three-wheeled Velocipede called

"THE RANTOONE,"

Which took a SILVER MEDAL as FIRST PRIZE FOR SPEED at the Races of the International Velocipede Exhibition at the Crystal Palace, on the 23rd of September, 1869.

PRICES.

	£	s.	d.
Driving-wheels, 2 feet 6 inches diameter, for Youths	8	8	0
Driving-wheels, 3 feet diameter, for Adults	10	10	0
Driving-wheels, 3 feet 6 inches diameter, for Adults	12	12	0

Terms to the Trade on Application.

Oct. 30, 1869.

Fig. 34 Bourne's patent of 1869 was perhaps the last attempt to manufacture a treadle-driven rear-driven bicycle. [Source: Andrew Ritchie]

Part Two - Sources

I have transcribed here as closely as possible the texts of newspaper and magazine articles, and other sources. My own comments on the sources have been included within square brackets

Fig. 35 Thomas McCall as a prosperous master-wheelwright in the mid-1890s. It shows him holding a hammer surrounded by his workmen. [Source: Royal Scottish Musems]

Sources - A

Glasgow Argus, 9 June 1842 (Thursday) [119]

Yesterday, a gentleman, belonging to Dumfries-shire, was placed at the Gorbals police bar, charged with riding along the pavement on a velocipede, to the obstruction of the passage, and with having, by so doing, thrown over a child. It appeared, from his statement, that he had, on the day previous, come all the way from Old Cumnock, a distance of 40 miles, bestriding the velocipede, and that he had performed the distance in the space of five hours. On reaching the Barony of Gorbals, he had gone upon the pavememt, and was soon surrounded by a large crowd, attracted by the novelty of the machine. The child who was thrown down had not sustained any injury; and under the circumstances, the offender was fined only in 5s. The velocipede employed in this instance was very ingeniously constructed - it moved on wheels turned with the hand, by means of a crank; but to make it "progress" appeared to require more labour than will be compensated for by the increase of speed. This invention will not supersede the railways

Glasgow Herald, 11 June 1842 (Saturday)

The Velocipede - On Wednesday, a gentleman, who stated that he came from Thornhill, in Dumfries-shire, was placed at the Gorbals police bar, charged with riding along the pavement on a velocipede, to the obstruction of the passage, and with having, by so doing, thrown over a child. It appeared, from his statement, that he had, on the day previous, come all the way from Old Cumnock, a distance of forty miles, bestriding the velocipede, and that he had performed the distance in the space of five hours. On reaching the Barony of Gorbals, he had gone upon the pavememt, and was soon surrounded by a large crowd, attracted by the novelty of the machine. The child who was thrown down had not sustained any injury; and under the circumstances, the offender was fined only 5s. The velocipede employed in this instance was very ingeniously constructed - it moved on wheels turned with the hand, by means of a crank, but to make it 'progress' appeared to require more labour than will be compensated for by the increase of speed. This invention will not supersede the railways.

Sources - B

English Mechanic, 14 May 1869 and 11 June 1869

(14 May 1869)

The Kilmarnock Velocipede.

Sir, - I enclose a photograph of a velocipede, which meets with great approval here (Kilmarnock). I have tried it, and find it very light and easy of motion. It is two-wheeled, the driving wheel 3ft 6in., and steering wheel 2ft 8in. The wheels are of wood, and are double disked. The maker (Mr. T. McCall, Langlands Street, Kilmarnock) has raced and beaten some of the ordinary two-wheeled velocipedes in Glasgow. If, Mr. Editor, you think this is worth engraving, I shall be glad to benefit some of my numerous brother readers. I may add that the price is £5 10s.

Mechanical Hawk

(11 June 1869)

The Improved Kilmarnock Velocipede.

Sir, - Since I last wrote, various improvements have been effected in the Kilmarnock velocipede. I now send you a photograph of it in its present stage. It has, as my brother readers will perceive, a far better steering handle, being fitted with a brake and gun-metal bearings; the connecting rods are also made alterable to a long or short leg. It is a remarkably safe velocipede, being so low and easily mounted. The speed is from 8 to 12 miles an hour, though I have gone downhill at what I should think a much greater speed. The price, through improved fittings, has risen to £7. The machine weighs about 58lb.

Mechanical Hawk

Sources - C

Cycling (Newcastle), August 1879

The First Bicycle – Histories of our iron horse will have to be re-cast. It was not a Frenchman nor an American that made the first bicycle after all, but a Scotchman named Gavin Dalzell, who ran about on a two-wheeler selling tea in Lanarkshire in 1836, beating His Majesty's mails, and outstripping everything and everybody. So writes "Bohemian" in one of our weekly contemporaries.

Bicycling News, 17 Dec. 1880

Does any one know where the first bicycle was made, and who the inventor was, and also the maker; or, failing this, the first velocipede, a pedal-motive machine? On receipt of information, I may have more to state thereupon, that is not generally known.

C.W.

. . . .

Bicycling News, 24 Dec. 1880

Correspondence

Sir, - In answer to "C.W." about the first bicycle made, I beg to quote the following, which I read in a contemporary about a year and a half ago: -

> "The first bicycle ever made and run successfully was constructed by Gavin Dalzell, a cooper, of Lesmahagow, Lanarkshire, in the year 1836, and it was used by him for years in travelling from village to village, he then being employed in selling tea. Now this vehicle was not a dandy horse, but a bicycle in the true sense of the word. The only material difference from the present machine consisted in its having the lesser wheel, by which it was steered, in front, and in the roughness of its make. The machine was still in existence, or was 2 years ago, when the writer saw it. Rough, however, and heavy as it was, Dalzell managed to travel at a great speed with it. On one occasion, indeed, he outran the King's Mail Coach, which, by Act of Parliament, was compelled to complete ten miles an hour, including all stoppages. Not only did he complete the ten miles before the coach, but, during the race he ran around it three times, much to the delight of the passengers, and the disgust of the guard and driver, who had bet on the race."

I have taken considerable pains in hunting up this information, and though I cannot guarantee its accuracy, yet I trust it is what "C.W." requires.

H.W.B.

A second letter was also published in the same issue, from "Clarion, Canonbury B.C., which is referred to in C. Wheaton's letter below. This letter discussed a Cruickshank hobby-horse caricature showing the Prince Regent pedalling with his hands to the front wheel of a hobby-horse, dated 1819, and asked whether that illustration could:

> "vitiate the American patent and so relieve our manufacturers from the heavy royalty they now have to pay on every machine exported to the United States….I fancy that I have read somewhere of a wonderful bicycle that used to be ridden in the wilds of Scotland some 30 or 40 years ago, but as there seems no definite information regarding it, I suppose that its rider was "Mrs. Harris.""

. . . .

Bicycling News, 7 Jan. 1881

First Bicycle and Velocipede

Correspondence

To the Editor of Bicycling News.

It is said that there is nothing news under the sun, and this seems to have been true, at least, in 1865, when our Parisian friends were said to have invented *the* bicycle. Everything, however, is supposed to have had a beginning, and there must have been a time when this *was* new, and probably all at once so: a sudden *leap*, as it were, from earth to air, giving *wings* to the wheel – rather *cranky*, this allusion to wings.

Though our researches may be limited, they will not be thrown away if we can remove the honour of this invention to our own shores, where, strange to say, it has attained such a development as to raise a strong suspicion that our steed has but returned to an indigenous soil, for nowhere else has it taken such deep root….

I will presume, then, to define the original bicycle as "a pedal motive machine, having two wheels running in one track, propelled by cranks on each side of the front wheel, which wheel is also made to turn to either side, thereby enabling the rider, when seated on the saddle, to guide and balance himself whilst in motion without any other support." If any one can put this into a single or even compound word, we shall have found a good name for our wheel-horse, or, as the French have it, *velhoss* (a slight connexion here).

When I solicited enquiry, it was not that I had got the "tip," but rather to invite opinions; also to compare and investigate. The Cruikshank (see "Clarion" B. N., Dec. 31st) is interesting as showing that the idea partly existed, if not carried out (?) The allusion to the "Wonderful Bicycle in the Wilds of Scotland" is more so; and "W.H.B.'s" further allusion to this, in a quotation, caused me to make enquiries in this direction, resulting in the following full and true particulars, for which I am indebted to Mr. Thos. Brown, of Lesmahagow: -

"The late Mr. Edwin Dalzell, merchant, Lesmahagow, Lanarkshire, was born on the 29th of August, 1811. Commencing business there in 1835, he carried it on uninterruptedly till his death, on the 14th of June, 1863.[119] He possessed, in common with several other members of the old Dumfriesshire family to which he belonged, a decided talent for the invention of contrivances of a mechanical and scientific character. More than one of their inventions have found their way to the Patent Office. Undoubtedly, the most interesting and important of the present day is that of the bicycle.

"It is a fact established incontrovertibly by written proof, that so far back as the summer of 1846 at the very latest, Dalzell had a bicycle of his own invention in almost daily use. And, according to the oral evidence of many people, and also to a statement made in a paragraph published in a newspaper widely circulated in the Upper Ward of Lanarkshire, and which was not contradicted, his bicycle had been constructed several years before 1846.

"Prior to his invention of the bicycle he had invented and constructed a tricycle, the propulsion of which was effected by its rider in a way both ingenious and unique. This tricycle, however, no longer exists, portions of it having been utilized in the construction of this bicycle, now at least thirty-four years old, which is still preserved by one of his family, T.B.Dalzell, at Lesmahagow.

"His bicycle went by the name of the 'Wooden Horse', and was so styled spontaneously by the people. John Leslie, the village blacksmith, who did the ironwork, called it the 'Horse', and the pedal movements the 'Stirrups' in the bill he rendered; and to this day no one, either old or young, seems to dream of giving it any other designation.

"It is constructed chiefly of wood, and is strong and substantial. The only material difference between it and the present ones is its having the steering wheel in front smaller than the other. The saddle, too, is so low that the rider starts himself with both feet on the ground. The stirrups, of iron, hang from the forepart, or croup, of the saddle, and are moved backwards and forwards alternately. They are connected by means of iron rods with the cranked axle of the driving wheel. The reins (handles) are bent back, so that they may be conveniently grasped by the rider. Another peculiarity which is very noticeable is that the upper part of the driving wheel is clad with wood from the saddle to rather beyond the highest part of the wheel. The rider is enabled by this contrivance to mount freight behind him, either living or the reverse. Frequently one, two, or even three lads perched behind the rider at one time, their arms clasped firmly round each other's waists, and all working as energetically as their strength would permit, the speed then attained being remarkable, and was secured by the lads assisting the rider, by resting their feet upon and assisting him in working the connecting rods already referred to. It had been proposed, though it was never carried out, to fix foot-pieces to these rods, and so to diminish the danger of the foot being crushed between the rods and the framework.

"The simultaneous balancing and propelling of a bicycle without the feet of the rider touching the ground are now so generally known that few think anything at all about them. Yet this was not always so. Indeed it is a fact.....that when Mr. Dalzell intimated his intention of making a second velocipede, that should only have two wheels, in place of three, and one wheel running before the other, and moreover that the velocipede would both be propelled and balanced without the rider's feet touching the ground, not one person could he find to believe such an incredible feat was possible till the thing was actually accomplished by him.

"As a natural consequence, therefore, the 'Wooden Horse' excited a marvellous interest wherever it made its appearance, and people travelled long distances to get a sight of it. To satisfy the larger curiosity of others, descriptions of it had to be sent. Measurements and a diagram were asked for occasionally, and were as frankly given as they were anxiously sought. On the 27th of November, 1848, Mr. Francis Forrest writes from Carnwath a letter which may be taken as a typical one:

" 'Sir, - As I did not see you when I was down to get a full account of your riding machine at that time, if you would be so good as to write me all about it – say, what rate you can go a mile easily, up hill, and if you would mark on this draught the lengths of the different parts, you will oblige me. Yours truly, Francis Forrest' "

"As a result of this courtesy on the part of the inventor, and of the advice and assistance he was always happy to give, numerous bicycles of a similar type, and tricycles with treadle action, came into existence in Scotland.

"As the fame of the "Wooden Horse" became widely spread, the circumstances of a foreign claimant stepping forward to take the honour of being the inventor of the bicycle is no matter of surprise. Natives of the district – the Upperward of Lanarkshire – in which it was so universally known, are to be found in every quarter of the known world. Besides, Mr. John Dalzell, already referred to – the only and younger brother of the inventor – was a practical engineer. In the pursuit of his business, he had to be in England, and about eight years altogether in the north and north-east of Europe. He died in Sweden, in the early months of 1851. Like his elder brother, he was also of an ingenious turn of mind, and, coming as he did into contact with many nationalities, it is quite probable that, with the open-hearted unselfishness so characteristic of him, he, too, may have instructed some how to make such a wonderful and hitherto unheard of machine. Bearing, then, these facts in mind, the wonder is that France alone has claimed the honour of inventing the bicycle, and that other countries with no better claim, though as good, have refrained from disputing the pretensions of La Belle France.

"Though the "Wooden Horse" differs from the modern bicycle in matters of detail, there is one grand principle that underlies all bicycles. And it consists in the invention of a two-wheeled velocipede, the rider of which should be able to propel and to balance without aid extraneous to the machine; or in other words, without his feet touching the ground, as in the case of the Celeripede or Dandy Horse."[120]

The Origins of the Bicycle

The subject of these notes would seem to be entitled to the credit, not only of having been the first to conceive the practicability of that principle, but to have invented and used a bicycle that conclusively proved that the principle was capable of being carried into practice.

To the Land O'Cakes, then, it appears, so far as is yet known, we may justly give the credit, if not of the whole idea, yet of putting it into practical shape. There still remains the idea in the Cruikshank caricature; but had this the steering front wheel? Without which it is but half an idea. (Nothing new, etc.)

Is it possible to obtain the loan of this wonder from the "Wilds of Scotland," and place it in our Stanley Exhibition? I am sure it would be treated "with care," and receive an honourable position as the father of the splendid family around him. If forwarded through me, in a strong crate, I would gladly undertake its safe delivery, and return it free of expense, though doubtless the club would gladly do so.

As regards the bicycle of Paris, I am informed by Mr. Scott, of the Waverley B.C., that this emanated from one Pierre Lallment, about 1864, in the employ of M. Michaux, with other information kindly sent me, but not touching, however, on first bicycles.

The first velocipedes (three or more wheels) have yet to be considered, but appears to have been disregarded under the all-absorbing interest taken here in the bicycle. I have information positive on these from a much earlier date, but time and space necessitate its postponement, so for this week I would say, "To be continued."

C. Wheaton, 35, Long Acre

Sources - D

Scottish American Journal, 27 Sept. 1883

The Inventor of the Bicycle - Forty years ago a man named Kirkpatrick Macmillan, a blacksmith in the parish of Keir, Dumfriesshire, made a bicycle on which he soon became a clever rider. On this "dandy horse", as it was called in the district, from the fact that over the wheels was placed a small wooden horse, on which the rider sat, he made among other trips a run to Glasgow, distant from Keir some sixty miles, and managed to keep in front of the mail coach all the way, much to the amusement of the passengers. He accidentally knocked down a woman on entering Glasgow, for which he was fined at the police court. We are not prepared to say that he was the actual inventor of the bicycle, but the machine must have been a novelty at the time, as some of the Buccleuch family, then resident at Drumlanrig Castle, sent for the "smith", with the request that he would ride up on the machine, which he did, greatly to their astonishment. It was constructed of wood, and was worked on the same principle as the bicycle of the present day - the wheels, however, being more of a size with the smaller one in front.

· ·

Scottish American Journal, 11 Oct. 1883

[Editorial]

Considerable discussion has taken place of late, both in the newspapers of this and of the Old Country, as to who was the inventor of the bicycle. The honour is really worth fighting for. As a means of conveyance it is truly revolutionizing the world. A riding horse – even the fleetest Arab – can scarcely "hold the candle" to it for speed, and for distance it is simply nowhere. Our reports of the number of miles covered by bicyclists in a single day or in a week would have almost astonished our forefathers more than either railways or telegraphs. But nowhere has the bicycle taken a firmer hold of the people than in Auld Caledonia. There it forms the great recreation of both youth and middle-aged. Every village and town almost have one or more bicycle clubs, and every county its association of them. Grand prize contests also take place throughout the country, the same as rifle shooting and athletics. But directly and indirectly the recreation simply cannot fail to be of great benefit to the nation in producing improved bone and sinew, and the inventor of the bicycle will throughout time be looked upon as one of our greatest public benefactors.

Then who was he? We are glad to be able to say that there is no doubt he was (like Stephenson, Watt, and a host of the world's other benefactors) a Scotchman. Many years before that little Frenchman, Pierre Lallement, in 1864, made a bicycle in Paris, one had been made in Scotland. Nearly twenty years before that the bicycle had been the wonder of the day there. Writing to a correspondent of the *Bicycle News*, Mr. Thomas Brown, of Lesmahagow, claims the honour of the invention as due to the late Mr. Gavin Dalzell, merchant, Lesmahagow, Lanarkshire, and says:-

> "It is a fact, established incontrovertibly by *written* proof, that so far back as the summer of 1846, at the very latest, he (Gavin Dalzell) had a bicycle of his own invention in almost daily use. And, according to the oral evidence of many people, and also to a statement made in a paragraph published in a newspaper widely circulated in the Upper Ward of Lanarkshire, and which has not been contradicted, his bicycle had been constructed several years before 1846." And that "prior to his invention of the

bicycle he had invented a tricycle, the propulsion of which was effected by its rider in a way both ingenious and unique."

There can be little doubt that Mr. Gavin Dalzell was the inventor of the bicycle. He was born on the 29th August, 1811, and carried on business at Lesmahagow from 1833 until his death on 14th June, 1863. Although a merchant he had a decided talent for mechanical and scientific contrivances. His "wooden horse" (as his bicycle was called) excited great wonder wherever it appeared. The speed which even it attained was remarkable, as it could easily outstrip the stage coach of the day.

It is, however, not surprising that there should now be foreign claimants to the invention. Gavin was the reverse of chary in giving full information about his invention to all who desired. Many on application received from him descriptions, measurements and diagrams. As a consequence several similar bicycles and tricycles soon appeared in various parts of Scotland. Besides, Gavin had a younger brother named John, who was a practical engineer, and who was familiar with the whole mechanism of the bicycle. John in pursuing his business was in England, and was about eight years in the north and north-east of Europe until his death in Sweden in 1851. He naturally was proud of his brother's invention, and would speak of it, and explain its principle and construction wherever he went. Mr. S.W. Dalzell, assistant engineer, Pittsburgh Division of the Pennsylvania Railroad Company, also is a son of the inventor – Mr. Gavin Dalzell.

There was money in this invention, had it been patented, and the right of production protected, but the failure of the Scotchmen to patent their inventions is proverbial. Murdock did not patent his invention of gas; and many others. Scotchmen naturally are not so selfish; they require to come into contact with those of other nationalities before the motto of "Mind Number One" is forced upon them.

. . . .

Scottish American Journal, 1 Nov., 1883

The Bicycle Invention

Cherry Valley, Oct. 15th, 1883

Dear Sir:- In your editorial of the 11th inst. you give the credit of the invention of the bicycle to Mr. Gavin Dalzell. Well, I very much doubt if he was the inventor. In the year 1830 two young men came from the village of Galston to the village of Howood, and remained there. They were hand-loom weavers. I went to work beside them thirteen years afterwards. One day, shortly after I commenced at work with them, one of them chanced to say that "the 'dandy horse' had gone completely out of fashion." I made inquiry as to what the "dandy horse" was, and they described it to me.

They said they used to meet Paisley chaps coming out on them every Saturday when they were going in with their cloth; but they had apparently given it up, as they had not seen any of them for seven or eight years.

Now, they must have seen the "dandy horse" sixty years ago, so that a man born in 1811 could not be the inventor. There must be plenty of old men belonging to Paisley, who can remember the time I am writing of. I could if I had been on the ground.

If you give this a place in our own paper I hope to hear from some of them. By the description of the "dandy horse" the principle was the same as in the bicycle, whatever different shapes it may have undergone.

Yours truly, D.L.

. . . .

Scottish American Journal, 22 Nov 1883

Inventor of the Bicycle

Allegheny, Pa., Nov. 12th, 1883

Dear Sir: - Your issue of 1st inst. contained a letter by "D.L." expressing a doubt as to Mr. Gavin Dalzell being the inventor of the bicycle, and giving the credit to the inventor of the Dandy Horse. Mr. Hugh McKay, writing on the same subject, gives Baron von Drais, the inventor of the Celefire, or speed-maker, that honour. Mr. McKay, in speaking of the Celefire, or velocipede as he calls it, says there is very little difference in the appearance of the bicycle of the present day and that of the Baron. The difference in shape is certainly very slight, but that in propelling is very great. On Mr. Dalzell's bicycle (as on those of the present day) the rider never touched the ground from the time he mounted the saddle until he dismounted, his mode of propulsion being by pedals connecting with the driving wheel. The motion of the Dandy Horse, and also of the Celefire, was obtained by placing the feet alternately on the ground and pushing the machine forward. In Harper's Monthly for July, 1881, there is a drawing of the Baron's invention, showing the method of propelling it.

Neither the owner of the Dandy Horse nor the Baron had any knowledge evidently that their machines could maintain their equilibrium whilst running without the riders using their feet on the ground, or that they could be wrought with cranks and attain a high rate of speed. Mr. Dalzell having solved these difficulties, and constructed a machine of his own design, which he used for many years, and which is still in existence, is, I think, fully entitled to the credit of being the inventor of the bicycle. There are many of your readers who have seen Mr. Dalzell's bicycle in operation, and probably a goodly number of them have been on it.

I hope you will excuse me for taking up so much of your space.

Yours truly, Wm. C. Dalzell

Scources - E

North British Daily Mail, 21, 22, 23, 27, 28 and 30 August 1884

21 August 1884

An Early Scotch Velocipedist

Sir, - A velocipede and its rider, said to have come from Dumfriesshire, passed Douglas, Lanarkshire, the rider halting at Douglas Mill for refreshments, and afterwards proceeding westward by way of Lesmahagow, in the month of October, 1846.[121] Can any of your readers give the name and address of the rider of this velocipede, or the name of the place where the velocipede was made?

I am, etc., N.F.

· ·

22 August 1884

An Early Scotch Velocipedist

Sir, - In answer to your correspondent 'N.F.' I remember, in the year 1845 or 1846, of a man coming from Carranbridge (in Dumfriesshire) to Old Cumnock on a velocipede. I well remember the circumstance. I was courting my wife at the time and happened to be out a bit late, or perhaps early. It was pretty dark, but I could see two wheels fly quickly past me, the one before the other, and a man sitting between them. I could not conceive what it was till the following day, when I saw a man riding through the town with a large crowd after him.[122] I don't remember his name, but you could easily get it by writing to his friend, Mr. William M'Kennell, draper, Cumnock. In that same year the men in the employment of Mr. George M'Cartney, mill wright, Cumnock, made several machines of the same pattern with some slight improvements. I may mention that they were all made of wood. I have also heard it stated that the first one that ever was made was the invention and handicraft of Wm. Murdoch, the inventor of gas. I believe the skeleton of it was about Lugar, the native place of the inventor, not long ago.

I am, etc., J.T.

Sir, - In answer to the note in today's *Mail* from 'N.F.' regarding an early Scotch velocipedist, the name of the rider who passed through Lesmahagow in Oct. 1846 was Kilpatrick M'Millan, who made the velocipede at Courthill, Parish of Keir, Dumfriesshire, and rode the same to Edinburgh from Dumfries by way of Lesmahagow, and I have no hesitation in saying that the humble village blacksmith from Courthill is the great

inventor and the originator of the velocipede originally called the "wooden horse."

I am, etc., W. Blackstock, 61, South Cumberland Street, Glasgow, Aug. 21.

Sir, - I cannot speak of 1846, but I can speak with perfect recollection of seeing in the workshop at Paisley, 35 years ago or thereby, of Mr. Dundas Smith Porteous, engineer, a velocipede built by himself, upon which he travelled to and from Glasgow frequently. Mr. Porteous's son continues the business and may be able to give additional information.

I am, etc., J.A.

Sir, - Your correspondent 'N.F.' wants to know the name of the man who came from Dumfriesshire to Glasgow via Douglas and Lesmahagow on a velocipede in the year 1846. His name was Kirkpatrick M'Millan, blacksmith, Parish of Keir, Dumfriesshire. He made the velocipede himself.

I am, etc., Thomas Wright, Slamannan, 21st August

p.s. He died several years ago.[123]

Sir, - Will you kindly allow me, in reply to your correspondent 'N.F.', to say that the velocipedist he wants to know about was Mr. Peter M'Millan, blacksmith, Keir Mill, by Thornhill, Dumfriesshire.[124] The machine was made of wood, and was called the "dandy charger" and was propelled at the same rate as the stage coaches running at that time.

I am, etc., A Dumfriesian.

· ·

23 August 1884

An Early Scotch Velocipedist

Sir, - Referring to the letters in *Mail* of 21ˢᵗ and 22d inst., I well recollect that about 35 years ago, *or more*, I saw frequently Mr. Gavin Weir, engineer, of Blackburn Mill, near Strathaven, riding a bicycle made by himself, which was known as the "wooden horse."[125] On it (he sat above the wheels) he went from home considerable distances on business, and it has a very good speed. Probably it is in his possession at Blackburn still. I am, however, unable to say whether he was the inventor of his machine.

I am, etc., Avon.

Sir, - Observing in your paper a correspondence in reference to a velocipede which passed through Lesmahagow from Dumfries in 1846, this is to say that velocipedes were used in Dumfries 30 years before that time. The young gentlemen of Dumfriesshire rode them from that town to Kirkbean and Colvend, and this must have been as early as 1816. The machines had two large wheels, the one before the other; the rider sat on a small saddle between them, and they were called the "Dandy Horse." An uncle of my own was nearly killed by one of them. He was travelling from Arbigland to Kirkbean, and when descending the Gillhead Brae, the machine ran off, he lost control, and was dashed to the ground, near the Lady well at the foot of the hill. I am quite certain as to the date I have named. 50 years ago this circumstance was told as a family story of the past.[126]

I am, etc., Kirkbean.

· ·

27 August 1884

An Early Scotch Velocipedist

Sir, - I see that several correspondents answer "N.F.'s" question about who an early Scottish velocipedist was. I knew him well, being brought up together. I have been in his father's smithy hundreds of times getting my clogs shod, as well as other things. He was born at Byreflat, on the estate of Waterside, parish of Keir, by Thornhill, Dumfriesshire. He made his first wooden horse when he was at Byreflat, and by and by he made another on an improved scale, and a very braw horse it was, with bridle and saddle and stirrups, with a brown mane and tail. His first run to Glasgow was about the years 1836 or 1837, He started from Thornhill with the mail coach, via Sanquhar, Cumnock, and Kilmarnock, and was in Glasgow before the coach. He met with a misfortune in Glasgow, having come against an old woman in the street and knocked down, and was fined 5s. He had many a run to Dumfries on his "wooden horse," when none of the farmers could beat him. I could tell a great number of incidents that I have seen and heard and know to be true, which if "N.F." wishes to know he could call on me and I would tell him, and he, if he chose, could give you for publication. His name was Kirkpatrick M'Millan, son of Robert M'Millan, a country blacksmith, parish of Keir. He was named Kirkpatrick for Sir Thomas Kirkpatrick, Capenoch,

Keir, the then Sheriff of Dumfriesshire.[128]
I am, etc., A Native of Keir.

Sir, - Pate M'Millan's velocipede was made by himself, and had two wheels of the same size. It had no treadles, and was propelled forward by just touching the ground with the point of his boot. He used to ride from his blacksmith shop to Dumfries before the coach, which was counted a great feat in those days. There are some great stories told about him and his riding.[129] If "N.F." wishes any more information about him I can easily get it for him. The address of the velocipedist is Courthill, Keir, Dumfriesshire.

I am, etc., James Smith, Jun., Townhead, by Thornhill, Aug. 26.

· ·

28 August 1884

An Early Scotch Velocipedist

Sir,- Kindly permit me to thank very cordially those who have contributed information on this subject. Would "Kirkbean" give the name of the maker of the velocipedes which he states were used in Dumfries in 1816?

I am, etc., N.F., 26th August.

· ·

30 August 1884

Invention of Velocipedes

Sir, - I doubt Dumfries cannot lay much claim to the honour of inventing the velocipede if it can go no further back than 1837. If any of your readers turn to Boswell's "Life of Johnson", Vol. 11, page 94 (Malone's 5th Ed.), they will find that a machine was known in London in 1769 which was moved by the rider. Besides, as one of your correspondents points out, the machine of K. M'Millan had no treadle, and was merely moved by the foot pressing against the ground.[130] I have read somewhere of a machine precisely similar, and very fashionable for a short time in London about the middle of the last century. It also had the same name, "the dandy horse".

I am, etc., D.B., Coatbridge, 28th August.

The Origins of the Bicycle

Sources - F

- *The Irish Cyclist and Athlete*, 28 Nov. 1888

- *Bicycling News*, 26 Jan. and 2 Feb. 1889

- *The Scottish Cyclist*, 12 Dec. 1888, 23 & 26 Jan., 20 Feb., 17& 24 April, 1889

(these entries have been included in chronological order)

The Irish Cyclist and Athlete, 28 Nov. 1888

I had a letter from a lady friend, the other day, who had visited the Glasgow Exhibition. In the course of her rambles there, she paid a visit to the Bishop's Palace, which was built for the occasion and devoted principally to a large collection of historical matters of the Stuart's family. My informant tells me that, among other things of interest on view, there was the first bicycle ever made, which she described as "a rickety affair". Is it possible, Mr. Editor, the bicycle dates back to the sixteenth century? I should rather think if this is truly the case, that the canny Scot, like his Irish fellow man, would not hesitate to claim his invention. Perhaps some of your Scotch readers would enlighten us on this question.

Hylas

· ·

The Scottish Cyclist, 12 Dec. 1888

"Hylos", writing in the *Irish Cyclist*, says a lady friend of his, who visited the Glasgow Exhibition, describes the first bicycle – made by Dalzell of Lesmahagow – as "a rickety affair". He asks – "Is it possible the bicycle dates back to the sixteenth century?" No, it is not. It was built "prior" to the year 1846. By the way, an enthusiastic friend of ours is now prosecuting investigations, with the object of proving that Dalzell's machine is not the first bicycle. He believes it will be found that Dalzell copied one made by a blacksmith down Thornhill way. Of this more anon.

· ·

The Scottish Cyclist, 23 Jan. 1889

Editorial – "En Passant"

Who invented and made the first velocipede? Is a question often asked, but, save in two or three standard works, not always correctly answered. We had an interview last Monday with Mr. J.B. Dalzell, son of the late Gavin Dalzell, merchant, Lesmahagow, who invented and made what we have always understood to be the first velocipede as distinguished from the "Draisienne" or "dandy-horse", propelled by striking the feet on the ground. This was immediately prior to 1846, up to which time no record, so far as we are

aware, exists of any two-wheeled machine propelled by pedals. But Dalzell, it would seem, did more than this, for his in a sense was a dual invention. Not only did he make the first velocipede, but his design must have been the actual prototype of the most popular machine of the day – the rear-driving safety. This is a big claim certainly, but we believe it can be substantiated, and are informed that Mr. Dalzell has documentary evidence of a conclusive character in his possession, proving the date mentioned of his father's invention. As regards the machine itself, visitors to the Bishop's Palace in the Glasgow Exhibition will remember seeing an ancient wooden structure on view, labelled "the first bicycle". This was of boneshaker appearance, the rear-wheel, which was the larger of the two, *being the driver*, by means of long levers attached to roughly made pedals. Mr. Dalzell is naturally desirous of putting the question of who was the inventor of the crude from of the earliest bicycle beyond doubt, and with the view of having the matter settled, we have done our best to induce him to exhibit his sample of the original machine, at the Stanley Show this week. We believe we have succeeded in doing this, and that Scotland's claim to the earliest honours in cycle construction will be demonstrated forthwith.

· ·

Bicycling News, 26 Jan. 1889

Editorial – "The First Bicycle"

Who invented and made the first velocipede? Is a question over which many mighty intellects have struggled in vain. In future it should be more easy to answer. On Monday last the editor of the "Scottish Cyclist" had an interview with Mr. J.B. Dalzell, son of the late Gavin Dalzell, merchant, Lesmahagow, who invented and made what has always been understood to be the first velocipede as distinguished from the "Draisienne" or "dandy-horse", propelled by striking the feet on the ground. "This", says our Glasgow friend, "was immediately prior to 1846, up to which time no record, as far as we are aware, exists of any two-wheeled machine propelled by pedals. But Dalzell, it would seem, did more than this, for his, in a sense, was a dual invention. Not only did he make the first velocipede, but his design must have been the actual prototype of the most popular machine of the day – the rear-driving safety. This is a big claim certainly, but we believe it can be substantiated, and are informed that Mr. Dalzell has documentary evidence of a conclusive character in his possession proving the date mentioned of his father's invention. As regards the machine itself, visitors to the Bishop's Palace in the Glasgow Exhibition will remember seeing an ancient wooden structure on view labelled 'the first bicycle'. This was of boneshaker appearance, the rear wheel, which was the larger of the two, *being the driver*, by means of long levers attached to roughly-made pedals. Mr. Dalzell is naturally desirous of putting the question of who was the inventor of the crude form of the earliest bicycle beyond doubt, and with the view of having the matter settled, we have done our best to induce him to exhibit his sample of the original machine at the Stanley Show".

. . . .

Bicycling News, 2 Feb. 1889

"The Stanley Show" (extract)

….In an out-of-the-way corner will be found the original bicycle, made in or before 1846, by one gavin Dalzell, of Lesmahagow, which was mentioned in Bicycling News last week. It is a fine old relic, and excites a good deal of interest. But, apparently, being exhibited at shows does it very little good. It was for a long while the occupant of a niche in the Glasgow Exhibition, and possibly it has been knocked about in travelling. At any rate it is fast falling to pieces, and it would be well if some provision could be made for the preservation of so historical an antiquity. It is even compared with the less ancient boneshaker, a clumsy old thing; the wheels are like those of a cart, and the handlebar is doubled like a pair of shears. Its chief claim to notice lies in its antiquity, and the fact that it is driven by crank levers attached to the rear wheel.….

. . . .

The Scottish Cyclist, 20 Feb. 1889

"The Original Bicycle. The Prototype of the Modern Rear-Driving Safety".

The vexed question of the date and honour of the actual invention of the modern bicycle has often been discussed in the columns of the cycling press, and as often left undecided. At the late Stanley Show in the Crystal Palace, we exhibited at our stand the veritable machine which we now purpose demonstrating to be *the* precursor of the modern type. The inventor and constructor of this machine was Gavin Dalzell, merchant, of lesmahagow, Lanarkshire, Scotland, who was born on 29th August, 1811 and died 14th June, 1863. He possessed – in common with several other members of that old Dumfriesshire family to which he belonged – a decided talent for the invention of contrivances of a mechanical and scientifc character. Many of these have had considerable merit, and more than one have found their way into the records of the Patent Office. To the

cyclist, the most interesting and important is undoubtedly that of the machine under notice.

From the written testimony of a letter, dated Glasgow, 17th June, 1846, the manuscript of which lies before us as we write, we are enabled to affirm that the machine we exhibited was in existence prior to that date. The accuracy of this letter Mr. J.B. Dalzell, son of the inventor, and present owner of the relic, has had supplemented by the oral evidence of actual eye-witnesses of his father's progress on the machine along the roads of Lanarkshire. A further testimony is given in the letter of Mr. Francis Forrest to the inventor, dated Carnwath, 27th September, 1848, which also lies before us, and in which he says:-

> Sir, - As I did not see you when I was down to get a full account of your riding machine at that time , if you would be so good as to write me all about it, say what rate you can go a mile easily uphill, and if you would mark on this draught the lengths of the different parts you will oblige me.

Yours truly, Francis Forrest.

On the genuineness of these manuscripts all this testimony hinges, and this is incontestibly proved by the post-marks on the outer side of the communications – envelopes, at that time, having been practically unknown. Prior to the invention of the bicycle he had constructed a tricycle, the propulsion of which was effected in an ingenious and unique manner, the details of which, unfortunately, have not been preserved, parts of the tricycle having been utilized in the construction of the bicycle, which, now at least 43 years old, is an object of antiquarian interest to more than the inquiring cyclist. At the Crystal Palace it attracted much attention from critical eyes, and was, undoubtedly, one of the curiosities of the Stanley Show for 1889.

In construction the machine is, singularly enough, the exact prototype of the now popular rear-driven safety – an apt illustration of the truth of the old adage – "There's nothing new under the sun". It is constructed chiefly of wood, which, though worm eaten, is still wonderfully strong, especially in the wheels, these seeming to have stood the ravages of time and rough usage much better than the frame-work. The rear wheel – the driver – is of wood, shod with iron, about 40 inches in diameter. The front wheel is of similar construction, but only of about 30 inches in diameter. From the front wheel hub the fork – straight, and with a rake which some of our modern makers could copy with profit – passes up, when joined together, through the forepart of the wooden frame-work. A pair of handles are then attached and bent backward into a V-shape to suit the rider, who sits about two feet behind the front wheel hub. These were commonly termed the "reins". The main frame is somewhat like that which is now termed the "dip" pattern, the design of which is applied in an extended form to ladies' safeties. A wooden mud-guard rises from this frame, covering about one-fourth of the circumference of the hind wheel; from this to the back forks, which are horizontal, and of wood, vertical flat stays run down, forming a dress-guard after the manner of those on the latest cycling devlopment – the ladies' safety. From the front curved portion of the frame to this mud-guard a horizontal bar runs, on which is placed the seat – we cannot call it a saddle. This is immoveable and made of leather, with slight padding underneath. The driving mechanism is by means of cranks fitted to the rear wheel hub, connected by rods to long levers hinged to the wooden frame close to the head; the connecting rods being joined to the levers at about one-third of their whole length from the pedals, which are merely projecting bolts affixed to the lever ends. The action thus obtained is not rotary, being a downward and forward thrust with return, the feet describing a small segment of a circle. That the gearing, which constitutes the chief wonder to the critical and historical reader, was actually on the machine while being ridden by Mr. Dalzell is proved by the receipted accounts of the blacksmith, John Leslie, who made all the iron work used in its construction. The accounts being evidently rendered at the beginning of each year, in accordance with the usual custom 50 years ago, are dated January 27, 1847, and February 10, 1847. These documents speak of the machine as "the horse", the expression of the simple country folk, to whom its construction was apparently suggestive of a hobby-horse. From the testimony of Mr. Dalzell's contemporaries, it would seem that he was ever willing to give directions and instruction as to the building of his "horse", and as a natural result of this courtesy, similar machines came into existence in other parts of Scotland. The fame of the "wooden horse" became widely known. Indeed, the circumstance of a foreign claimant stepping forward to take the honour of being the inventor of the bicycle, is no matter of surprise. Natives of the upper Ward of Lanarkshire, in which it was so widely known, are to be found in every quarter of the globe. Besides this, the only brother of the inventor, Mr. John Dalzell, was an engineer, and in the pursuit of his business, he travelled and resided in England, and in North Eastern Europe, for several years dying in Sweden in 1851. It is quite possible that he might have given such information as would have enabled several similar machines to be constructed abroad. Bearing these facts in mind, the wonder is that France only has claimed the merit of its invention. However, to our mind the fact is indisputively (sic) proved that to Scotland – through Mr. Gavin Dalzell – must henceforth be given the honour of the birth-place of the modern cycle.

The honour has not been without its claimants in this country, the most credible of these claims being that of Kirkpatrick M'Millan, a native of Courthill, parish of Keir, Dumfriesshire, for whom it is asserted that he rode from Thornhill to Glasgow, about the year 1836 or '37. This word "about" is what damns the claim in our eyes, as anyone who has had experience of the unreliability of hearsay evidence in the matter of dates will readily concur in, and no documentary evidence has yet been forthcoming to support this shadowy claim.

It was one of the objects deemed worthy of a place in the Bishop's Palace at the late Glasgow International Exhibition, where it attracted much notice, and is now, we hear, to be sent to the Paris Exhibition for a similar purpose.

. . . .

The Scottish Cyclist, 24 April 1889

"The Original Bicycle"

The extract which follows appeared in last week's *Bicycling News*. B. N., it will be remembered, gave an illustration of the machine exhibited by us at the Stanley Show:-

> "The First Rear-Driving Safety. The following reaches us from S. James, Trevlyn, Mill Lane, W. Hampstead, N.W., under the date of April 8th, 1889: - "I had thought I was the inventor of the rear-driving safety, or its bone-shaking predecessor......but I am now confronted by one Gavin Dalzell, hailing also from Scotland, who is said to have invented such a bicycle in 1846. I would like to ask a question or two about this to clear up natters of doubt. I saw it at the Show, in a good state of preservation certainly, and my wonder was how it came to be kept in existence so long a time. I sent you a drawing of mine in the *English Mechanic*, Feb. 4, 1870, but although more than one was made, I do not believe I could produce a machine as evidence after these years, although plenty of witnesses as to the reality. Unless in constant use during the forty years, I cannot understand how such a machine could avoid being broken up by some of the numerous forces that would tend to its destruction – rust, ill-use, etc., etc. I cannot but think that it would be much more satisfactory if some evidence could be produced about the use of the machine, otherwise, although there were other drawings in the *English Mechanic* about that time, I cannot hear of any rear-driving machine besides my own having actually been made and used before 1870..."

Anyone who has seen the machine will be surprised at "S. James's" lack of understanding. We are afraid we must set him down as a maker of things "cheap and nasty". The *original rear-driven bicycle* is a good and substantial piece of wood and iron work, and will, we believe, last 100 years more. There is nothing more peculiar in its present condition than there is in the thousand and one articles of curiosity saved from the ravages of time and preserved in our museums. For many years the original bicycle has occupied a place of honour and security in the house of the inventor's son, J.B. Dalzell, Esq., of Hamilton....

Sources - G

The Wheel and Cycling Trade Review, 15 March 1889

"The Original Bicycle"

At the late Stanley Show was exhibited the machine which is now generally conceded to be the original bicycle. We present a cut of the machine reproduced from the *Scottish Cyclist*, also a representation of the features of the inventor, one Gavin Dalzell, a merchant of Lesmahgon (sic), Lanarkshire, Scotland. Dalzell was born August 29, 1811, and died June 14, 1863. He possessed decided talent for mechanical inventions. Fron the written testimony of a letter, and the testimony of J.B. Dalzell, son of the inventor and present owner of the machine, it is proven that it was in use previous to 1846, and there are eye-witnesses who recollect the inventor riding his bicycle over the roads of Lanarkshire.

In construction the Dalzell bicycle is the exact prototype of the now popular rear-driving safety. It is constructed chiefly of wood, which, though worm-eaten, is still wonderfully strong, especially in the wheels, these seeming to have stood the ravages of time and rough usage much better than the frame-work. The rear wheel – the driver – is of wood, shod with iron, about forty inches in diameter, and has twelve spokes, each about an inch in diameter. The front wheel is of similar construction, but only of about thirty inches in diameter. From the front wheel hub the fork – straight, and with a rake which some of our modern makers could copy with profit - passes up, when joined together, through the fore-part of the wooden frame-work. A pair of handles are then attached and bent backward into a V- shape to suit the rider, who sits about two feet behind the front wheel hub. These were commonly termed the "reins". The main frame is somewhat like that which is now termed the "dip" pattern, the design of which is applied in an extended form to ladies' safeties.

A wooden mud-guard rises from this frame, covering about one-fourth of the circumference of the hind wheel; from this to the back forks, which are horizontal, and of wood, vertical flat stays run down, forming a dress-guard after the manner of those on the latest cycling devlopment – the ladies' safety. From the front curved portion of the frame to this mud-guard a horizontal bar runs, on which is placed the seat – we cannot call it a saddle. This is immoveable and made of leather, with slight padding underneath. The driving mechanism is by means of cranks fitted to the rear wheel hub, connected by rods to long levers hinged to the wooden frame close to the head; the connecting rods being joined to the levers at about one-third of their whole length from the pedals, which are merely projecting bolts affixed to the lever ends. The action thus obtained is not rotary, being a downward and forward thrust with return, the feet describing a small segment of a circle. That the gearing, which constitutes the chief wonder to the critical and historical reader, was actually on the machine while being ridden by Mr. Dalzell is proved by the receipted accounts of the blacksmith, John Leslie, who made all the iron work used in its construction.

Sources - H

Bicycling News, 6 Feb. 1892

The Origin of the Rear-driven Bicycle. Gavin Dalzell's claim disputed.

Although it is probable that the great question of the origin of the bicycle will never be satisfactorily settled, it has now been generally conceded for some years past that the first rear-driven bicycle was the invention of the late Gavin Dalzell, a blacksmith of Lesmahagow, Scotland. His machine was made in 1846, or the year previous, and the motive power was communicated to the rear wheel by means of roughly-made pedals attached to long swinging levers. This bicycle was exhibited at the Stanley Show at the Crystal Palace in 1889, and there attracted a great deal of attention.

Within the last few weeks we have received an interesting letter from a Mr. Thomas McCall, of Kilmarnock, who, although he advances no claims on his own account, throws a new light on to those which have been made on behalf of Gavin Dalzell. The letter is of considerable interest, so we make no apology for printing it in full. It runs as follows:-

"January 12th, 1892

"At the outset I may say that I lay no claim to being the inventor of bicycles, or velocipedes as they were first named, but perhaps have had something to do in improving and introducing them.

The first idea in the way of a bicycle was simply a pair of wheels, a backbone to connect them, a seat between the wheels, so low that the rider's feet rested on the ground,

The Origins of the Bicycle

and a cross-bar on which the rider rested his breast and arms.

There was no driving gear whatever, but the rider propelled himself and machine forward by leaning on the cross-bar and kicking behind with his feet on the ground.

On one occasion two men went away with a machine of this description; on reaching the top of a hill on the road they both got on to have a ride down the hill. This road lay at right angles to another road at the foot of a very steep decline. On coming down the hill, being without a brake of any description, they were totally unable to turn on to the other road, dashed across it, and stuck fast into a thorn hedge. Had it been a stone wall instead of a hedge the consequences would have been serious.

I now come to the next improvement in velocipedes, viz., driving gear.

This was done by a blacksmith of the name of Peter McMillan, who wrought at Drumlanrig Castle for some time, and latterly on his own account at Pierpont, Dumfriesshire.[131] This would be about 1845.

I remember, when a boy, on coming out of school one day, seeing him with his velocipede. I followed him as he led it up a long hill and made a thorough inspection of it. On gaining the top of the hill the man got on and rode away. I ran for over half-a-mile, but he outstripped me.

It was after this principle that I made velocipedes years after, of which I will give account.

When I was an apprentice to the joiner and millwright trade, I commenced to make one in my spare time. On hearing, however, that a smith eight miles off had the remains of an old velocipede, without gearing (in all probability the one with which the two men had the escapade), I proceeded thither, bought it for 5s., and set out for home. On the way, however, the wheels broke down. I made new wheels, put cranks, connecting rods and pedals on, and for the first time owned a velocipede.

One day I rode 70 miles on this rude affair, from Sanquhar to two miles past Kilmarnock and back, but was well-nigh tired out. I disposed of that machine.

A few years after, at New Cumnock, I made an entirely new one without any drawings or reference, which was the one to which Mr. Galbraith refers, and which was in use over 20 years.

In 1871 I exhibited my machine against some boneshakers, which were in vogue at that time in Kilmarnock. I also rode into Glasgow, and received an order from a house for half-a-dozen of my sort. I made them along with some others. A clerk in connection with that firm in Glasgow (who was the best rider in Glasgow at that time), highly approved of my machine. I also made one for a surgeon in England.

I was advised to advertise it in an English journal, which I did, and sent a photograph of machine with rider, which was also inserted (*English Mechanic*).

Some years afterwards, I received a letter from a man in England stating that a certain party was copying off my design, which he thought was not fair.

Of course I had no claim or letters patent, and as I was unwell at the time, I took no notice of it.

The present safety bears a strong relationship to my design, to which many testify. The machines I made were safe and easily balanced, owing to the angle and formation of the shears (forks - AR) of the front wheel, and which the safety has. In this respect the velocipedes which I made were unique from all other boneshakers or high bicycles.

The only radical difference between my make and the safety is this: the power was conveyed to the rear wheel by means of swinging pedals, connecting rods and cranks, instead of, as in the safety, a chain.

This is a rough sketch of my machine. The wheels and backbone were all of wood.

On searching among my old papers I have come across one of the photographs which I got done 25 years ago, and which I enclose. There is a breast board on it, as you will see, but which I afterwards abandoned. You might please return the photograph when it has served your end.

Thos. McCall. 1, High Street, Kilmarnock, N.B."

It will be seen that Mr. McCall gives the credit of first adding driving gear to machines, which has hitherto been awarded to Dalzell, to Peter McMillan, also a blacksmith, "who wrought at Drumlanrig Castle", and fixes the date of the latter's invention as "about 1845". It may also be noted that he knew the man, and that seeing him with his velocipede, he "followed him up a long hill, and made a thorough inspection of it." - an inspection which was so thorough that he remembered the details well enough a few years later to be able to construct a machine on the same plan. For the satisfaction of our readers, we publish illustrations bearing on the subject. These include a sketch of Gavin Dalzell's bicycle which was made at the Stanley Show in 1889, and two drawings of the machine made by Mr. McCall - the one taken from his letter, and the other from the photograph, which he also sends us - a faded print bearing the name of Bruce and Howie, photographers, John Finnie Street, Kilmarnock. The resemblance between the two machines, one made several years after the other, is distinctly striking. At the same time it lends us no aid in the solution of the problem. Who made the first rear-driven bicycle? On the evidence before us both Gavin Dalzell and Peter McMillan seem to have made machines of this description about the years 1845 or 1846. Perhaps some of our readers can throw some further light on the subject.

. . . .

Bicycling News, 13 Feb. 1892

The first gear-driven bicycle. Gavin Dalzell's claim further disputed.

Mr. James Johnston, late sub-captain Glasgow Tricycling Club, writes: -

"As a Dumfriesian and a cyclist, and also being related in a far off way to the late *Kirkpatrick McMillan*, blacksmith, Courthill, near Penpont, in the parish of Keir, Dumfriesshire, I have been very much interested in the letter you publish from Mr. Thomas McCall, 1, High Street, Kilmarnock, in your issue of the 6th inst., also your editorial comments. Like Mr. McCall, I am inclined to dispute the claim of the later Gavin Dalzell, cooper, in Lesmahagow, as being the inventor of driving-gear on the old hobby-horse, or dandy-horse, in the year 1846. For some considerable time past I have, when opportunity occurred in visiting Thornhill, Penpont and Dumfries districts, been engaged in collecting information to prove that Kirkpatrick McMillan (not *Peter* McMillan, although often called *Pate* McMillan by his friends) was the first and real inventor, and that Dalzell's is only a copy as regards the driving power. McMillan's machine had a fancy horse's head and a breast-plate, as spoken to by McCall, and everyone who knew McMillan's horse confirms these points.

After such a lapse of time it is exceedingly difficult to get hold of real tangible or documentary evidence. There were so few letters and newspapers in those days, and I am still busy collecting all I can bearing on the subject. To publish details of all the letters I have received from those who remember having seen and known McMillan personally would occupy many pages. Amongst others I have interviewed and have evidence from are: –

1. John Findlater, blacksmith, Carronbridge, near Thornhill, a hale, hearty old fellow, who wrought in the late Duke of Buccleuch's smithy on Drumlanrig Estate with McMillan, and who was on intimate terms with him. He is positive McMillan put driving gear on on (sic?) or before 1840.

2. Samuel Dalzell, blacksmith, Drumlanrig Mains, letter dated 12th Sept. 1888.

3. John Brown, merchant, Penpont, trustee in winding up McMillan's affairs.

4. Thomas Haining, Farmer, Laight, Tynron, by Thornhill.

5. Robert McMillan, blacksmith, a nephew of McMillan's.

6. Jas. Black, oatmeal miller, Dumfries (now unfortunately stone blind), a most intelligent man, who lived for years near McMillan.

All these parties are positive that McMillan had driving gear on his old dandy horse for some years before 1846, the date fixed on by Dalzell's friends when the latter made his bicycle.

Last week I received a most interesting letter from a gentleman named Thomson, near Blantyre, who saw McMillan and his bicycle twice in Glasgow, about 1838, and also in 1845.

During the last eight days there have also been several letters in the *Glasgow*

Evening Times backing out the claims of McMillan *versus* Dalzell's. I annex a copy of the very latest, which appeared in that paper on the evening of 6th inst. which will speak for itself.

> The principle of driving is identical on both machines – of that there seems no doubt. Finally, I may add McMillan stood over 6ft., and was a powerful and fearless rider, and repeatedly covered 14 miles in an hour. He made several machines, the last one after his death falling into the possession of a nephew in Liverpool, who ultimately sold it to a family of the name of Gladstone, relations of the present ex-Premier".

The following is the letter from the *Glasgow Evening Times* of February 6th: -

> Sir, - I read with interest in Thursday's issue Mr. Johnston's letter anent (about – AR) the invention of the bicycle. In further confirmation of our common opinion, he naturally desiderates documentary evidence in preference to hearsay, if such could be obtained. No doubt such evidence, if it existed at all, would be very satisfactory, especially in establishing the year in which a particular event was said to have happened. Nevertheless, your correspondent must not under-estimate the high value of so called hearsay in a matter of this kind, especially when the report is so general as it is. It may be said that the evidence on which I myself mainly rely is that of one of Kirkpatrick Macmillan's own sisters, Mary Grierson Macmillan, for a considerable number of years, Mrs. ———. She remembers her brother making the dandy-horse in the smithy sometime about 1834. This machine was a bicycle without the cranks. A few years later he improved his machine by adding cranks. On this improved machine Kirkpatrick Macmillan made his famous ride to Glasgow, leaving Courthill one evening about 8 p.m. after his day's work in the smithy. Many stories are current as to Macmillan's adventures on the dandy-horse. Passing through Old Cumnock on his way to Glasgow, as he was going down a well-known incline in the village about midnight at a terrific rate, he met a young man on his way home from seeing a sweetheart. This man, being somewhat superstitious, got a terrible fright, and reported upon reaching home that that he had "seen the deill fleeing through the air". Your

correspondent must be aware that writing was not so common in those days as now.

I am, etc, Ben Jubal

Bicycling News, 20 Feb. 1892

More about the origin of the rear-driven bicycle.

Following up the interesting letter which appeared in our issue of a fortnight ago, the Glasgow representative of *Bicycling News* recently called upon Mr. Thomas McCall, of Kilmarnock. To him we are very greatly indebted for the courteous manner in which he and his family entertained our news searcher, and the considerable trouble to which he has put himself in consequence of our quest for information as to the genuine inventor of the rear-driver. Mr. McCall has long past given up riding on wheels. He has a wife and grown up family, including a son who possesses a safety of more modern pattern than the machine on which his father one day covered no less than seventy miles. The following letters, which have, within the last few days been received by our Kilmarnock friend and forwarded to us, show, we think, almost beyond question that the claim set up for Kirkpatrick or Patrick McMillan, that he came before Dalzell in the originating of the safety, has been made out. The earliest date with which Dalzell seems to have been credited with riding his machine is 1845, and we here give proof of McMillan being in the field four or five years earlier than that.

The first of the letters we publish is from Mr. James Geddes, who purchased McMillan's machine in 1851, and the second is from Mr. John Findlater, who is upwards of 80 years of age, and who has been in the neighbourhood of Dumfriesshire all his days. These are followed by an extract from the *Dumfries Standard* of the 6th of this month: -

[Letter from James Geddes to Thomas McCall]

"Bellstane, Feb. 9th, 1892.

"Mr. Thomas McCall,

"Dear Sir, - I received yours this morning, and am not sure if I can give any additional information regarding the origin of the gear-driven bicycle. But I am older than you, and it strikes me forcibly that Kirkpatrick McMillan made and used his gear-driven bicycle prior to the year 1845. I bought his machine in 1851, and the wheels were creaky, having been out of use for a long while. I am not aware if ever McMillan made another. There is an old man, also a blacksmith, over 80 years of age, still active and doing a little work, who was with McMillan when he wrought at Drumlanrig Mains, who crossed a bicycle driven by the kicking process. His name is John Findlater. If you write to him, he can give you more information than I can. I remember on one

occasion McMillan, Findlater and Wm. Nichol[132] went to Sanquhar on a trip, each having a machine, McMillan only having driving gear, and they agreed to keep together, but being challenged by some weavers to a race, they freed McMillan of the bond, and away he went, leaving the weavers reeking and sweating far behind. I am not sure whether McMillan told me or not – I think he did – that in the days of the stage-coach he went to Glasgow, and amused a crowd of students, etc., by cutting the "figure eight" on the Green with his gear-driven bicycle, and came home before the coach. He might have gone to Glasgow some other route than that by which he returned. I cannot say, but I know of no man more likely to give the date of McMillan's invention than John Findlater, Carronbridge, and I see in the Dumfries Saturday *Standard*, a letter, signed James Johnston, which it seems is distinctly relative to K. McMillan, who states the date of his friend's invention to be 1840 or 1841, which I do think is very near the mark.

"Hoping that you are all well, and that you will reach the truth bye-and-bye, I am, your truly,

(Signed) James Geddes.

"P.S. – I have returned your printed letter, thinking you may have to use it."

[Letter from John Findlater to *Bicycling News*]

"Carranbridge, 12th February, 1892

"Dear Sir, - I received your letter last night about the old dandy-horse. I wrought along with Mr. McMillan for some years both at Mallyford and Drumlanrig Mains. Now, the smithy was removed from Mallyford to the Mains, I think, about the year 1840 or 1841. I had my house at Burnhead, a little more than a mile from the smithy, but the Mains was 3½ miles from Burnhead, and I removed from Burnhead to the Alton to be near my work. Now, here are dates which I have. I removed from Burnhead to Alton on Whit-Sunday, 1844, and Mr. McMillan had cranks on his dandy-horse before that date, but how long I cannot say, but I think this paper which I enclose from the Dumfries Standard of February 6th, 1892, must be very correct.

Be so good as to let me know how you got on with the Lesmahagow cooper.

Yours truly, (Signed), John Findlater.

"Carranbridge, by Thornhill, Dumfriesshire."

Extract from *Dumfries Standard*, of 6th February, 1892.

Who Invented the Bicycle? The following letter appears in the *Evening Times*, dated 12, Carment Drive, Shawlands, Glasgow, February 2nd, 1892: - "As a Dumfriesian and a cyclist, and also being related in a far off way to the late *Kirkpatrick McMillan*, blacksmith, Courthill, near Penpont, in the parish of Keir, Dumfriesshire, I may inform your correspondent, 'Ben Jubal', and others interested in cycling matters that I have for some considerable time been engaged in collecting information to prove that McMillan was undoubtedly the first in the field to put driving-gear levers and cranks on the old hobby-horse or dandy-horse, and not the late Gavin Dalzell, cooper, in Lesmahagow. To enter into the details would occupy too much of your valuable space, but, briefly, I may say the evidence I have secured in Penpont, Keir, Thornhill, and Dumfries districts shows that it was about 1840-41 that McMillan brought out his invention. I hope to publish full particulars very soon. Meanwhile I will be glad if 'Ben Jubal' or any other gentleman can furnish any further news on the point, documentary evidence as against hearsay being preferable. The date of Dalzell's bicycle is 1846 not 1836.

"I am, etc., James Johnston."

It does not seem at all improbable that, Lesmahagow being between Carronbridge and Edinburgh, a road sometimes ridden by McMillan, Dalzell may have seen the machine used on these journeys, and made a copy of it. McMillan had occasionally some curious adventures. On one occasion he was laid hold of by some policemen, in Edinburgh, for footpath riding – not because they considered his machine a carriage, but on account of his endangering the lives of the lieges – but on his doing some fancy riding they let him off. McCall himself put in a lot of riding on his machine, which he broke up but a year or two ago, and which weighed probably about 60lbs. The feat he accomplished of riding seventy miles in one day was a wonderful one. Still there must have been some semblance of speed in the machine, as he timed himself to do a mile in five minutes, and could do about ten miles in one hour.

. . . .

Bicycling News, 5 March 1892

More about the origin of the rear-driven bicycle.

Mr. Jas. Johnston, of the Glasgow Tricycling Club, writes:-

Referring to my letter to you of the 13th inst. on this subject, and also to further information in your later issues, I beg now to hand you annexed matter, as also a photo of Macmillan (please return same), which I hope you will be able to publish in an early issue of *Bicycling News*.

I have published in a Scottish contemporary of yours, on 17th ult. (see *Scottish Cyclist* of that date), copies of letters from the following parties, all extremely strong in favour of Macmillan as being the pioneer of gear-driving on the old hobby-horse or dandy-horse: -

- 1. Letter from Mr. Samuel Dalzell, Drumlanrig Mains, Thornhill, to Robert Macmillan, Dumfries, a nephew of Kirkpatrick Macmillan, dated 12th Sept., 1888.

- 2. Letter from Mr. John Findlater, blacksmith, Canonbridge (sic?), by Thornhill, to James Johnston, Glasgow, dated 26th Jan., 1889.

- 3. Letter from Mr. Thomas Haining, farmer, Laight, Tynron, Dumfries-shire, to James Johnston, Glasgow, dated 30th Jan., 1889.

- 4. Letter from Mr. John Brown, merchant, Penpont, to James Johnston, Glasgow, 30th Jan., 1889.

- 5. Letter from Mr. Robert Hamilton, Castlebank, Dumfries, to James Johnston, Glasgow, 6th February, 1892.

- 6. Letter from Mr. Robert Macmillan, blacksmith, Pleasance, Dumfries to James Johnston, Glasgow, 5th February, 1889.

- 7 and 8. Copies of letters which appeared in *North British Daily Mail*, 21st August, 1884.

- 9 and 10. Copies of letters from *Glasgow Evening Times*, dated 5th and 6th February, 1892.

- 11. Extracts from letters from Mr. W. Auchennraith, Blantyre, to James Johnston, Glasgow, February, 1892.

Since these letters have been exhibited to the public, especially in the Dumfries, Thornhill, Keir, and Penpont districts, through the kindness of the respective editors of *Dumfries Herald* and *Dumfries Standard*, I have been fairly overwhelmed with a mass of correspodence, quite positive in asserting Macmillan to be the gear inventor. To publish the whole of it is an impossibility. I can only refer to a few letters briefly, and ask you to publish one or two important ones. The evidence daily grows stronger in favour of Macmillan. Link by link, in the interests of truth, I am discovering further proofs that he was on the road with his driving gear many years prior to 1846. I hope to send you a summary of the whole evidence I have collected for an early issue, and also the letter [sic? – 'letters'?] for your perusal. After which I will be glad to read your editorial comments.

Mrs. E.....B......writes from Academy Street, Dumfries, under date Feb. 9th, 1892, as follows: -

    "Mr. Johnston,

The Origins of the Bicycle

"Dear Sir, - I noticed in the *Dumfries and Galloway Courier and Herald*, of Saturday, 6 an article on "Who Invented the Bicycle?" and information wanted in regard to it from any gentleman. Although I am only a *woman* I flatter myself that what I can say on the subject will be accepted, *and it is truth*. To begin with, when I was a little girl I sat many a time on Kirkpatrick Macmillan's shoulder holding on by his head while he drove his dandy-horse (as it was then called) from where my father and mother lived to Mr. Shaw, the gamekeeper's at Drumlanrig Castle. Macmillan was lodging with us at the time, and wrought in the smithy at Drumlanrig Mains. *That was in the years 1842-43. How I remember the dates so exact is that my father got a situation near to Dumfries in May, 1843. We left Drumlanrig then, and Macmillan was with us till the day we left.* He may have been with us in '41, but I am not sure as to that. At all events his dandy-horse must have been made before he came to stay with us so he must have been the first to invent that mode of conveyance so far as Dalzell is concerned. *Had it not been that I did not want the credit of the invention to be given to one who had no right to it*, I, being a woman, would not have written to you on the subject, but I thought it would only be doing justice to the memory of the old friend of my girlhood. You are at liberty to use what I have said if it will in any way help you in what you wish to prove, but not to publish my name. Hoping you will succeed, I am, etc.

(Signed), E…..B…..

A day or two later this lady sent me the following postscript to add to above, viz.: -

"P.S. – Mr. Johnston. In reading your article on the bicycle in Saturday's *Herald* I thought then that I had omitted to say anything about how Macmillan propelled his bicycle. I am sorry I cannot remember very clearly the construction of it, but certainly there was driving gear on it. There were places he put his feet on to move it along, and not on the ground. I remember that perfectly well, and seeing others trying to work it but could not, as they always got their feet off and on to the ground, and also something above that he held with his hands, but I think that would be to guide it, as he sometimes used his left to hold me when it was going at a great speed. As far as I can remember his position on it, and the working of it, had much the same appearance as they have at the present time, but the bicycle itself was a very different machine, that you have heard described already. The head is correct – I can see it in my mind's eye as distinct as if it were before me. I may say, that I can prove the date to be correct from a Bible that I got in a present the year after we left Drumlanrig. My name is on it and May, 1844. Sorry for troubling you with so much, and I doubt to no purpose. I am, etc.,

(Signed), E……B……"

Referring to the above, I have, after considerable persuasion, got this lady's consent to publish her name, viz., Elizabeth Fingland or Bailey, and she has also sent me her Bible to prove her statements. Her father held a situation on Drumlanrig estate, under the late Duke of Buccleuch, and the *Bible was presented to her by the niece of her father's new master, about a year after they removed from Drumlanrig*. The inscription on the bible is: - "Elizabeth Fingland. With best wishes. Bromrig House, 20 May, 1844".

Mr. William Brown, son of Mr. John Brown, merchant, Penpont, trustee on Macmillan's estate, in letters dated 15 and 19 ult., writes: -

"Mr. Willian Brown, dyker, and Mr. Walter McKinnell, Penpont, old residenters, are both certain it is upwards of fifty years since Macmillan had driving gear on his dandy-horse.

Mr. Robert Mathieson, grocer, Bankhead, Caerlaverock, by Dumfries, a Penpont native, on visiting the Glasgow Exhibition, and looking at Dalzell's old bicycle and the date, 1846, exclaimed to some friends, He had seen Macmillan *on one many years before that*.

Mrs. McWhir, widow, Penpont, was married forty-five years ago (the ladies generally don't forget the date of their marriage), and says Macmillan was scouring the country long before that event.

Mr. William Brown, smith, Townhead, Penpont, aged sixty-seven, says Macmillan exhibited his riding powers in the presence of the Dowager Duchess of Buccleuch and company in front of Drumlanrig Castle in 1844."

Mr. John Findlater, Carronbridge, corroborates this incident. I could add some more names from the Penpont district, but these should suffice.

Mr. Thomas Wright, station, Slammanan, aged sixty-six, in letters of 16 and 25 ult., says: -

"I would be about twelve years of age when I went to be "Pate's" nearest neighbour. He had his first horse then; it had no driving gear…..It would be in 1838, or early in 1839, when he made his second horse….He made the gear himself. I was often at the smithy, and saw him working at it. He also improved the spring of the saddle. The first one had a single spring, his second had two springs made in a long oval shape, perhaps three or four inches apart at the centre and tapering at each end; it was a decided improvement. I left the district at Martinmass, 1840….I think it probable his first trip to Glasgow would be in 1841….I returned to Keir in 1844. I resided there seven years, about half-a-mile from Courthill."

Robert Brydon, Cample House, Thornhill, writing on the 24 Feb., says John Martin, blacksmith, Closeburn Mill, served his apprenticeship with Macmillan, and used to ride home frequently on his (Macmillan's) machine, in 1843, when going to see his father. He thinks Macmillan had driving gear on as early as 1839.

Letter from Rev. John Henderson, M.A., North Newton Manse, Newton-on-Ayr, Feb. 19, 1892: -

"Dear Sir, I duly received yours yesterday morning, and have to thank you for the same. Referring to the subject of your communication, it may be stated that until less than a month ago we were not aware of the fact that a bicycle with a driving gear had been exhibited in the Glasgow

International Exhibition as the first gear-driven bicycle in Scotland, much less that it purported to have been made by one Gavin Dalzell, of lesmahagow. Had we been aware of that, you may be well assured that for the honour of my uncle, the late Kirkpatrick Macmillan, and for the love of justice we would have challenged the claim at once. You may make whatever use of this letter you please.

Yours sincerely, (Signed) John Henderson."

This gentleman is a son of Mrs. Henderson (Mary Grierson Macmillan), sister of Kirkpatrick Macmillan, and she is now residing as above at Newton-on-Ayr.

Mrs. Henderson, in a former issue of *Bicycling News* (13th ult.), is referred to by 'Ben Jubal', who states that Macmillan, one night after work was over in the smithy at Courthill, started for Glasgow. He stayed at Old Cumnock over the night with an old acquaintance of his, a school-master named McKennell, and left next day for Glasgow. This is referred to more particularly in the annexed letter, which I cut out of the *Evening Times*: -

"Sir, - Allow me to so state a few facts which came under my own observation in reference to above.

Previous to the year 1843 (the year of the Disruption) Kirkpatrick McMillan, blacksmith, Dunscore, Dumfriesshire, rode into Old Cumnock late one summer's night or early in the morning. He called at the residence of his cousin, Mr. John M'Kinnell, the then parish school-master, where he was kindly welcomed and hospitably entertained. In the morning, at the breakfast hour, M'Millan came out with his horse, and rode up and down the town to the great amusement of the crowds who ran after him. I saw him do what I have never seen another do since, except in a circus. Standing on the saddle and guiding the front wheel with his hand, he came down what was then called M'Kinley's Brae at full speed. About that time several imitations of M'Millan's machine, with some improvements, were made in the engineering works of George M'Cartney, Cumnock, and for several years were in great vogue. The drawings you gave in Saturday's *Times* are, on the whole, pretty accurate, but, as far as I remember the wheels were both one size.

I am, etc., John Templeton."

In riding down McKinlay's Brae at midnight he (Macmillan) nearly frightened a young man out of his senses who had been away seeing his sweetheart. I have just discovered this man's name, who shortly afterwards got married. He was a fellow apprentice of John Templeton's, and some of his family are still about Old Cumnock. I hope, therefore, to fix pretty definitely the date of Macmillan's visit to Old Cumnock on his first trip to Glasgow. Mr. Templeton makes two slight inaccuracies in his letter. 1. Courthill is in the parish of Keir; Dunscore is a neighbouring parish. 2. McKennell was only an intimate acquaintance, not a cousin.

· ·

Bicycling News, 19 March 1892

Editorial - The first rear-driven bicycle

The thanks of the historian of the future, and those of cyclists generally, are due to Mr. James Johnston, of Glasgow, who, after an infinite amount of correspondence and research, has undoubtedly succeeded in proving that the first rear-driven, or gear-driven, bicycle was made by Kirkpatrick Macmillan some time between 1835 and 1840. Hitherto the credit has been awarded to Gavin Dalzell, of Lesmahagow, who made his first machine in 1845 or 1846, bu the evidence collected by Mr. Johnston distinctly proves the justice of the claim made for Macmillan. We have, during the last few weeks, been able to publish a good deal of this evidence, and a concluding portion appears in our issue of today. Besides this we have received from Mr. Johnston the originals of the various documents, and having perused and examined them carefully we have no hesitation in pronouncing in favour of Macmillan's claim. The proof is, to our mind, overwhelming, and especial stress may be laid on the evidence of John Findlater, a fellow apprentice of Macmillan's, who made a machine of the same fashion but without gear, and the very conclusive statement of Wm. Fergusson, a nephew of Gavin Dalzell. Henceforth, therefore, the credit of having made the first rear-driven bicycle must be given to Kirkpatrick Macmillan.

· ·

Bicycling News, 19 March 1982

More about the origin of the rear-driven bicycle. Kirkpatrick Macmillan's claim substantiated.

Mr. Jas. Johnston, of the Glasgow Tricycling Club, writes us, concluding his arguments in favour of Macmillan, thus: -

I left off in B. N. of 5th inst. saying I had found out the name of the young man who got such a fright on seeing Macmillan on wheels riding into Old Cumnock after midnight. This was James Kennedy, a shoemaker, who told the story to his shopmates, and they made fun of him until they witnessed the unwonted spectacle of seeing Macmillan riding about the town next day. He (Macmillan) appears to have engaged in conversation with many of the residents from the fact that immediately after his visit a copy of his bicycle with levers and cranks was made at Macartney's Millwright and Engineering Works, a business still successfully carried on.

I visited Old Cumnock on Saturday, 6th inst., furnished with an introduction to Mr. A. B. Todd, the local correspondent of the *Glasgow Herald*. In company of Mr. Todd we first called on Mr. George Goldie (about 76), the principle partner of Macartney's business already referred to. Mr. Goldie remembers distinctly

The Origins of the Bicycle

Macmillan's visit to Old Cumnock prior to the Disruption in 1843, when he stayed with McKinnell, the schoolmaster, and then proceeded for Glasgow. Mr. Goldie is positive of the time, because McKinnell left the school when the Disruption took place. (McKinnell died in America two years ago). We then proceeded to Macartney's workshops, where Mr. Goldie showed us a small copy of a horse's head, which belonged to the last bicycle made (on Macmillan's principle) made at the shop. Mr. Goldie has been in Old Cumnock all his life, and is now at the head of the business in which he served his apprenticeship.

We next called on Mr. D. Smith, Inspector of Poor (shoe-maker in his younger days), who spoke confidently of seeing Macmillan and his horse before the Disruption of 1843. As a schoolboy, along with a number of his mates, he was too late for school on account of running after Macmillan, but the teacher (McKinnell) did not punish them, as he threatened to do, when they explained how they were late for school. We next interviewed Miss Sarah Kennedy, housekeeper at Hillside House, and daughter of James Kennedy already mentioned, who was returning from seeing her sweetheart when frightened by Macmillan. Her father was married in 1842. I subjoin a copy of his marriage certificate: -

"That James Kennedy and Jean Vallance have been proclaimed in order to marriage in the Parish Church here, and that no objections have been offered is attested at Cumnock, the 18th day of August, 1842, by – (Signed) John McKinnell, Sess. Clerk."

"The above pair were married at Cumnock by me, on the 19th day of August, 1842.

(Signed) Robert Brown, Minister."

In addition to those who have already spoken of Macmillan's first ride to Glasgow, the *Dumfries Standard* of 24th ultimo publishes a long interview by their reporter to another sister of Macmillan's, presently residing in Dumfries, viz., Mrs. Marchbank, widow, aged 72, who details graphically all she knows about her brother and his geared velocipede. She is positive of the time of her brother's ride to Glasgow from the fact of one of her daughters, now over 49 years of age, being at the time a baby at the breast. This confirms the Old Cumnock information as above very strongly.

Having read the above, your readers can guess the surprise I experienced when a nephew of the late Gavin Dalzell, of Lesmahagow, called at my residence, and has since handed me the following statement for publication, which will speak for itself: -

"In the year 1846 I was staying at Lesmahagow with my uncle, Gavin Dalzell – that year he made his velocipede. He told me he had seen a man the year before riding a velocipede down the Glasgow and Carlisle Road. He said

this man was a blacksmith, from Thornhill, but he could not give me his name.

Some years ago, when his son J.B.D. was writing about his father being the inventor of the velocipede, I wanted him to go to Thornhill and make search of the blacksmith his father told me of. I fear J.B.D. never took the trouble of going in search of the inventor, but wished it to be believed his father was the inventor of driving gear, viz., cranks and levers.

(Signed) Wm. Fergusson, 6, Kenmure Street, Glasgow, March 12th, 1892."

The above information is so startling that it may be asked why it has never been proclaimed to the world till now. I make answer and say simply because no one appears, to use an old Scottish phrase, "to have fashed their thoom aboot Macmillan", and it is only now, when his claims have been brought prominently before the public by the aid of the cycling papers and the Glasgow and Dumfries newspapers, that the truth has come out at last. Mr. Fergusson says a friend sent him some Dumfries newspaper, and after reading what was said about McMillan, he determined at once to pay me a visit and state the truth about his uncle, Gavin Dalzell. The initials "J.B.D." stand for his cousin, Mr. J.B. Dalzell, of Hamilton, the son of Dalzell. Mr. Fergusson is now about 65 years of age, and at the time he was staying with his uncle he was an assistant-teacher in a Lesmahagow school. His uncle was on foot, going his rounds selling tea, when he saw Macmillan on his geared velocipede. Whether the two men engaged in conversation or not, I leave your riders to judge. At all events, Dalzell afterwards had many a consultation with his friend, John Leslie, the Lesmahagow blacksmith, with the result that they managed to make a copy of Macmillan's machine, with lever and crank driving. That Gavin Dalzell copied from Macmillan is further testified to in some Lesmahagow evidence now in my possession, but which, I regret, I am not allowed to publish.

Summing up all the evidence I have collected in abstract form, I now draw attention to the following: -

1. Mrs. Henderson and Mrs. Marchbank (sisters of Kirkpatrick Macmillan), Messrs. Thomas Wright (Slammanon), John Findlater (Carronbridge), Robert Hamilton, B. Irving and I. Murray (all of Dumfries), are of opinion he had no driving gear on his dandy-horse prior to about 1840 (the date of Dalzell's bicycle is 1846).

2. B. Irving (Cintra Villas, Dumfries), and I. Murray (Dumfries), say that Macmillan's first experiment with levers and cranks was applied to a tricycle he made prior to or in the year 1835, but finding the work of propelling it too laborious, he set to and made his second dandy-horse with levers and cranks attached. Irving is positive on this point, as he had a ride on this tricycle before he left Keir Parish (when he was very

intimate with Macmillan) and went to Dumfries Academy, at 15 years of age, where Macmillan's brother John, at the time, was rector.

3. John Templeton, (Glasgow, native of Old Cumnock), Geo. Goldie and D. Smith (Old Cumnock), remember distinctly seeing Macmillan and his geared velocipede in Old Cumnock prior to the Disruption in 1843.

4. Mrs. Bailey (Dumfries) states positively in a long letter that as a girl she sat perched on Macmillan's shoulder whilst he drove his geared dandy-horse in 1842-3. At that time Macmillan lodged with her father and mother on Drumlanrig Estate. Her father left Duke of Buccleuch's employ in 1843, which she confirms by producing a Bible she got presented to her in May, 1844.

5. Messrs. James Black, Robert Macmillan, and Mrs. Bailey (Dumfries), also Thomas Haining (Laight), W. Thomson (Blantyre), and Thomas McCall (Kilmarnock), describe his bicycle similarly as having the horse's head, and also the levers and cranks. The Old Cumnock witnesses also refer to the horse's head, and a nice copy of same is to be seen now at Macartney's Works there.

6. At least thirty persons still alive can be produced to testify what they know of Macmillan and his bicycle, but not one of them can say that they ever heard or knew of such a man as Gavin Dalzell until this discussion started, or, at all events, until a few of them cast their eyes on his bicycle in the late Glasgow international Exhibition.

7. When Mr. Thomas McCall (Kilmarnock), met Macmillan with his bicycle in 1845, he must have had a lengthened conversation with him, and examined his bicycle very carefully so as to be able to build a copy of it for himself and take orders for several more from both Scotch and English customers.

8. Macmillan was at least twice in Glasgow with his bicycle, and once at Edinburgh. His first ride to Glasgow was in 1841 or '42, when he stayed overnight with his friend McKinnell at Old Cumnock. This is the occasion on which he raced on the road with the Dumfries and Glasgow coach, and gave it the go-by for a short distance. At this time he would be about 28 or 29 years of age.

9. He also rode to Glasgow in 1845, via Dalveen Pass, Elvanfoot, Lesmahagow, and Douglas. Mr. McCall (Kilmarnock), and Mr. W. Thomson (Blantyre), saw him that year. This also is supposed to be the year referred to by several correspondents in letters to *N. B. Daily Mail*, in 1884.

10. 1845 is the year Dalzell saw Macmillan on the Carlisle road. Whether the two men were actually acquainted or not I cannot make out. Dalzell is known to be an old Dumfries-shire name.

11. Having satisfactorily proved that Macmillan was the inventor, and Dalzell an imitator, I may now leave the matter in the hands of the jury – your readers – to say whether I have proved my case or not.

12. I may conclude by saying Kirkpatrick Macmillan was a splendid tradesman; anything he put his hand to was well done, and as a proof of his ability, his son informs me, he made several ploughs without even a screw in them – two of these were to the order of Mr. Gladstone, of Capenoch, near Penpont, a brother of the ex-Premier. Macmillan was of undoubtable pluck – once he set himself to any piece of complicated work, he persevered until success crowned his efforts. He belonged to a clever family. His brother John was at one time tutor to the late Mr. John Bright, M.P., and afterwards successively Rector of Dumfries Academy, Glasgow High School and Edinburgh High School. Another brother, George, was second master of Hutchinson's Schools, Glasgow, whilst a third was a clerk in that city. He was of a kindly disposition – one of the hail-fellow-well-met sort – a lively companion, and a man devoid of any pride. This is shown by his willingness to exhibit his bicycle, and to assist anybody to make one for themselves. He stood over six feet, a fine specimen of an athlete, and was admittedly a powerful and fearless rider, in fact, one of our earliest trick riders. On market days, when he frequently rode from Courthill to Dumfries – 14 miles – he appeared to have had no difficulty in keeping up with the farmers in their gigs. He died on 26 june, 1878, in his 65th year. Two of his family now survive – a son in Liverpool and a daughter married in Walsall.

13. At the time he made his first bicycle we must not forget newspapers were scarce. In Dumfries in 1833 a local paper was sold at 7d., and the postage of a letter from Thornhill to London was 1s. 1½d., and to Edinburgh and Glasgow about 8d. People therefore at that time read few newspapers, and wrote as few letters as possible.

14. Many old acquaintances of Macmillan are under the impression that he was the first man to even make a dandy-horse (without cranks), but that is a mistake. Such machines were in existence before he was born.

I beg to call your attention to several typographical errors in my contribution on this subject in B.N. of 5th inst. The words (1) "Perepont" should have been *Penpont*; (2) "Dumfries and *Glasgow* Courier" should read "Dumfries and *Galloway* Courier; (3) "Smithy at *Dumfries* Mains" is inserted in place of *"Drumlanrig* Mains"; and (4) "McKennell" is substituted for *McKinnell*.

We refer in another paragraph to the evidence collected by Mr. Johnston. The portraits we give here are those

The Origins of the Bicycle

of Macmillan and Thomas McCall, who made a machine copied from Macmillan's in 1846

. . . .

Bicycling News, 26 March 1892

Our Letterbox - The first rear-driven bicycle.

Sir, - I have read with great interest your papers on the origin of the rear-driver. I may say in further proof of Macmillan's claim that my late uncle, William Nicol, of Drumlanrig Mains, made the woodwork for Macmillan's machine, he (Macmillan) making the ironwork for my uncle necessary to convert his "dandy horse" into a rear-driver. My uncle's machine was still in good condition in 1880, when I used to ride it on Drumlanrig Castle Road. The power was communicated to the driving wheel by means of long levers. (Diagram – copy this). The lever working on a ratchet at B, C representing the centre of the driving wheel, and A the pedal. Unfortunately, it has since gone to pieces.

My father used to frequently ride Macmillan's machine when a youngster, and he says that his shins are still marked by tumbles received from that refractory animal.

A true anecdote of Macmillan may interest you. He was riding through the streets of Edinburgh when he unfortunately collided with an ancient piece of petticoated humanity, for which offence he was hauled before the baillie. He, "douce mon", fined Macmillan 5s. for, said this Solomon, "It's no possible for flesh and bluid tae sit on the tap o' a wheel without coupin". This sage would not believe that he was any other being than "Sawtan". This proves that the dislike shown by magistrates to cyclists is by no meanas original, but has descended from generation to generation.

Andrew Macmillan Todd, North Road C.C., Hitchin

P.S. W. Nichol's machine must have been in existence some time before McCall's.

. . . .

Bicycling News, 23 April 1892

The First Gear-Driven Bicycle. Kirkpatrick Macmillan's claim admitted to be correct.

On 19th ult., having the courage of our convictions, *Bicycling News* was the *firs*t paper to declare its opinion that the claim of the late Kirkpatrick Macmillan, blacksmith, Courthill, Keir, near Penpont, Dumfriesshire, to be the first inventor of crank and lever driving to the old dandy-horse or velocipede was so genuine it could not be disputed. These claims were very ably set forth by Mr. James Johnston, of the Glasgow Tricycling Club, and we are informed that within the last few days Mr. Johnston has received a private communication from the immediate representative of the late Mr. Gavin Dalzell, of Lesmahagow, acknowledging in the most honourable manner possible that Macmillan was first in the field with his invention. We have pleasure, therefore, in publishing the annexed letter from Mr. Johnston as a fitting conclusion on this now well thrashed-out subject, which we trust has proved interesting to many of our readers:-

To the Editor of "Bicycling News".

Macmillan v. Dalzell

Sir, - Referring to my former contributions on this subject, and with the view of finally bringing all further discussion to a satisfactory conclusion, I have in the most friendly way possible had two interviews with Mr. J.B. Dalzell, of Hamilton, son of Mr. Gavan (sic) Dalzell, of Lesmahagow. Our first meeting took place on the 19th ult., and our second on 16th inst. We have discussed the whole matter in all its bearings, and whilst Mr. J.B. Dalzell frankly acknowledges from the perusal of all the evidence he has read about Kirkpatrick Macmillan that Macmillan's application of cranks and levers to drive the old dandy-horse, or hobby-horse, or velocipede, is of a prior date to that of his father's, yet we think, after carefully comparing notes and reading various letters, that his father's invention, although unquestionably of a later date than Macmillan's, appears to be quite distinct and apart from Macmillan's. There are certainly points of considerable similarity in the two machines, although the many points of *dis*-similarity confirm the independent conceptions – for instance, the frame of Macmillan's bicycle is different, and has a longer steering stalk; it had also a horse's head and a breast board, specialities which were wanting in Mr. Dalzell's machine, and which go to shew clearly that the two inventions were not exact copies of each other. The remarkable likeness of the two bicycles, however, can readily be explained by the sources from which apparently it is believed the two parties derived their ideas of crank and lever driving – Macmillan, either from the first steamboat successfully tried at Dalswinton Loch, or from the Steam Road Engine, and Dalzell, according to traditional stories in the neighbourhood of Lesmahagow, and from a conversation with one of his own family, a brother of Mr. J.B. Dalzell, that he conceived the idea of mechanical driving from watching the movements of the old Scotch spinning wheel. Dandy-horses without driving gear came out at the end of last century, and an odd copy of the same was to be seen in various parts of Scotland from 1820 to 1830, but Mr. J.B. Dalzell cannot trace out that his father ever saw one of them, although it is quite probable that he may have seem a drawing or sketch of one through being a great reader and possessor of a grand library. As a matter of fact, in 1819 quite a series of illustrated caricatures of riders on dandy-horses were published in London that year, and one of the best copies of same which I have come across is now in the possession of Mr. J.J. Clark, the enterprising cycle agent of Dumfries.

With regard to Mr. William Ferguson's statements that his uncle, Gavin Dalzell, *saw* "a man the year before (1845) riding a velocipede down the Glasgow and

Carlisle Road", Mr. J.B. Dalzell denies the veracity of this, while frankly admitting that his father had heard or been told of a man (presumably Macmillan) being seen on a velocipede on Carlisle Road. It is also quite evident that Mr. J.B. Dalzell, from the amount of newspaper extracts, letters, etc, he has in his possession, has spared no efforts to make his information complete in regard to his father's machine, and the invention of the bicycle generally (a better collection is not in existence), *his only apparent oversight being that he did not go personally down (as I did) to Penpont district, and search out further particulars about Macmillan and his geared velocipede.* In 1884, a number of letters appeared in the *North British Daily Mail* on the subject of early velocipedes, one of them being signed by J. Smith, jun., Townhead, Thornhill, dated 27th August of that year, and from the reading of it, and the meaning it conveyed, he (J.B.D.) naturally concluded that Macmillan's machine was only a dandy-horse, pure and simple, viz., that it had no driving gear, and it was no use, therefore, paying any more attention to the matter. All's well, however, that ends well. The verdict of the jury now reads – *first* Macmillan, and Dalzell a good *second.* I cannot conclude without complimenting Mr. J.B. Dalzell on the gentlemanly and honourable way he has acted all through this matter, his sole desire being, like myself, to get at the truth, and award honour to whom honour is due. Truth is mighty and will prevail.

Jas. Johnston, Glasgow Tricycling Club.

. . . .

Bicycling News, 28 May 1892

"James Johnston, Glasgow T. C."

The name of Mr. James Johnston, of the Glasgow T. C., is by this time well known to most of our readers who are familiar with his recent success in proving to the satisfaction of all concerned the origina of the rear-driven bicycle. In Scotland Mr. Johnson is known as being just as keen and enthusiastic in his cycling as he has shown himself to be persevering in his researches. The *Scottish Cyclist* recently gave his portrait, and completed the sketch by the following pen picture: -

"Born at Dalswinton, in the county of Dumfries, Mr. Johnston was early apprenticed to the law, but finding little charm in the pursuit, he entered the employ of an uncle who was entensively engaged in the bacon-curing industry in Dumfries, and spent two and a half years there, before coming to Glasgow in 1868. Since then he has continuously represented one of the principal Glasgow firms in the corn trade, his travels extending from Glasgow to Carlisle and from Stranraer to Berwick. Our friend'' burly form is therefore "weel kent"''all over Southern Scotland.

"It is now ten years since, acting upon medical advice, Mr. Johnston adopted tricycling in the endeavour to rid himself of nervous rheumatism, contracted by a damp hotel bed. Cautioned to pursue the exercise in moderation and with a due observance of hygenic principles, Mr. Johnston is now almost wholly rid of his old enemy, and in consequence is a staunch advocate of rational cycling as a health restorer. Tricycling, a decade back, being almost in the zenith of popularity – men engaged in the sober affairs of life had then no choice between the uncanny ordinary and thesafe, if ponderous, three-wheeler – our friend joined the Glasgow Tricycling Club, of which he is still a member. For several years he held the office of sub-captain, and had to decline higher honours owing to the nature of his business.

"Mr. Johnston is a true "knight of the road" both in a commercial and a sporting sense, and if he is well known in the market towns of Southern Scotland, he is also a familiar figure on its roads. If we mistake not, he was the first to introduce the old pattern "Humber" tricycle in Galloway. Of course, he changed to the "Cripper" in time, but more recently he has transferred his affections to the "R. and P." machine. He is an ardent supporter of the tricycle, even as it is a faithful support to him, believing that no man over a certain weight can be satisfactorily mounted on a safety.

"A constant reader of cycling literature, our friend has dabbled to some extent in contributions to the press. Under the nom de plume "St. Mungo", he contributed a series of articles to the old *Scottish Athletic Journal* (parent of *Scottish Sport*) on "The Tricycle and Tricycling", besides being a constant supplier of gossip to its columns. To him *The Scottish Cyclist* is frequently indebted for little tit-bits of information, and we always welcome the envelope that carries an enclosure from "St. Mungo". Of his assiduous labours in the cause of right, in connection with the origin of the rear-driven bicycle, our readers are well aware. For that alone would our worthy friend deserve a niche in the temple of cycling fame".

Sources - I

The Scottish Cyclist, 10 Feb., 1892

The First Rear-Driven Bicycle. A Revival of the Question of Origin.

Within the last week or two correspondence has been rife in the *Glasgow Evening Times* on the ever-recurring topic which provides the heading to this article.

It will be remembered by most of our readers that we entered into an exhaustive inquiry of the subject in the winter of 1888, in conjunction with Mr. J.B. Dalzell, of Hamilton, a relative of the now-famous Gavin of that ilk. The result of that was our complete satisfaction of the *bona fides* of the claim that Gavin Dalzell, of Lesmahagow, was the adaptor of driving gear to the old hobby-horse. It was placed beyond dispute by the production of correspondence (one letter actually bearing the dated post-mark), and accounts for the iron forgings used in the machine, that it had been constructed probably prior to 1846 – the proofs showing that it had been in use that year. By permisson of Mr. J.B. Dalzell, we exhibited the "original" at the Stanley Show of 1889, and, having been entrusted with the documentary evidence for that purpose, we convinced the editors of our contemporaries of the legitimacy of the claim.

About the time of our investigations in 1888, a respected friend and contributor to these columns, Mr. James Johnston, of the Glasgow Tricycling Club, was engaged in obtaining evidence to support the theory that a Dumfriesshire blacksmith named Kirkpatrick M'Millan was the real inventor, and that Gavin Dalzell had copied the machine made by M'Millan. We referred to Mr. Johnston's investigations in our issue of December 12, 1888, and later, when dealing exhaustively with the Dalzell proofs, we expressed the opinion that the claim in favour of M'Millan was not substantiated by any satisfactory evidence, but rested merely on hearsay. Mr. Johnston, however, has never relaxed his efforts, and during the intervening years has travelled many miles, and conducted a deal of correspodence, in the pursuit of his object. From time to time he has shown us the fruits of his labours, but, whilst these have borne a promising appearance, they have generally fallen short of positive proof. Be that as it may, we think the time has now come when the results of Mr. Johnston's assiduous and disinterested labours in the cause of truth may be published. Mr Johnston begins his campaign as follows:-

Who Invented the First Gear-Driven Bicycle? Gavin Dalzell's Claim Disputed

On Feb. 20, 1889, you published an article headed "The Original Bicycle", setting forth the claims of the late Gavin Dalzell, cooper in Lesmahagow, as being the first man to put on driving gear – levers and cranks – on the old dandy horse or hobby horse – "about" the year 1846. This machine was exhibited in the Bishop's Palace of the late Glasgow International Exhibition, and also at the Stanley Show in 1889.

As a Dumfriesian and a cyclist, and being related by marriage in a far off way to the late Kirkpatrick M'Millan, blacksmith, Courthill, near Penpont, in the parish of Keir, Dumfriesshire, I have, as you know, since the time you published Dalzell's article been engaged in trying to solve the vexed question of the date and honour of the actual invention of the modern bicycle. This honour, I think, from the evidence I have gathered, belongs to M'Millan, and not to Dalzell. Surely the evidence of a Considerable Number of Living Witnesses, who frequently saw and knew M'Millan, is quite as strong and good as that of Dalzell. Unquestionably, documentary or tangible evidence,

when it does exist, is most satisfactory in establishing the year in which a particular event was said to have occurred, and Dalzell's friends, although they produce certain documents, cannot fix on any particular date. About 1846 is the nearest they can name. In the absence of documentary evidence – newspapers and letters in those days were not so common – we must not underestimate the high value of oral or hearsay evidence in this matter from people satill living in the district who have seen M'Millan on his machine hundreds of times.

To publish details of all the interviews I have had, and letters I have received from these witnesses in Penpont, Keir, Carronbridge, Thornhill, and Dumfries districts would occupy too much space. The letters I send for your perusal. These all go to show that M'Millan was First in the Field, before 1840, with his driving gear, which is identically the same in principle as Dalzell's.

Your contemporary, *Bicycling News*, in issue of 6th inst., publishes a letter from Mr. Thomas M'Call, 1 High Street, Kilmarnock, who backs up the claim of M'Millan as being the great inventor, who met him on the road with his machine in 1845, and who describes its appearance correctly. Mr. M'Call is a joiner, and built a lot of machines similar to M'Millan's. Two details in M'Millan's machines are very carefully noted, points which have also been told me over and over again by old residenters in Dumfriesshire. These are, an imitation horse's head on the front of the bicycle, and a breast-plate for the rider to lean on whilst propelling the machine.

During the past week or two there have also been some interesting letters in *Evening Times* on this subject. A correspondent signing himself "Ben-Jubal" says, on 6th inst.., "the evidence on which I myself mainly rely is that of one of Kirkpatrick M'Millan's own sisters, Mary Grierson M'Millan, for a considerable number of years Mrs...... She remembers her brother making the dandy horse in the smithy sometime about 1834. This machine was a bicycle without the cranks. A few years later he improved his machine by adding cranks. On this improved machine Kirkpatrick M'Millan made his famous ride to Glasgow, leaving Courthill one evening about 8 p.m. after his day's work in the smithy."

This letter is already too long, and I conclude by adding The Names of People Still Alive who are positive in the belief that M'Millan is the pioneer of gearing, viz.:

(1) John Findlater, blacksmith, Carronbridge, near Thornhill – a hale, hearty fellow of most wonderful memory – who wrought for many years along with M'Millan in the smithies on the late Duke of Buccleuch's estate, before M'Millan went to Courthill. He is quite positive M'Millan put driving-gear on the dandy horse before 1840. This point is further confirmed by M'Millan's sister; also by

(2) James Black, oatmeal miller, Dumfries (now unfortunately stone blind), a most intelligent man, who went to live near Courthill smithy in 1843, and who has run after M'Millan and his horse scores of times. He says driving-gear was on his machine in 1843, and long before that.

(3) Thomas Haining, farmer, Laight, Tynron, by Thornhill. He went to school at Penpont in 1843, and describes the driving-gear very correctly, and also refers to the horse's head on the front of it.

(4) Samuel Dalzell, blacksmith, Drumlanrig Mains.

(5) John Brown, grocer, Penpont, trustee in winding up M'Millan's affairs.

(6) Robert M'Millan, blacksmith, Pleasaunce, Dumfries, a nephew of M'Millan's

(7) B. Irving, Cintra Villas, Dumfries.

(8) Thomas M'Call, 1 High Street, Kilmarnock.

(9) W. Thomson, Auchenwraith, Blantyre, who saw M'Millan and his machine in Glasgow in 1845, and who conversed with him whilst visiting his (Thomson's) brother at 94 Thistle Street. He also refers to the incident of M'Millan being interviewed by the police, and taken before one of the bailies for causing such a crowd on the streets. The bailie told him (M'Millan) "no tae be frichted; they didna mean tae put him in the police office, but jist wanted tae see what the deevilish-lookin thing was like." This is a traditional story in Penpont district, which is confirmed 47 years afterwards by this gentleman.

Dalzell's friends admit M'Millan had a dandy horse, but pooh-pooh the idea that he ever invented driving gear. There is no doubt he had a machine for some years previous to inventing levers and cranks. It is scarcely possible he would undertake the journey to Glasgow, and push the machine by his feet on the road. He made a considerable number of machines with the gear on – one in particular for the old Duke of Buccleuch, who was charmed with M'Millan's performance as a rider one night in front of Drumlanrig Castle, in the presence of a select company. The last machine he rode came into the possession of a nephew, who died in Liverpool, and it was ultimately sold to a family there of the name of Gladstone, relations of the ex-premier.

Next week we will publish the various letters bearing on the subject which have been collected by Mr. Johnston.

It should be pointed out that Mr. Johnston is slightly in error in saying that no particular date has been fixed in the case of Dalzell. The evidence clearly proved that the lever-geared machine was in use in 1846, other less conclusive testimony pointing to the probability that it had been constructed prior to that. On the other hand, all that Mr. M'Call, of Kilmarnock, has adduced in favour

of M'Millan's claim is that he saw M'Millan riding his machine "about 1845".

. . . .

The Scottish Cyclist, 17 Feb. 1892
The First Gear-Driven Bicycle.

[One of the crucial articles published by James Johnston regarding Macmillan, this *Scottish Cyclist* article is printed here in full, even though it contains several texts of articles which I have also printed elsewhere. As well as letters sent to him personally by witnesses, Johnston also chose to publish here two of the letters from the *North British Daily Mail* from 1884, and two of the letters sent in to the *Glasgow Evening Times* during the discussion of the origins of the bicycle that was currently going on there.

With the exception of the letters from the *North British Daily Mail* and *Glasgow Evening Times*, the letters were addressed to James Johnston either following interviews with the writers or after written requests to them. The letters were written in 1888-9. It is impossible to know to what extent they were edited or changed from the originals. Writing to *The Scottish Cyclist* of the correspondence he had been collecting, Johnston wrote – "I have now pleasure in handing you copy of a portion of the correspondence". *The Scottish Cyclist* did not confirm in this article that they had indeed seen the originals of these letters, but earlier said that Johnston had "from time to time shown us the fruits of his labours". (10 Feb. 1892)

The italicized passages are all as in the original article.]

"St. Mungo" writes: - As promised, I have now pleasure in handing you copy of a portion of the correspondence to show that the late *Kirkpatrick M'Millan, blacksmith, Courthill, Parish of Keir (near Penpont), Dumfriesshire*, was the inventor of *driving-gear* on the old hobby horse or dandy horse, and not the late Gavin Dalzell, cooper, in Lesmahagow.

(1) Letter from Mr. Samuel Dalziel, blacksmith at Duke of Buccleuch's smithy, Drumlanrig Mains, to Mr. Robt. M'Millan, blacksmith, Dumfries, a nephew of Mr. Kirkpatrick M'Millan:-

Drumlanrig Mains, Sept. 12, 1888.

Sir, - It must be 50 years since your uncle made his dandy horse. He took the pattern from one that belonged to Charters, a turner or joiner at the Millhole, Dumfries.

(Signed) Samuel Dalziel

The Origins of the Bicycle

(2) Letter from Mr. John Findlater, blacksmith, Carronbridge, by Thornhill, to James Johnston, Glasgow

Carronbridge, by Thornhill, January 26, 1889.

Dear Sir, - Supplementing the conversation I have just had with you in reference to the first bicycle, said to have been invented by Mr. Gavin Dalzell, cooper, Lesmahagow, and which was exhibited in the Bishop's Palace of the late Exhibition, I make the following statement, and believe that the *first* and real inventor of applying driving gear to the dandy horse was an old fellow-apprentice of mine, named Kirkpatrick M'Millan, blacksmith, Courthill, Keir, near Penpont, Dumfriesshire. Dalzell, you say, claims to have invented his gear about 1846, but M'Millan had put it on many years before; I am positive, not later than 1839 or 1840. What makes me so sure is that I have lived in this district all my days, working at my trade of blacksmith. I commenced my apprenticeship in 1826, and went to Mallowford smithy in 1833, on the Duke of Buccleuch's estate of Drumlanrig, and wrought there till 1840; then that smithy was abolished, and another new one erected by the Duke at Drumlanrig Mains, where I continued in his employment till 1848. I neighboured M'Millan at both these places, and think he came to Mallowford about 1835 or 1836. That one day he was at Carronbridge and saw a dandy horse in the village which had been ridden from Dumfries by a Mr. Charters, a turner in wood by profession, who had come by this mode of conveyance to see his sweetheart - or he got a copy of Charters' horse one day he was at Dumfries. I am not quite positive which is correct. It had no driving gear at all - he (Charters) just propelled it by sitting stride legs and pushing it with his feet on the road. M'Millan, working from the sketch, made one for himself, and I made another. M'Millan got tired of pushing it along by his feet on the road, and invented the driving gear, which consisted of two long rods fastened on the cranks of the axle of the rear wheel, the other end of the rods being fixed to stirrups which hung on each side of the fore part of the machine. The body and the wheels were made of wood, and the wheels were hooped, of course, with iron. I have not seen Dalzell's machine, but, from the description you have given me of it, I am certain it must be just a copy of M'Millan's. I can remember of M'Millan once riding his bicycle before the Dumfries and Glasgow coach all the way to Glasgow, and carrying luggage. The coach driver was anxious to relieve him of his luggage, but he declined. On coming to Glasgow he was surrounded by a perfect multitude of old and young folks anxious to get a look at him and his horse. In the excitement he unfortunately knocked down a child and got himself into trouble with the authorities, but on explaining that it was a pure accident he was set at liberty. Possibly, on returning home, he would vary the route, and take the Hamilton and Lesmahagow road via Abington, Elvanfoot, and Dalveen Pass to Carronbridge, and it is also quite possible he may have rested at Lesmahagow, when Dalzell might have seen the famous rider and his horse. He was a big, strong man, and a fearless rider. I have tried to mount his machine often, but could never get my feet into the stirrups in time to balance myself. I preferred to get on to my own steed and push it on the road by my feet. This is what impresses the fact so well in my memory that he had driving gear on his one when we wrought together at Mallowford from 1835/6 to 1840. On another occasion he performed on his horse on the lawn in front of Drumlanrig Castle in the presence of the present Dowager Duchess of Buccleuch and a number of lady visitors. These anecdotes may help your cause, and I think it is quite clear that Dalzell was not the first man to propel the velocipede by machinery. -

I am, yours truly, (Signed) John Findlater

(3) Letter from Thomas Haining, farmer, Laight Tynron, Dumfriesshire, to James Johnston, Glasgow, dated January 30, 1889

Dear Sir - In reply to your letter, and referring to the conversation I had with you in the train from Dumfries to Thornhill the other day about Kirkpatrick M'Millan, blacksmith, and his velocipede. I have much pleasure in saying that I believe he was the first to invent driving gear to propel it.

I was born at Laight in the year 1836, and went to Penpont school in 1843. The school was within one mile of M'Millan's smithy, and it was not many days until this wonderful wooden horse came under my notice. To me it was a perfect wonder, but to the natives it was nothing new, as "Pate" and his dandy horse had pranced through the village long before I had gone to school. From memory his bicycle had a long wooden body, wheels of same material shod with iron, and he appeared to drive it with a pair of stirrups or pedals hanging from the fore part of the frame, which were connected by an iron rod to the cranks or axle of hind wheel. In front of the wooden frame was the imitation of a horse's head, and in my boyish wonder I was lost in admiration of the noble steed, but in after years and frequent inspections of said horse, I got into the secret of its wonderful powers. M'Millan was a tall, strong, powerful man, and an expert rider.

Since meeting with you I have been making inquiries about M'Millan. A neighbour of mine was in the farm of Holm, a short distance from the smithy, where he got his work done. Mr Brown tells me that 47 years ago when he and his father went to that farm that M'Millan's horse had been in existence many years before that date. He remembers him riding the dandy horse down the Main Street of Thornhill (a gentle declivity) at full speed, springing on to the saddle and standing upright. Such being the case the horse must have had a good amount of training, and also the rider, to be able to perform in that manner.

You speak of a Mr. Dalzell, of Lesmahagow, who is supposed by many to be the first man who put on machinery to drive the bicycle. I never heard of such a man, and if his friends or relations claim that he did so about 1846, they will stand a poor chance of proving their case, as M'Millan was on the road many years before that date. I think if you make inquiries in the Glasgow Police Court you will find that M'Millan and his horse were both *fined* and *confined* in the Glasgow prison prior to 1846, for causing an obstruction on the streets.[133] You will have no difficulty in getting information from plenty of the old people in the neighbourhood of Thornhill, Carronbridge, Keir Mill, or Penpont, who will corroborate all that I have stated, and be able to give you earlier information than I can do. Trusting that you may get at even the birth of the dandy horse, and wishing you all success.

I am, yours truly, (Signed) Thomas Haining.

---

(4) Letter from Mr. John Brown, merchant, Penpont, to Mr. James Johnson, Glasgow.

Penpont, January 30, 1889.

Dear Sir, - I beg to acknowledge receipt of yours about Kirkpatrick M'Millan and his bicycle, and in reply have not the slightest hesitation in stating that he was the first man to ride such a machine that I ever saw or heard tell of. He had some sort of way of propelling it by machinery but I regret I cannot exactly say how at this distant date. I knew M'Millan well, as I have lived in Penpont all my lifetime, and am now about 60 years of age. As a boy at school here about 1839-40, I remember of often running after M'Millan when on his machine in the company of a lot of my schoolmates, but found it impossible to outrun him, he got along so quickly. My wife also knew him well.

In reference to the claim of Mr. Dalzell, of Lesmahagow, as being the inventor of the first bicycle in1846, I know nothing, but I am certain M'Millan was long before him. There are a lot of old folks in this village who can confirm this, and I could easily get half-a-dozen certificates to that effect.

M'Millan died about ten years ago, aged about 65 years, and I was appointed trustee for the family. I cannot recollect of coming across any papers in reference to his dandy horse amongst his effects. -

Yours truly, (Signed) John Brown.

In reference to above letter, I personally saw Mr. Brown two weeks ago, and he promised to have another look through old documents in his possession, and see if he could find anything in reference to M'Millan's bicycle.

Mr. Brown's wife, however, at the same time was certain they were all burned many years ago.[134]

(5) Letter from Mr. Robert Hamilton, Castlebank, Dumfries, to James Johnston, Glasgow, Feb. 6, 1889.

Kirkpatrick M'Millan Velocipede

Dear Sir - Referring to conversation with you *re* above, I have pleasure in writing you to say I am confident he was the first man to put on driving gear on the dandy horse. I was born in 1819 and wrought as a journeyman miller at Keir Mill, near Penpont, from 1849 to 1859, and remember of Kirkpatrick M'Millan and his bicycle well, as he and I were intimate friends. He made several dandy horses. I took a fancy to have one, too, and at my odd time made the body of one, whilst a joiner of my acquaintance of the name of Lawson helped me with the wheels. Then I got M'Millan to put on the driving gear same as his machine. This was in the year 1849, but, from what people said in the district when I went to it, he had had this gear for a number of years previously. At the moment I cannot recollect to whom I sold my bicycle. Wishing you success in your search after the inventor of driving gear to the bicycle,

I am, yours truly, (Signed) R. Hamilton.

P.S. I was born and brought up in the parish of Closeburn, about four miles from Keir Mill, and had frequent opportunities of seeing him (M'Millan) years before I went to work at Keir Mill. I am positive M'Millan put on his driving-gear on or about 1840. The gear consisted of cranks attached to the axle of rear wheel, fixed to levers which were fastened to stirrups or pedals dropped from the shoulders of the dandy horse. The front wheel was left free to steer with, and was the smallest of the two.

(Signed) R. Hamilton.

(6) Letter from Mr. Robert M'Millan, blacksmith, Pleasance, to James Johnston, Glasgow

Pleasance, Dumfries, Feb. 5, 1889.

Dear Sir, - I am a nephew of the late Kirkpatrick M'Millan, of Courthill, Keir, Dumfriesshire, and I can well remember seeing him riding on his dandy horse when I was at school (more than fifty years ago); in fact my earliest recollections of the man are associated with the queer machine. It was made of wood, with the lesser wheel in front, over which was the figure of a horse's head (hence the name, dandy horse), and was worked with cranks. His first production in that way may not have had cranks, but I never saw one without them. *The last one he made fell into the hands of a*

The Origins of the Bicycle

younger brother of mine, who ultimately sold it to a Liverpool gentleman just thirty-two years ago. I think my uncle travelled to Glasgow on one when I was at school, and as he was then a capable rider, it must be between fifty-five and sixty years since he made his first one. -

I am, yours truly, (Signed) Robert M'Millan.

The following are copies of letters which appeared in the *North British Daily Mail*: -

(7) (To the Editor "N.B. Daily Mail.")

21 August 1884

Sir, - A velocipede and its rider, said to have come from Dumfriesshire, passed Douglas, Lanarkshire, the rider halting at Douglas Mill for refreshments, and afterwards proceeding westward by way of Lesmahagow, in the month of October, 1846.[135] Can any of your readers give the name and address of the rider of this velocipede, or the name of the place where the velocipede was made?

I am, etc., N.F.

(8) Reply – (To the Editor of "N.B. Daily Mail.")

Sir, - In answer to the note in today's *Mail* from 'N.F.' regarding an early Scotch velocipedist, the name of the rider who passed through Lesmahagow in Oct. 1846 was Kilpatrick M'Millan, who made the velocipede at Courthill, Parish of Keir, Dumfriesshire, and rode the same to Edinburgh from Dumfries by way of Lesmahagow, and I have no hesitation in saying that the humble village blacksmith from Courthill is the great inventor and the originator of the velocipede originally called the "wooden horse."

I am, etc., W. Blackstock, 61, South Cumberland Street, Glasgow, Aug. 21, 1884.

The annexed correspondence I had beside me for many months past, and for want of time I put off copying it out. Within the last few weeks, however, as you know, an amount of correspondence has been going on in the Evening Times, headed, "Who Invented the Bicycle?" and I sent a letter to the Times stating that I had for some time been collecting evidence to prove that M'Millan was the man, and not Gavin Dalzell.

The following are the most interesting letters which have appeared, and which I must ask you to re-publish, viz: -

(To the Editor of the Evening Times.)

"February 5, 1892.

Sir, - Between 50 and 60 years ago - if I remember aright it was 1838 - great excitement was caused in Glasgow by the appearance of something speeding through the streets that nobody could understand. No one could determine nearer what it was than that it resembled the Devil, of whom no trustworthy picture had ever been taken. The bailies cried "Catch him" and the police ran with all their might; but all was of no avail. Orders were issued that if ever it appeared again stronger efforts were to be made. Some believed the Devil was amongst them, and old and young wives declared "something was sure to happen". They were true prophetesses. The next time the "queer" thing appeared, the Dumfries or Thornhill blacksmith, who bestrode it, surrendered to satisfy the public curiosity; for if he had chosen he could have eluded both the police and the bailies. One of the latter told him "no tae be frichtet, they dinda mean tae put him in the polis offis but just tae see what the devilish-lukin' thing was like". In 1845 the blacksmith - I cannot recall his name - spent some days with my brother at 94 Thistle Street and I lodged in Cleland Street opposite. He showed me the machine. It was neatly made and it was oramented with a horse's head. Its body was hollow, and he told me that he could pack it in two stones weight and travel at the rate of 14 miles an hour. He had made several of the machines - one as a present and one to order of the Duke of Buccleuch. I am inclined to think these were the first bicycles in Scotland.

I am, etc., W.

(To the Editor of the Evening Times.)

February 6, 1892.

Sir, - I read with interest, in Thursday's issue, Mr. Johnston's letter anent the invention of the bicycle. In further confirmation of our common opinion, he naturally desiderates documentary evidence in preference to hearsay, if such could be obtained. No doubt such evidence, if it exists at all, would be very satisfactory, especially in establishing the year in which a particular event was said to have happened. Nevertheless, your correspondent must not under-estimate the high value of so-called hearsay in a matter of this kind, especially when the report is so general as it is. It may be said that the evidence on which I myself mainly rely is that of one of Kirkpatrick M'Millan's own sisters, Mary Grierson M'Millan, for a considerable number of years Mrs...... She remembers her brother making the dandy-horse in the smithy sometime about 1834. This machine was a bicycle without the cranks. A few years later he improved his machine by adding the cranks. On this improved machine Kirkpatrick M'Millan made his famous ride to Glasgow, leaving Courthill one evening about 8 p.m., after his day's work in the smithy. Many stories are current as to M'Millan's adventures on the dandy-horse. Passing through Old Cumnock on his way to Glasgow, as he was going down a well-known incline in the village about midnight at a terrific rate, he met a young man on his way home from seeing a sweetheart. This man, being somewhat superstitious, got a terrible fright, a reported on reaching home that he had "seen the deil fleein' through the air." Your correspondent must be aware that writing was not so common in those days as it is now.

I am, etc., - Ben-Jubal.

The letter initialled "W." is written by a most intelligent elderly gentleman, Mr. W. Thomson, Auchenwraith, Blantyre, who has since written me several letters, which have only one fault – they are too long for copying out. Here are a few extracts: -

I had intended for many years past to have sent the papers an account (referring to M'Millan's bicycle) after I saw the clumsy thing in the Glasgow Exhibition (Dalzell's bicycle)...... The impression Mr. K. M'Millan left on me was that he was a good, rare individual, very mild tempered, and sympathetic...... I think he stayed about a week in Glasgow (1845) at that time, mostly about our house through the day......At that time I had shown an aptitude for shipbuilding, etc......On M'Millan hearing that he took me over to see his horse in the coal-house, so that I could make one from it.

The beautiful carved head of the horse was the first thing that took my attention – after, he showed me its interior (for carrying luggage) – then my curiosity how he got it to run was excited and I remember taking a broadside view of it which still clings to me like the following (here is drawn an illustration of the bicycle), which shows the driving rod and cranks, of course, but the wheels were nearer each other than the rough sketch shows, but cannot remember how he applied his feet, but he could not have ridden at the speed of fourteen miles an hour if he had not had the crank, besides I remember my brother saying he had made some great improvement. I think that is all I can say, further than it was prettily made, and the crank on the hind wheel was what I thought would puzzle me to make......I wish you to understand that the machine in 1845 was not new, neither was it his first trip to Glasgow on it.

· ·

The Scottish Cyclist, 9 March, 1892

The First Gear-Driven Bicycle – Macmillan *versus* Dalzell

Mr. James Johnston again writes –

Referring to my former contributions on this subject, in your issues of 10th and 17th ult., I fully expected to have wound up in today's *S. C.*, but since the re-publication of a portion of the correspondence in the columns of the *Dumfries Herald* and *Dumfries Standard*, I have been overwhelmed with a mass of letters, all positive in asserting that Macmillan is *the* inventor. To publish all the letters would be an impossibility; I can only refer to a few of them very briefly, and ask you to publish one or two important items. I hope to conclude what I have to say in your next or following issue.

[The text which follows is exactly the same as that published in *Bicycling News*, 5 March 1892, beginning with the letter from Mrs Elizabeth Bailey, and it would therefore be superfluous to include it again (**see Sources H.**)

· ·

The Scottish Cyclist, 23 March, 1892

Editorial - Macmillan v. Dalzell

Those of our readers who visited the Glasgow International Exhibition of 1888 will remember, if they entered the "Bishop's Palace" and peered closely into a dark corner of one of the chambers, seeing an ancient wooden structure in the early stages of decay, which possessed all the characteristics of the "hobby horse". But its chief claim to distinction lay in the application of a primitive form of driving-gear, by means of which the rider propelled the vehicle, instead of in the "hobby horse" fashion by pushing with the feet on the ground. This gear was in the form of cranks and levers with stirrup pedals.

At the time of exhibition, it excited enough curiosity to cause us to investigate its origins and antiquity; and some time after we sufficiently interested Mr. J.B.Dalzell, of Hamilton, who had lent the machine for exhibition, to cause him to search for proofs of the date of its construction.

The result was that he was enabled to lay before us documentary evidence of a very conclusive character proving that the machine, so fitted with the driving-gear, was in existence in the year 1846, and had been constructed probably prior to that date by his father, Gavin Dalzell, of Lesmahagow. We therefore published the facts, and exhibited the relic at the Stanley Show, January, 1889, at the same time showing the letters and proofs to fellow-pressmen. These were unanimously accepted as conclusive, and no other claim having been established, Gavin Dalzell was hailed as the inventor of driving-gear for bicycles.

But even then another Richmond was in the field, and in our article on the Dalzell claim we mentioned that a friend had been investigating the claims of Kirkpatrick Macmillan, of Courthill, Dumfriesshire. (See *Scottish Cyclist* of Dec. 12 1888; also of Feb.20, 1889.) This friend was none other than Mr. James Johnston, Glasgow Cycling Club. At that time, we dismissed as insufficient the only evidence which Mr. Johnston had collected, and which consisted simply of such oral testimony as could be derived from certain individuals who had taxed their memory upon events of fifty years back. Since then, as our readers are aware, Mr. Johnston has been assiduously gathering his forces, and in these columns and elsewhere, he has showered down a mass of evidence which demands the closest consideration.

Looking through the various letters which have appeared in our pages, and which are supposed to furnish the weightiest testimony, we have dismissed much that is irrelevant, and retained the following statements as bearing most distinctly on the question. A sister of Macmillan remembers him making the machine about 1834, and "a few years later" adding the cranks. John Findlater is positive that the gearing was put on before 1840, because he (Findlater) worked with Macmillan from '36 to '40, and during that time he tried to ride the machine, but could never manage it because of the "stirrups". This is very strong testimony, because it is improbable that Findlater would forget at what period he was employed with Macmillan - when he came to the village, and when he left.

He is supported by James Black, who is certain the gear was on the machine in 1843, and "long before that"; and by R.Hamilton, who is positive Macmillan put the gearing on his hobby-horse on or about 1840. Several witnesses testify that Macmillan rode to Glasgow in 1845. This might have been done on the old hobby-horse, without the gear, but we find one, W.Thompson, assert that he carefully examined the machine then, and remembers distinctly the rods and cranks, which greatly puzzled him. Then we have Mrs. Bailey recalling how, when a child, she sat perched on Macmillan's shoulders whilst he propelled the machine by means of the stirrups; and she reckons the date by the time her father left Drumlanrig estate as 1843.

However corroborative all this evidence may be, it would be hardly conclusive to the ultra-judicial mind. When it is remembered that Macmillan and his hobby-horse were familiar to the several witnesses both before and after the gear was fitted, it will be admitted that to recall the exact date of transition from the ungeared to the geared condition is taxing the memory pretty severely. Certainly, corroborative circumstances help the witnesses to fix the dates.[136]

So far have we got when a nephew of Gavin Dalzell's steps in and declares that he stayed with his uncle at Lesmahagow in 1846, the year Dalzell made his velocipede; also that his uncle told him he had seen a blacksmith from Thornhill go down the road the year before on a velocipede. This witness, Mr. Fergusson, gives us no details of the making of his uncle's machine, as one might suppose it possible for him to furnish, but he tells how when Mr.J.B.Dalzell was engaged in establishing his father's claim, he (Fergusson) tried to persuade him to find out all he could about the Thornhill

blacksmith. We think it is reasonable to expect further information from Mr. Fergusson regarding the construction of Dalzell's velocipede, if he was there when it was being made. Otherwise his letter is but an accusation against Mr. J.B. Dalzell. Mr. Johnston refers to Lesmahagow evidence that he is not allowed to publish, which testifies that Dalzell copied from Macmillan. It would be very satisfactory to see this evidence.

Summing up the whole evidence it seems to us that Mr. Johnston has made out a strong *prima facie* case for Macmillan; but we question if he will get the cycling world to reject Dalzell's proofs in favour of the combined testimoney of living witnesses who, comparatively aged now, seek to carry their memories back fifty years, probably in the *desire to support* Macmillan's claim. So far, the evidence has been circumstantial, though very strong. We think Macmillan's claim is a good one. It seems certain that he possessed a hobby horse for many years before gearing was introduced; and what more likely than that he, a blacksmith, with a smattering of mechanical knowledge, should apply lever and crank driving gear? Did Dalzell copy Macmillan? - that is the question. Meantime we think Mr. Counsel Johnston could strengthen his case by a further examination of Mr. Wm. Fergusson; and we fancy that that gentleman's reflections upon Mr. J.B. Dalzell call for a reply. The case, to our mind, is not yet concluded, and we accordingly remain neutral.

The First Gear-Driven Bicycle (separate article)

"St. Mungo" now concludes his contribution in favour of Macmillan thus:- "I left off in *Scottish Cyclist* of 9th inst., saying I had found the name of the young man who had got such a fright in seeing Macmillan on wheels riding into Old Cumnock after midnight. This was James Kennedy, a shoemaker, who told the story to his shopmates, and they made fun of him until they witnessed the unwonted spectacle of seeing Macmillan riding about the town next day. He (Macmillan) appears to have engaged in conversation with many of the residenters from the fact that immediately after his visit a copy of his bicycle with levers and cranks was made at Macartney's Millwright and Engineering Works, a business still successfully carried on. I visited Old Cumnock on Saturday, 5th inst., furnished with an introduction to Mr. A.B. Todd, the local correspondent of the *Glasgow Herald*. In company of Mr. Todd we first called on –

Mr. George Goldie (about 76), the prinicipal partner of Macartney's business already referred to. Mr. Goldie remembers distinctly of Macmillan's visit to Old Cumnock prior to the Disruption in 1843, when he stayed overnight with M'Kinnell, the schoolmaster, and then proceeded to Glasgow. Mr. Goldie is positive of the time, because M'Kinnell left the school when the Disruption took place. (M'Kinnell died in America two years ago.) We then proceeded to Macartney's workshops, when Mr. Goldie showed us a small copy of a horse's head which belonged to a bicycle made (on Macmillan's principle) at the shop. Mr. Goldie has been in Old Cumnock all his life, and is now at the head of the business in which he served his apprenticeship.

We next called on Mr. D. Smith, Inspector of Poor (shoemaker in his younger days), who spoke very confidently of seeing Macmillan and his horse before the Disruption in 1843. As a schoolboy, along with a number of his mates, he was too late for school on account of running after Macmillan, but the teacher (M'Kinnell) did not punish them as he threatened to do when they explained how they were late for school.

We next interviewed Miss Sarah Kennedy, house-keeper at Hillside House, and daughter of James Kennedy, already mentioned, who was returning home from seeing his sweetheart when frightened by Macmillan. Her father was married in 1842. I subjoin a copy of her marriage certificate ["The above pair were married at Cumnock by me, on the 19th day of August, 1842, John MacKinnel, Session Clerk." – AR]. This satisfactorily proves, of course, the time of Macmillan's visit to Old Cumnock, en route for Glasgow, as occurring in 1841 or 1842.

In addition to those who have already spoken of Macmillan's first ride to Glasgow, the *Dumfries Standard* of 24 ult. publishes a long interview by their reporter to another sister of Macmillan's, presently residing in Dumfries, viz., Mrs. Marchbank, widow, aged 72, who details graphically all she knows about her brother and his geared velocipede. She is positive of the time of her brother's ride to Glasgow, from the fact that one of her daughters, now 49 years of age past, being at the time a baby at the breast. This confirms the Old Cumnock information as above very strongly.

Having written above, your readers can guess the surprise I experienced when a nephew of the late Gavin Dalzell of Lesmahagow, called at my residence, and has since handed me the following statement for publication which will speak for itself.:-

"In the year 1846 I was staying at Lesmahagow with my uncle, Gavin Dalzell. That year he made his velocipede. He told me he had seen a man the year before riding a velocipede down the Glasgow and Carlisle Road. He said this man was a blacksmith from Thornhill, but he could not give me his name.

"Some years ago, when his son, J.B.D., was writing about his father being the inventor of the velocipede, I wanted him to go to Thornhill and make search of the blacksmith his father told me of. I fear J.B.D. never took the trouble of going in search of the inventor, but wished

it to be believed his father was the inventor of driving gear, viz., cranks and levers.

Wm. Fergusson
6 Kenmure St. Glasgow.
March 12, 1892."

The above information is so startling that it may be asked why it has never been proclaimed to the world till now. I make answer, and say simply because no one appears, to use an old Scottish phrase, to have "fashed their thoom" about Macmillan, and it is only now, when his claims have been brought prominently before the public by the aid of the cycling papers, and the Glasgow and Dumfries newspapers, that the truth has come out at last.[137]

Mr. Fergusson says a friend sent him some Dumfries newspapers, and after reading what was said about Macmillan, he determined at once to pay me a visit and state the truth as regards his uncle, Gavin Dalzell. The initials "J.B.D." stand for his cousin, Mr. J.B. Dalzell, of Hamilton, the son of Dalzell. Mr. Fergusson is now about 65 years of age, and at the time he was staying with his uncle he was an assistant teacher in a Lesmahagow school. His uncle was on foot going his rounds selling tea when he saw Macmillan on his velocipede. Whether the two men engaged in conversation, or not, I leave your readers to judge. At all events, Dalzell afterwards had many a conversation with his friend, John Leslie, the Lesmahagow blacksmith, with the result that they managed to make a copy of Macmillan's machine with lever and crank driving.

Summing up all the evidence I have collected in abstract form, I now draw your attention, Mr. Editor, to following:-

1. Mrs. Henderson and Mrs. Marchbank, sisters of Kirkpatrick Macmillan; Messrs. Thomas Wright, Slamannan; John Findlater, Carronbridge; Robert Hamilton, B. Irving, and J. Murray, all of Dumfries, are of opinion he had driving-gear on his dandy-horse prior to or about 1840. (The date of Dalzell's bicycle is 1846.)

2. B. Irving, Cintra Villas, Dumfries, and J. Murray, Dumfries, say that Macmillan's first experiment with levers and cranks was applied to a tricycle he made prior to or in the year 1845, but finding the work of propelling it too laborious, he set-to and made his second dandy-horse, with levers and cranks attached. Irving is positive on this point, as he had a ride on this tricycle before he left Keir parish (when he was very intimate with Macmillan) and went to Dumfries Academy at 15 years of age, where Macmillan's brother John at the time was Rector.

3. John Templeton, Glasgow (native of Old Cumnock), George Goldie, and D. Smith, Old

Cumnock, remember distinctly of seeing Macmillan and his geared velocipede in Old Cumnock prior to the Disruption in 1843.

4. Mrs. Bailey, Dumfries, states positively in a long letter that as a girl she sat perched on Macmillan's shoulder whilst he drove his geared dandy-horse in 1842-3. At that time Macmillan lodged with her father and mother on Drumlanrig Estate. Her father left Duke of Bucleuch's employ in 1843, which she confirms by producing a Bible she got presented to her in May, 1844.

5. Messrs. James Black, Robert Macmillan, and Mrs. Bailey, Dumfries; also Thomas Haining, Laight, W. Thomson, Blantyre, and Thomas McCall, Kilmarnock, describe the bicycle similarly as having the horse's head, and also the levers and cranks. The Old Cumnock witnesses also refer to the horse's head, and a nice copy of same is to be seen now at Macartney's works there.

6. At least thirty persons still allive can be produced to testify what they know of Macmillan and his bicycle, but not one of them can say that they ever heard or knew of such a man as Gavin Dalzell until this discussion started, or, at all events, until a few of them cast their eyes on his bicycle in the late Glasgow International Exhibition.

7. Mr. Thomas McCall you dismissed rather summarily in your issue of 10th ult. In addition to seeing Macmillan in 1845, he must have had a lengthened conversation with him and examined his bicycle very carefully, so as to be able to build a copy of it for himself and take orders for several more from both Scotch and English customers.

8. Macmillan was, at least, twice in Glasgow with his bicycle, and once at Edinburgh. His first ride to Glasgow was in 1841 or 1842, when he stayed overnight with his friend, M'Kinnell, at Old Cumnock. This is the occasion on which he raced on the road with the Dumfries and Glasgow coach, and gave it the go-by for a short diatance. At this time he would be about 28 or 29 years of age.

9. He also rode to Glasgow in 1845, via Dalveen Pass, Elvanfoot, Lesmahagow, and Douglas. Mr. M'Call, Kilmarnock, and Mr. W. Thomson, Blantyre, saw him that year. This also is supposed to be the year referred to by several correspondents in letters to *North British Daily Mail*, in 1884.

10. 1845 is the year Dalzell saw Macmillan on the Carlisle Road. Whether the two men were actually acquainted or not I cannot make out. Dalzell is known to be an old Dumfriesshire name.

11. Having satisfactorily proved that Macmillan was the inventor, and Dalzell an imitator, I may now leave the matter in the hands of the jury – your readers – to say whether I have proved my case or not.

12. I may conclude by saying that Kirkpatrick Macmillan was a splendid tradesman; everything he put his hand to was well done, and as a proof of his ability, his son informs me that he made several ploughs without even a screw in them – two of these were to the order of Mr. Gladstone of Capenoch, near Penpont – a brother of the ex-Premier's. Macmillan was of indomitable pluck. Once he set himself to any piece of complicated work, he persevered until success crowned his efforts. He belonged to a clever family. His brother John was at one time tutor to the late Mr. John Bright, M.P., and afterwards successively rector of Dumfries Academy, Glasgow High School, and Edinburgh High School, whilst a third was a clerk in that city. He was of a kindly disposition – one of the hale-fellow-well-met sort – a lively companion, and a man devoid of any pride. This is shown by his willingness to exhibit his bicycle, and to assist anybody to make one for themselves. He stood over six feet – a fine specimen of an athlete – and was admittedly a powerful and fearless rider, in fact, one of our earliest trick riders. On market days, when he frequently rode from Courthill to Dumfries – 14 miles – he appears to have had no difficulty in keeping up with the farmers in their gigs. He died on 26th January, 1878, in his 68th year. Two of his family now survive, a son in Liverpool and a daughter married in Walsall.

13. At the time he made his first bicycle we must not forget that newspapers were scarce. In Dumfries, in 1883, a local paper sold at 7d, and the postage of a letter from Thornhill to London was 1s. 1½d., and to Edinburgh and Glasgow about 8d. People, therefore, at that time read few newspapers, and wrote as few letters as possible.

14. Many old acquaintances of Macmillan are under the impression that he was the first man to *even make* a dandy-horse (without cranks), but that is a mistake. Such machines were in existence before he was born.

· ·

The Scottish Cyclist, 27 April 1892

Editorial - Macmillan v. Dalzell - A satisfactory conclusion.

In our exhaustive consideration of the evidence on the above question, in our issue of March 23, we argued for still further inquiry on several points. There was nothing to gain, while there might be some injustice done in forming a hasty conclusion; and bearing this in mind, we conceived it to be wise to endeavour to bring the two gentlemen most particularly interested in the matter together to compare notes. In this we were successful, and the result of two interviews between Mr. James Johnston and Mr. J.B. Dalzell is concisely outlined on another page.

Since the last evidence was published much more of a convincing nature has been adduced in Macmillan's favour - some of it private. All has been placed in our hands, but considering the deliberations that were being conducted between the two gentlemen referred to, we refrained from publishing anything else, and now no reason exists for doing so.[138] It is satisfactory to us to know that our delay in giving a verdict has been the means of eliciting the conclusive document which may be taken as bearing the assent of both parties, and also that it has been the means of reserving a certain modicum of honour to the memory of Gavin Dalzell. Justice has thereby been done. The opposing "counsel" have privately come to an agreement, and it only remains for us to "withdraw a juror", and compliment both parties on the happy conclusion. So far as we can ascertain, Mr. J.B. Dalzell, at the time he was engaged in establishing his father's claim to the first application of driving-gear to velocipedes, investigated all other known claims as thoroughly as seemed then necessary, and no blame attaches to him that since then contrary evidence that finally assumed indisputable proportions was gathered.

To Mr. Johnston chiefly belongs the great honour of having collected that evidence, and having demonstrated even to the satisfaction of the other side that Macmillan was before Dalzell. He has won "hands down". Few can estimate the enormity of the task Mr. Johnston set himself. The letters we have received from him, and the documents that have been placed in our hands by him, but weakly illustrate the amount of his work in the interests of justice. That he has been instrumental in fixing the honours upon Macmillan is his reward; but, added to that, the thanks of cycling historians and antiquarians are his proper due.[139] His name will be forever associated with the elucidation of the evolution of the bicycle from the hobby-horse. To the making of history these facts are now contributed, - that in the early forties Kirkpatrick Macmillan, presumably having obtained his idea from the first steamboat experimented with on Dalswinton Loch, applied driving gear to the hobby-horse; and that a year or two later Gavin Dalzell built a similar machine, but presumably obtained his idea from the spinning-wheel.[140] There is no clear evidence that Dalzell copied Macmillan's idea, and the points of dissimilarity are such as lead both parties to the conclusion that the conceptions were quite independent of each other. To the happy conclusion arrived at, we have but to add the hope that no further claims will arise which seek to rob Scotland of the honour bestowed on her by such worthy sons.[141]

· ·

The Scottish Cyclist 27th April 1892

The First Gear-Driven Bicycle – Messrs Johnston and Dalzell Compare Notes and Arrive at a Satisfactory Conclusion. Macmillan's Claim to Priority Admitted.

Mr James Johnston now writes:- Referring to what I have already written in your columns on this subject, and with the view of finally bringing this discussion to a satisfactory conclusion, I have in the most friendly manner possible had two interviews with Mr. J.B. Dalzell of Hamilton, son of the late Mr. Gavin Dalzell of Lesmahagow. Our first meeting took place on 19th ult., and our second on 16th inst. We have discussed the whole matter in all its bearings, and while Mr. Dalzell frankly acknowledges from the perusal of all the evidence he has read, that Macmillan's application of cranks and levers to drive the old dandy horse or hobby horse or velocipede is of a prior date to that of his father (as per private letter from Mr. J.B.D. to myself to that effect) [*We have seen a copy of this letter and confirm the acknowledgement. – Ed. *S.C.*]; yet we conclude, after carefully comparing notes and reading various letters, that his father's invention, although unquestionably of a later date than Macmillan's, appears to be **Quite Distinct from Macmillan's.**[142]

There are certainly points of similarity in the two machines, but the many points of dissimilarity confirm the theory of independent conception. For instance, the frame of Macmillan's bicycle was different, and had a longer steering stalk; it had also a horse's head and a breast board, specialities which were awanting in Mr. Dalzell's machine. The remarkable likeness of the two bicycles, however, can be readily explained by the sources from which it is believed the two parties derived their ideas of crank and lever driving – Macmillan either from the first steamboat successfully tried at Dalswinton Loch, or from the steam road engine; and Dalzell, according to tradition in the neighbourhood of Lesmahagow, and also from a conversation with one of his own family (a brother of Mr. J.B. Dalzell), that he conceinved the idea from watching the movements of The Old Scotch Spinning Wheel.

Dandy horses, without driving gear, were introduced at the end of the last century, and several were to be seen in various parts of Scotland from 1820 to 1830, but Mr. J.B. Dalzell cannot trace that his father ever saw one of them, although it is quite possible that he may have seen a drawing or sketch of one through being a great reader and the possessor of a grand library. As a matter of fact, in 1819 a series of illustrated caricatures of riders on dandy horses was published in London, and one of the best copies of same which I have come across is now in the possession of mr. J.J. Clark, the enterprising cycle agent of Dumfries.

With regard to Mr. William Fergusson's statement that his uncle, Gavin Dalzell, saw "a man the year before riding a velocipede down the Glasgow and Carlisle road", Mr. J.B. Dalzell denies the veracity of this, while frankly admitting that his father had heard, or been told, of a man (presumably Macmillan) having been seen on a velocipede on the Carlisle road. It is also quite evident that Mr. J.B. Dalzell, from the amount of newspaper extracts, letters, etc., he has in his possession, has spared no efforts to make his information complete in regards to his father's machine, and the invention of the bicycle generally (a better collection, I believe, is not in existence), His Only Apparent Oversight being that he did not go personally down (as I did) to Penpont district and search out further particulars about Macmillan and his geared velocipede. In 1884 a number of letters appeared in the *North British Daily Mail* on the subject of early velocipedes, one of these being signed by J. Smith, jun., Townhead, Thornhill, and dated 27th August of that year; and from the reading of it and the meaning it conveyed he (J.B.D.) naturally concluded that Macmillan's machine was only a dandy-horse, viz., that it had no driving gear, and that it was no use, therefore, paying any more attention to the matter. All's well, however, that ends well. The verdict of the jury now reads – *First* Macmillan and Dalzell a good *second*.

I cannot conclude without complimenting Mr. J.B. Dalzell on the gentlemanly and honourable way he has acted, his sole desire being, like myself, to get at the truth, and award honour to whom honour is due. *Magna est veritas et praevalebit.*

. . . .

The Scottish Cyclist, 27 April, 1892

With Lens and Pen

Mr. James Johnston, Glasgow Tricycling Club

It is meet that at this time, when the subject of our sketch has been brought so prominently before the public in connection with cycling history, his portrait should be handed down to generations yet unborn, who will point to him as the "discoverer" of Macmillan. Mr. Johnston has reached that stage of ripened manhood when it is difficult to determine how many winters have passed over his head. He is neither old nor young – old, perhaps, in experience, but certainly young in spirit. The affairs of the world have pressed lightly on our friend; or rather, we might say, having pressed, they weighed but lightly, finding a temperament ready to combat and repel them. We would diagnose our friend as a man "without a liver"; consequently jovial and good natured, and prone to the accumulation of adipose tissue. Hence it takes a sound and well-constructed cycle to carry our heavy-weight, and for many years 'Humber' Johnston, as he was called from his unstinting advocacy of the Beeston firm's work, was no small advertisement of the mount he affected.

Born at Dalswinton, in the county of Dumfries, Mr. Johnston was early apprenticed to the law, but finding little charm in the pursuit, he entered the employ of an uncle who was entensively engaged in the bacon-curing industry in Dumfries, and spent two and a half years there, before coming to Glasgow in 1868. Since then he has continuously represented one of the principal Glasgow firms in the corn trade, his travels extending from Glasgow to Carlisle and from Stranraer to Berwick. Our friend'' burly form is therefore "weel kent""all over Southern Scotland.

It is now ten years since, acting upon medical advice, Mr. Johnston adopted tricycling in the endeavour to rid himself of nervous rheumatism, contracted by a damp hotel bed. Cautioned to pursue the exercise in moderation and with a due observance of hygenic principles, Mr. Johnston is now almost wholly rid of his old enemy, and in consequence is a staunch advocate of rational cycling as a health restorer. Tricycling, a decade back, being almost in the zenith of popularity – men engaged in the sober affairs of life had then no choice between the uncanny ordinary and thesafe, if ponderous, three-wheeler – our friend joined the Glasgow Tricycling Club, of which he is still a member. For several years he held the office of sub-captain, and had to decline higher honours owing to the nature of his business.

Mr. Johnston is a true "knight of the road" both in a commercial and a sporting sense, and if he is well known in the market towns of Southern Scotland, he is also a familiar figure on its roads. If we mistake not, he was the first to introduce the old pattern "Humber" tricycle in Galloway. Of course, he changed to the "Cripper" in time, but more recently he has transferred his affections to the "R. and P." machine. He is an ardent supporter of the tricycle, even as it is a faithful support to him, believing that no man over a certain weight can be satisfactorily mounted on a safety.

A constant reader of cycling literature, our friend has dabbled to some extent in contributions to the press. Under the nom de plume "St. Mungo", he contributed a series of articles to the old *Scottish Athletic Journal* (parent of *Scottish Sport*) on "The Tricycle and Tricycling", besides being a constant supplier of gossip to its columns. To him *The Scottish Cyclist* is frequently indebted for little tit-bits of information, and we always welcome the envelope that carries an enclosure from "St. Mungo". Of his assiduous labours in the cause of right, in connection with the origin of the rear-driven bicycle, our readers are well aware. For that alone would our worthy friend deserve a niche in the temple of cycling fame.

Sources - J

Dumfries and Galloway Standard and Advertiser, 24 Feb.1892

"The Inventor of the Bicycle – M'Millan's Claim Fully Established"

[The first part of the following article contains original material which, it should be emphasized, was the result of an independent investigation carried out by this newspaper. It is extraordinary that Johnston himself does not appear to have talked to Macmillan's sister, Mrs. Marchbank, or to her daughter, Mrs. Watret, as did the writer of this article. The second part of the article contained extracts from the interviews James Johnston had conducted with various eye-witnesses, taken from the article which had been published by *The Scottish Cyclist* on 17 Feb. 1892. Thus, these duplicate in part the text of *The Scottish Cyclist* article (17 Feb. 1892) which is printed in Sources I.]

There is at present living at Kingholm, Dumfries, an old lady of 72 years of age whose evidence in the present controversy as to the invention of bicycle driving gear throws considerable light on the subject. This is Mrs Marchbank, a sister of the late Mr Kirkpatrick M'Millan, blacksmith, Courthill, Penpont, for whom Mr James Johnston, Glasgow, with no little show of reason, claims the invention. On Saturday evening a representative of the *Standard* called on Mrs Marchbank, at the residence of her brother-in-law, Mr Anderson, Kingholm. Mrs Marchbank appears a woman of marked intelligence, and not only readily complied with the request that she should state what she recollected of her brother's famous dandy-horse, which aroused so much wonder wherever seen at the time, but favoured our reporter with some details of -

The M'Millan family.

Mr M'Millan, her father, for many years carried on the blacksmith's business at Courthill, to which, on her father's death, Kirkpatrick succeeded. Though not much enamoured with what he regarded as the less useful, if not as the useless, branches, he gave his children an excellent education, and had the satisfaction in after-life of seeing the male members make excellent use of the instruction received at the parish school. Through the instrumentality of the mother, John, the eldest son, attended the university with a view of qualifying for the ministry. He abandoned that idea, however, and became successively the rector of Dumfries Academy, Glasgow High School, and Edinburgh High School. At one time he officiated as tutor to John Bright.

His brother George rose to the position of second master of Hutchison's Hospital, Glasgow, while a second, Robert, became a clerk in that city. Before taking over the management of the business at Courthill, Kirkpatrick for a short period served in the "Vulcan" Foundry, Glasgow. He was, it appears, a man of indomitable pluck; once he set himself to any complicated piece of work he persevered until he had successfully mastered it.

Mrs Marchbank's recollections.

Mrs Marchbank's first remembrance of the "dandy-horse" dates back about 56 or 57 years. She was at that time employed as a servant at Moniaive; and one evening, on the occasion of a visit from her brother, she was surprised on going to the door to see him surrounded by a great crowd of people, who manifested keen interest in the "uncany" machine. M'Millan naturally took not a little pride in his "horse", and boasted its superiority over the quadruped in that it neither required corn nor water. To which one of the onlookers replied retorted, "No, but it'll need oil". As the visit was made in the evening, and M'Millan had to return to Courthill the same night, a distance of seven miles, Mrs Marchbank had not an opportunity of minutely inspecting the bicycle; and she is therefore unable to say how it was propelled or to furnish any account of its construction.

But when two or three years later she removed to Thornhill on her marriage to George Marchbank, she was frequently in the habit of seeing her brother ride through the town on a "dandy-horse" of a more approved pattern to that on which he made the journey to Monaive. This machine she is quite positive was driven by means of gear attached to the back wheel with stirrups for the feet. In height the machine might be about four feet; the shape was that of a horse, the name of the owner being painted on the head; and the seat for the rider was a saddle resting on a spring.

She remembers well of his starting on his memorable trip to Glasgow when he out-distanced the stage-coach, and the accounts he gave of his exploits are also even now quite fresh on her mind. M'Millan strictly refrained from taking strong drink; and when passing through Cumnock on his way to the capital of the West, he appealed to one of the good wives for a drink of milk; but mistaking him for a cutler, she declined to supply it at any price. He jumped on his "horse" and rode away, much to the amazement of the woman, who summoned her husband to "see the devil runing awa' on horseback". The old man did come, with the result that M'Millan was called back and well provided for; and on the return journey he spent the night under the family's roof. At Glasgow he was met by two if not three of his brothers. They were anxious to see him ride

The Origins of the Bicycle

the machine on the pavement. According to Mrs Marchbank's narrative, one of the "Baillies" asked that they should induce him to do so, and on condition that his name was not mentioned, he undertook the responsibility of defraying any expense to which M'Millan's conduct might expose him. A crowd was of course attracted, and two policemen interfered. One seized M'Millan and removed him to the Police Office, and the other endeavoured as best he could to push the machine along the street. Robert M'Millan, Kirkpatrick's brother, no doubt to the great relief of the officer, took charge of the offensive "horse". Kirkpatrick was liberated on bail; and on the following morning appeared before the magistrate. He was fined 2s 6d; but what the exact nature of the offence libelled was remains doubtful. The "Baillie", to whom we have referred, refunded M'Millan the amount of the penalty. While he readily conversed upon other features of the journey, M'Millan was always very reticent in alluding to this incident.

The journey, Mrs Marchbank distinctly remembers, was performed at the time one of her daughters, now 49 years of age, was still a child at the breast. And the occasion is further impressed upon her memory by the facts that it was about the time of the Disruption in 1843, and that four years after removing to Thornhill her husband was appointed precentor to Keir Church, upon which the family took up their residence at Bridge End, in that parish. Now, her brother's journey to Glasgow was made, she has no hesitation in saying, during her four years' stay at Thornhill.

But though 1843 may be regarded as about the year in which the memorable trip was performed, the gear-driven machine and its rider had, it is evident, become quite familiar on the roads in the district for a considerable time previous. It was before that event that the Duke of Buccleuch secured him to perform on the bicycle in presence of a company of guests at Drumlanrig Castle. That to Glasgow was the only long journey M'Millan attempted. He was, however, often in the habit, after the labours of the day were over, of proceeding from Courthill round by the Auldgirth Bridge, up the Closeburn side of the Nith to Thornhill, round by Penpont, and back to Courthill - a distance, it is estimated, of 12 miles - without exhibiting any signs of fatigue. As shewing his dexterity, M'Millan would set the "horse" in motion at a good rate and then stand in the saddle. This feat was invariably done for the delectation of the many visitors who called to see the "horse". Shortly after his marriage, M'Millan became possessed of a pony and trap, and thereafter discarded the "dandy horse". During the years he rode the bicycle he effected various improvements upon it. He did not, however, devote his attention, as might be expected, to the manufacture of cycles for customers; but he assisted his apprentices in constructing similar machines for their own use.

Confirmation

Mrs Watret, wife of Mr Watret, mason, 79 High Street, Dumfries (Mrs Marchbank's eldest daughter), is able, from personal recollection, to corroborate her mother's statement on the most material points. She was born at Courthill, and for the first 15 years of her life she resided, with the exception of about 12 months spent in Glasgow, solely with her grandfather and uncle, Kirkpatrick. She has a faint recollection of her uncle having another velocipede prior to the construction of the improved machine; but, like her mother, she can give no description of it.

Regarding the gear-driven machine, however, she remembers quite clearly. Her uncle, she says, brought home a tree from a neighbouring wood and set to work to construct the "horse". When the machine was about completed, she remembers asking where the legs were and her uncle showing her two iron levers with stirrups. The machine was steered by the first wheel. In front of the plate, which served as a rest for the breast, there was a cross lever with horn handles, by which the machine was guided. M'Millan's visit to Glasgow was the next incident that fixed itself upon her memory. She can recall his departure, his return, and the stories he related regarding his experiences. At Kilmarnock, he used to relate, an old woman cried, "Here's a bit of an engine run awa' wi' a man". With reference to the Glasgow incident, Mrs Watret says her uncle denied that he had knocked down a little girl, and was of opinion she must have fallen from fright. When at the police office, either on the night of the arrest or next morning, some of the authorities took him into a back court in order that he might demonstrate to them how the machine worked; and he "formed the figure eight with it". At this period, she believes, she was six years of age or so, and she can confirm her mother's view that it was about the time of the Disruption. At all events she is convinced that the date of the journey was considerably prior to to opening of Virginhall Free Church, which she attended while it was in an unfinished state, and long before she was, at the age of 9, taken to reside with an uncle and aunt in Glasgow, with whom she remained for nearly a year.

During the first portion of her stay at Courthill, Kirkpatrick frequently, when exhibiting the cycle to visitors, held her in one arm while on the machine, and guided it with the other hand. Another of his clever achievements with it was to "form the figure eight" on the public road. The machine was afterwards handed over to a nephew, who employed it going between Penpont and Dumfries - a run repeatedly accomplished by M'Millan himself.

The foregoing statements were given with wonderful precision; and although the mother and daughter were interviewed at different times and places, without, so far as our reporter is aware, any consultation on the subject during the interval, there is entire agreement on almost every essential detail. Their evidence, taken in conjunction with that of independent witnesses mentioned in Mr Johnston's correspondence, may, we think, be reasonably held to prove that three or four years prior to that in which there is any record of the existence of Dalzell of Lesmahagow's gear-driven velocipede (1846), Kirkpatrick M'Millan had not only applied driving gear to his "dandy horse", but had become an expert rider. There is, we understand, resident in or near Ayr, another sister of the Courthill blacksmith, who can, there is reason to believe, fully confirm her sister and niece's evidence.

Mr Johnston's Researches

The last issue of *The Scottish Cyclist* contains letters which Mr James Johnston, Glasgow, has received from various persons on the subject, and from these we give below a number of extracts:

From Mr R. M'Millan, blacksmith, Pleasance, Dumfries:

"Dear Sir - I am a nephew of the late Kirkpatrick M'Millan, of Courthill, Keir, Dumfriesshire, and I can well remember seeing him riding on his dandy horse when I was at school (more than 50 years ago); in fact, my earliest recollections of the man are associated with the queer machine. It was made of wood, with the lesser wheel in front, over which was the figure of a horse's head (hence the name, dandy horse), and was worked wth cranks. I never saw one without them. The last one he made fell into the hands of a younger brother of mine, who ultimately sold it to a Liverpool gentleman just thirty two years ago (ie, 1860). I think my uncle travelled to Glasgow on one when I was at school, and, as he was then a capable rider, it must be between 55 and 60 years since he made his first ones."

Mr M'Millan (ie, the above, not Kirkpatrick - AR) had communicated on the subject with Mr S. Dalziel, blacksmith at Drumlanrig Mains, and from him received the following note:

"It must be 50 years since your uncle made his dandy horse. He took the pattern from one that belonged to Charters, a turner or joiner in the Millhole, Dumfries."

From Mr John Findlater, blacksmith, Carronbridge:

"I believe that the *first* and real inventor of applying driving gear to the dandy horse was an old fellow-apprentice of mine - Kirkpatrick M'Millan. Dalzell, of Lesmahagow, you say, claims to have invented his gear about 1846, but M'Millan had put it on many years before; I am positive, not later than 1839 or 1840. What makes me so sure is that I have lived in this district all my days, working at my trade of blacksmith. I commenced my apprenticeship in 1826, and went to Mallowford smithy in 1833, on the Duke of Buccleuch's estate of Drumlanrig, and wrought there till 1840; then that smithy was abolished, and another new one erected by the Duke at Drumlanrig Mains, where I continued in his employment till 1848. I neighboured M'Millan at both these places, and think he came to Mallowford about about 1835 or 1836. One day he was at Carronbridge and saw a dandy horse in

the village which had been ridden from Dumfries by a Mr Charters, a turner in wood by profession, who had come by this mode of conveyance to see his sweetheart - a girl of the name of Gracie - or he got a copy of Charters' horse one day he was at Dumfries. I am not quite positive which is correct. It had no driving gear at all - he (Charters) just propelled it by sitting stride legs and pushing it with his feet on the road. M'Millan, working from the sketch, made one for himself and I made another. M'Millan got tired of pushing it along by his feet on the road, and invented the driving gear, which consisted of two long rods fastened on the cranks of the axle of the rear wheel, the other end of the rods being fixed to stirrups which hung on each side of the fore part of the machine.

The body and wheels were made of wood, and the wheels were hooped, of course, with iron. I have not seen Dalzell's machine, but, from the description you have given me of it, I am certain it must just be a copy of M'Millan's. I can remember of M'Millan once riding his bicycle before the Dumfries and Glasgow coach all the way to Glasgow, and carrying luggage. The coach-driver was anxious to relieve him of his luggage, but he declined. On coming to Glasgow he was surrounded by a perfect multitude of old and young folks anxious to get a look at him and his horse. In the excitement he unfortunately knocked down a child and got himself in trouble with the authorities, but on explaining that it was a pure accident he was set at liberty. Possibly, on returning home, he would vary the route, and take the Hamilton and Lesmahagow road via Abington, Elvanfoot, and Dalveen Pass to Carronbridge, and it is also quite possible he may have rested at Lesmahagow, when Dalzell might have seen the famous rider and his horse. He was a big, strong man, and a fearless rider. I have tried to mount his machine often, but could never get my feet into the stirrups in time to balance myself. I preferred to get on to my own steed and push it on the road by my feet.

This is what impresses the fact so well in my memory that he had driving gear on his one when we wrought together at Mallowford from 1835-6 to 1840. On another occasion he performed on his horse on the lawn in front of Drumlanrig Castle in the presence of the present Duchess of Buccleuch and a number of lady visitors."

From Mr T. Haining, farmer, Laight, Tynron.

"I was born at Laight in the year 1836, and went to Penpont school in 1843. The school was within one mile of M'Millan's smithy, and it was not many days until this wonderful wooden horse came under my notice. To me it was a perfect wonder, but to the natives it was nothing new, as "Pate" and his dandy horse had pranced through the village long before I had gone to school. From memory, his bicycle had a long wooden body, wheels of same material shod with iron, and he appeared to drive it with a pair of stirrups or pedals hanging from the fore part of the frame, which were connected by an iron rod to the cranks or axle of hind wheel. In front of the wooden frame was the imitation of a horse's head, and in my boyish wonder I was lost in admiration of the noble steed, but in after years and frequent inspections of said horse, I got into the secret of its wonderful powers. M'Millan was a tall, strong, powerful man, and an expert rider. Since meeting with you I have been making inquiries about

The Origins of the Bicycle

M'Millan. A neighbour of mine was in the farm of Holm, a short distance from the smithy, where he got his work done. Mr. Brown tells me that 47 years ago, when he and his father went to that farm, that M'Millan's horse had been in existence many years before that date. He remembers him riding the dandy horse down the Main Street of Thornhill (a gentle declivity) at full speed, springing onto the saddle and upright. Such being the case the horse must have had a good amount of training, and also the rider, to be able to perform in that manner.

From Mr R. Hamilton, Castlebank, Dumfries:

"I was born in 1819, wrought as a journeyman miller at Keir Mill from 1849 to 1859, and remember of Kirkpatrick M'Millan and his bicycle well, as he and I were intimate friends. He made several dandy horses. I took a fancy to have one too, and at my odd time made the body of one, whilst a joiner of my acquaintance of the name of Lawson helped me with the wheels. Then I got M'Millan to put on the driving gear same as his machine. This was in the year 1849, but, from what people said in the district when I went to it, he had had this gear for a number of years previously. I was born and brought up in the parish of Closeburn, about four miles from Keir Mill, and had frequent opportunities of seeing him (M'Millan) years before I went to work at Keir Mill. I am positive M'Millan put on his driving-gear on or about 1840. The gear consisted of cranks attached to axle of rear wheel, fixed to levers which were fastened to stirrups or pedals dropped from the shoulders of the dandy horse. The front wheel was left free to steer with, and was the smallest of the two."

Mr John Brown, merchant, Penpont, writes that as a boy at school about 1839-40 he remembers running after M'Millan when on his bicycle along with many of his school mates, and they found it impossible to out-run him. M'Millan died about ten years ago, aged about 65 years, and Mr Brown was appointed trustee for the family, but cannot remember finding among his effects any papers relating to the invention.

Sources - K

Glasgow Evening Times, 4 Feb., 1892

Who Invented the Bicycle?

12, Carment Drive, Shawlands, Glasgow, Feb. 2, 1892

Sir, - As a Dumfriesian and a cyclist, and also being related by marriage in a far-off way to the late Kirkpatrick M'Millan, blacksmith, Courthill, Kier, Dumfriesshire, I may inform your correspondent "Ben Jubal" and others interested in cycling matters, that I have for some considerable time been engaged in collecting information to prove that M'Millan was undoubtedly the first in the field to put driving gear – levels and cranks - on the old hobby horse or dandy horse, and not the late Gavin Dalzell, cooper in Lesmahagow. To enter into details would occupy too much of your valuable space; but briefly, I may say the evidence I have secured in Penpont, Keir, Thornhill and Dumfries districts, shows that it was about 1840-41 that M'Millan brought out his invention. I hope to publish full particulars very soon. Meantime I will be glad if "Ben Jubal" or any other gentleman can furnish any further news on the point – documentary evidence against hearsay being preferable. The date of Dalzell's bicycle is 1846, not 1836.

I am etc, Jas. Johnston.

· ·

Glasgow Evening Times, 6 Feb., 1892

Who Invented the Bicycle?

Sir, - I read with interest, in Thursday's issue, Mr. Johnston's letter anent the invention of the bicycle. In further confirmation of our common opinion, he naturally desiderates documentary evidence in preference to hearsay, if such could be obtained. No doubt such evidence, if it exists at all, would be very satisfactory, especially in establishing the year in which a particular event was said to have happened. Nevertheless, your correspondent must not under-estimate the high value of so-called hearsay in a matter of this kind, especially when the report is so general as it is. It may be said that the evidence on which I myself mainly rely is that of one of Kirkpatrick Macmillan's own sisters, Mary Grierson Macmillan, for a considerable number of years, Mrs .... She remembers her brother making the dandy-horse in the smithy sometime about 1834. This machine was a bicycle without cranks. A few years later, he improved his machine by adding cranks.

On this improved machine Kirkpatrick Macmillan made his famous ride to Glasgow, leaving Courthill one evening about 8 pm after his day's work in the smithy. Many stories are current as to Macmillan's adventures on the dandy horse.

I am, etc, Ben Jubal.

· ·

Glasgow Evening Times, 8 Feb., 13 Feb., 16 Feb., 17 Feb. and 20 Feb. 1892

Letters to the Editor.

Monday, Feb. 8, 1892

Sir, - The question as to who invented the bicycle might easily be settled it if can be proved whether the first known velocipede was built of wood or iron. In cycling parlance the former is called a "boneshaker" and the latter a "settler"

I am, etc, Reddy.

Sat., Feb. 13, 1892

The Invention of the Bicycle (To the Editor of the *Evening Times*)

Sir, - With reference to the invention of the bicycle, may I be allowed the favour of a parting word. Your many readers will be aware that the essential idea involved in the word "bicycle" is that of a two-wheeled machine. Now, on the testimony of hundreds, Kirkpatrick Macmillan's dandy-horse was such a machine. His adding cranks and other gear later made the machine rather more nor less than this. Accordingly, it appears to me that the issue has been slightly confounded by some of your correspondents. Mary Grierson Macmillan informs me that her brother was certainly not long in adding cranks to his original dandy-horse, and that all was completed midway between 1830 and 1840. I saw the blacksmith myself frequently, and he always appeared to me to move about in an atmosphere of mechanical thought and invention. He was only one member of a highly talented and at the same time historical family. His sister, it appears, was not aware till just recently that her brother's claims had ever been disputed.

On all the available evidence, therefore, I have no doubt that Kirkpatrick Macmillan was the inventor of the bicycle in both forms – without the driving-gear and with the driving-gear. Macmillan's famous ride to Glasgow between 1830 and 1840 made his machine public enough. After that there were many imitators.

I am, etc, Ben Jubal.

Mon., Feb 16, 1892

Who Invented the Bicycle?

12, Carment Drive, Shawlands, Glasgow, Feb., 13 1892

Sir, - Since writing to you ten days ago I have received a great amount of correspondence to prove that the late K. Macmillan was the first man supposed to have put on driving gear on the old dandy-horse. On 20th Feb., the *Scottish Cyclist* published an article on the "Original Bicycle", and maintained from documentary evidence that this honour belonged to …..Dalzell. In endeavouring to substantiate the claims of Macmillan, I have published a reply in the *Scottish Cyclist* of 10th

inst. I have yet to follow on with a copy of the correspondence and the names of a great number of people who saw and knew Macmillan.

I have read with pleasure Ben Jubal's letter in tonight's *Evening Times*. When he asserts, however, that K. M. "was the inventor of the bicycle in both forms, without the driving gear and with the driving gear", he treads a dangerous ground. I have information in my possession to prove that Macmillan got a copy or sketch of the dandy-horse without cranks from a Mr. Charters, boot-turner, Dumfries, about 1830, and who used to ride on it from Dumfries to Carronbridge to see his sweetheart. Besides, anyone well read in cycling history knows that neither Dalzell nor Macmillan invented the dandy-horse (without cranks), this machine having been brought out…..by Drais….

On this point, finally, I may say there was exhibited in the late Glasgow International Exhibition by a firm of Newcastle coachbuilders a very fine specimen of the dandy-horse….An elderly shoemaker named James Dargavel, who was alive in 1889, and who had lived in Keir all his life, said he remembered seeing Macmillan riding his dandy-horse before the great cholera in Dumfries and district in 1832. I can assure Ben Jubal, if he will exercise Job's virtue a little longer, that I hope to solve beyond any doubt that Macmillan was the gear inventor, and not Dalzell.

I am, etc, Jas. Johnston.

Feb., 17, 1892

Who Invented the Bicycle?

Feb. 16, 1892

Sir, - I was rather amused, as well as interested, while reading Mr. Johnstone's letter in Monday's issue on the subject of the bicycle. He seems to fear I am "treading on dangerous ground"……However, it may be remarked that I have always been in the habit of very carefully examining my own ground before treading on it…..

I would recommend Mr. Johnstone carefully to sift the information as to Charter's relation to Kirkpatrick Macmillan, He seems to me in general to be on the right track concerning Kirkpatrick Macmillan's gear claims, but, pursuing his wide-spread and serious investigation, he may reasonably expect to receive a little unreliable chaff in the midst of an abundance of substantial and wholesome grain……In the face of the accumulated probable evidence in favour of Kirkpatrick Macmillan, the claim put forth on bahalf of Dalzell seems to me to be peculiarly flimsy and weak.

Macmillan was characteristically the very reverse of an imitator. He built on no man's foundation with regard to mechanics. There was a tinge of scorn in his nature which usually accompanies genius, and which made him abhor imitation. To modify the old Latin saying, *Nihil tetigit quod non ornavit*, it may be said of Kirkpatrick Macmillan that he touched nothing that he did not at least improve.

I am, etc, Ben Jubal.

20 Feb. 1892

Who Invented the Rear-Driven Bicycle? The Rival Claimants.

The interest taken in the discussion on the question "Who Invented the Bicycle?" induces us to publish the portraits of the two Scotch claimants, Gavin Dalzell, of Lesmahagow, and Kirkpatrick Macmillan, of Dumfries, with sketches of the types of machines attributed to them.

For Dalzell's portrait we have to thank the editor of the *Scottish Cyclist*. Macmillan's is enlarged from a *carte-de-visite* (by T. Douglas, photographer, Thornhill) kindly supplied by our correspondent "Ben Jubal". The two machines are reproduced from the *Bicycling News*.

· ·

Glasgow Evening Times

22 Feb., 1892

The Inventor of the Bicycle

573, Gallowgate, Feb. 20, 1892

Sir, - Allow me to state a few facts which came under my own observation in reference to above.

Previous to the year 1843 (the year of the Disruption) Kirkpatrick M'Millan, blacksmith, Dunscore, Dumfriesshire, rode into Old Cumnock late one summer's night or early in the morning. He called at the residence of his cousin, Mr. John McKinnell, the then parish schoolmaster, where he was kindly welcomed and hospitably entertained. In the morning, at the breakfast hour, M'Millan came out with his horse, and rode up and down the town to the great amusement of the crowds who ran after him. I saw him do what I have never seen another do since, except in a circus. Standing on the saddle and guiding the front wheel with his hand, he came down what was then called M'Kinlay's Brae at full speed. About that time several imitations of M'Millan's machine, with some improvements, were made in the engineering works of George M'Cartney, Cumnock, and for several years were in great vogue. The drawings you gave in Saturday's *Times* are, on the whole, pretty correct, but as far as I remember the wheels were both one size.
I am, etc, John Templeton.

Glasgow Evening Times, 23 Feb. and 27 Feb 1892

Tues, Feb 23, 1892

The Inventor of the Bicycle

21st Feb., 1892

Sir, - In my young days I was domiciled in Stonehouse, and well remember Mr. Dalzell and his dandy horse. He used to sell tea, I think. If my memory is correct, he first appeared in Stonehouse with his machine in 1845. Stonehouse, I may say, can claim the honour of seeing the first tricycle that, I believe, was ever made. It was made by a cartwright named Hamilton, to the order and design of a Mr. Walker, a master tailor. It was run on the roads about Stonehouse four months or so after Dalzell appeared with his dandy horse.

I am, etc, W.

22 Feb. 1892

Sir, - I read with interest Mr. Templeton's letter in today's *Times*. His letter contains two slight inaccuracies, which I may be allowed to correct. 1. Courthill is in the Parish of Keir, not Dunscore, which is a neighbouring parish. 2. John M'Kinnell was not a relative of the late Kirkpatrick Macmillan. I fancy Mr. Templeton would be under this impression from the fact that Macmillan spent a day or two with M'Kinnell at Old Cumnock, and from the fact of the close intimacy which long existed between John M'Kinnell and the Macmillan family.

I am, etc., Ben Jubal.

27 Feb 1892

Who Invented the Bicycle?

Sir, - After the letters that had appeared up till the 20th, I thought no person would have attempted to dispute Macmillan's just claim. I am therefore much surprised to see in your issue of the 23d, Mr. G. Lacy Hillier attempting to disprove the evidence of so many living witnesses. Inventors, as a rule, make the job as complete and near perfection as possible, which copyists fail to do. Prominent in Dalzell's machine is the eleven or odd-spoked wheel; sufficient to mark him as the copyist and not the inventor. Nor is your Stonehouse correspondent any nearer the mark. There was a steam tricycle made before the end of the last century by Symington, the builder of the first steamboat, but he was not the inventor. Millar of Dalswinton, and another gentleman, were the two immediately concerned. The latter's name I cannot recall, but the one was the inventor and the other the financier; Symington being the builder and improver in some respects only.

I am, etc., B.

Sources - L

Dumfries and Galloway Saturday Standard, 15 June 1895

[The headline of this account appears to suggest that the article is continuing an ongoing story, or that at least it is a story with which readers are expected to be familiar. A search of the newspaper a month before and a month after the appearance of this article failed to find any further mention of research into the origins of the bicycle. It is also an account which contains very little new information, and we can only take this Mr Brown's word for it that his meeting with Macmillan was actually true.]

More about the first bicycle and its inventor

Mr William Brown, blacksmith, Woodhead, Glencairn, throws more light on the inventor of the first bicycle and the wonderful article itself. He was acquainted with Kirkpatrick Macmillan, and "Pate", as he was familiarly called, was not infrequently a visitor at his house at Woodhead. He presented a somewhat unusual and striking appearance, and this in part explains how it was that when some saw him mounted on his "wood horse", which was the term then used to denote the bicycle, and careering along the road, they imagined that there was something uncanny about him. Nor is this to be wondered at, as "Pate's" own father had been heard to remark that he was "daft". Whether that was so or not, he was a character of much originality - of which his invention bore simple witness - and rather more than ordinary intelligence, while the other members of the family bore a scholarly reputation. So much for Macmillan.

Mr Brown has something to say about the first bicycle, of which he has a distinct recollection. In the year 1844, which was some time after the invention, Mr Brown, who then followed the occupation in which he is still engaged, together with his brother George, who was a watchmaker in Dunscore, resolved to visit Macmillan with the avowed purpose of inspecting his "dandy horse", as it was also called. On reaching Courthill they were received by "Pate's" father, who informed them that the inventor was from home on his "wood horse". The one that he was riding was, however, his second machine, and they had an opportunity of inspecting the one first invented.

This was an article of rude design and roughly executed. It consisted of a piece of a tree, forming the body of the machine, with two wheels attached. The primitive character of the machine is shown by the method of propulsion - the rider seated astride, scraping the ground first with the one foot and then the other, an operation which soon came to tell on the rider's boots and tended to divest locomotion of both speed and pleasure. Seeing

the necessity for some mechanical means of driving, "Pate" set himself to overcome this difficulty, and as a result his second bicycle was much superior to his first attempt. A part of a tree was again used for the body of the horse, which was fitted with a head and a mane in imitation of the real animal. The mouth being open, the teeth were displayed - the intention evidently being to give the idea that the horse was panting after hard runing. A spring rising from the neck of the horse was attached to the front of the saddle, another spring being beneath it, crosswise at the back. The front wheel, which was about two feet in diameter, ran immediately below the "horse's" neck to which it was attached. The back wheel ran in a groove cut for it in the body of the "horse", and it was a good deal larger than the front one, being about three feet eight inches in diameter. The driving was managed in the following manner. An iron pin ran through the shoulders of the "horse", and at each side a stirrup hung down. This was composed of a small piece of wood four inches long, on which the foot rested. Then to the back wheel a crank was attached at each side, and this again was connected to the stirrup by a rod. When the crank was down at one side of the machine it was up at the other, and thus by the successive forward movement of first one foot and then the other the machine was propelled.

Guiding was managed somewhat similarly as now. The handle-bars were shorter than they generally are at the present time, and Pate was even more considerate than the bicycle-makers of the present day, as he provided a rest for the fore-arm by fixing a small piece of wood across the neck a little behind the handle-bars. The saddle was about four feet three inches from the ground, and the feet in the stirrup about six inches. The wheels were made of wood, hooped with iron, similarly to carriage wheels. But the iron was rounded, and it was impossible to ride the bicycle when the roads were slippery.

Mr William Brown and his brother paid a second visit to Courthill shortly afterwards and took precise measurements of Macmillan's second machine, with a view to constructing one similar. This they did at odd times, William doing the iron work and George the wood work. Well skilled in the handling of smaller instruments, the watchmaker furnished the "horse" with a splendidly finished head and neck, showing a much better appearance than did the copy.

Mr Brown chose a straight part of the road a short way from his house to learn to ride, and with a view to avoid spectators gathering he took out his "wood horse" at night when traffic had ceased. It, however, happened that when he was going to practice the news somehow leaked out, and there was generally about half-a-dozen boys present on these interesting occasions, his machine, naturally, being regarded with a good deal of curiosity. The roads in those days were rougher than now, and Mr Brown was never able to travel at any considerable speed, except perhaps downhill; and in fact it was only in that case that his "wood horse" was of advantage, except perhaps when he was fortunate to be going the same way as a gig, in which case he caught hold of it by one hand and got pulled along with little exertion on his part.

For a long while he did not use his "wood horse", and several years ago disposed of it to Mr John Maxwell, mill-wright, Blackwood, for the modest sum of five shillings. In his hands it afterwards went to pieces, and the merest fragments only now remain. Mr Brown has a good recollection of "Pate" coming up to Woodland and telling them of his many wondrous escapades on his bicycle. He was able to drive it standing, and sometimes took on a boy in front of him, and he had also been known to treat a lady to a ride. Once he started from Moniaive just a little before the coach and arrived in Glasgow before it; but that the ride proved eventful on more than one account. He ran down a pedestrian on Glasgow pavements, and was taken before a magistrate of St Mungo and fined in the sum of half-a-crown, Mr Brown thinks.

Another incident he remembers well, which took place when Pate was returning from a trip to Ayr. The day was late, and he divested himself of his jacket and laid it across the neck of his "horse". Riding in this way down the road, he approached a place called Ballinie, where a man was at work mowing at the side of the water near the road. Though it was broad daylight, such was the appearance of "Pate" that the rustic momentarily threw down his scythe on catching a glimpse of the approaching figure and made off through the fields as hard as he could, evidently mistaking for one from the dark regions the inventor of the bicycle while out showing to the world his wonderful invention, which in after years, with transforming improvements affected, was destined to find a high place in public favour.

Sources - M

Dumfries and Galloway Standard and Observer, 2 June 1897

The Origin of the Cycle - A talk with an old Dumfriesian about this and other things.

We had the other day an interesting conversation with Mr. David Johnston, a worthy Dumfriesian, who long carried on a clothier's establishment in one of the most fashionable parts of London, and is now enjoying a dignified repose after the cares of a busy and prosperous business career. An annual visit to his native place is one of the pleasures in which Mr Johnston indulges himself. He is brimful of reminiscences of the town in his early years, which he can relate in vivid narrative.....

Mr. Johnston was the nephew of James Charteris, wood turner, whose name has often been mentioned in connection with the first inception of the bicycle, and it was on this subject that our conversation chefly turned.

It has been commonly stated and accepted that Mr Charteris was the maker of a bicycle of a very crude form, the rider of which simply placed his feet on the ground, and by pushing with them alternately carried the machine and himself along. This is entirely at variance with the recollection of Mr. Johnston, who as a boy in the early thirties was a frequent rider of the "dandy horse" as it was called. Mr Charteris, he says, was not the maker of the machine, but purchased it in Glasgow about the year 1829, and the method of propulsion was quite different from that stated.

We reproduce below the substance of his statement, throwing our talk into continuous narrative form for the reader's convenience.

"We lived at No. 16 English Street. The Charteris boys, John and Robert, were my intimate companions. The English coach at that time left the town at a quarter to two. John Charteris and I used to ride after it on the dandy horse along the Annan Road as far as the first stage, which would be about nine miles. There was room for two of us on the machine. Charteris got onto it, and I somehow squeezed myself in behind him.

"I am sorry my recollection is not distinct enough to enable me to give you anything very tangible about the propelling power, but it was certainly not propelled by setting the feet on the ground. They were placed on pedals or stirrups just much the same as in the modern bicycle, but I think it was the front wheel that was propelled, and I do not remember any connection between it and the second. I have seen a statement that there was an iron belt attachment, and Charteris being accustomed to the use of belts and shafting it is not improbable that he may have adopted some such contrivance. There were handle bars on the front to guide or turn the wheel......

> "The bicycle had little light wooden wheels, built on the principle of a cart wheel, with a slight iron tire - just such a one as you would now hoop a cask with. A blacksmith named William Smart lived in Irish Street, almost at the back of where the Mechanics Hall now is. As soon as the bicycle wanted new tires - which I don't mind telling you was very often, in consequence of the usage it got - my

uncle would say, "Just take it round to Willie Smart and let him put a pair of new tires on."

"My uncle himself, to the best of my knowledge, never crossed his legs on the machine; it was bought for the amusement of the boys......The history of his "dandy horse", which was told to me by my mother (Mrs Johnston, the sister of Mr.Charteris) in the year 1835 or 1836, is very clearly imprinted on my memory. He was a wood turner, and had his machinery driven by water power; but his experience in "the dry summer" of 1826, when the water failed, made him resolve to get a steam engine, which could be used n the summmer months. He set to making the engine himself, getting the castings at Caldow's foundry in Maxwelltown, and he made it all but the boiler. For this he had to go to Glasgow. It was there that he bought "the dandy horse", and he had it sent on to Dumfries by carrier's cart along with the boiler. He never made any of the machines himself. This one was destroyed long before "the forties" and it had no successor in Charteris' possession.

"James Charteris was a wonderful man. Whenever he had seen a piece of machinery, no matter how complicated the mechanism, he could go home and reproduce it. He was no inventor; but as a copyist he was perfection. He was the only wood-turner in the town of Dumfries, and often worked as long as eighteen hours a day, having the help of his two sons and a man whom they employed. The water power that drove his turning lathes he turned to practical account in other

ways. His place of business was in what we then called "the Mill Hole"; it is now Mill Street. In a room above his wood-turning shop he had two carding machines and a small flour-mill, all driven with shafts and belting from the same water-wheel.

"He made, as I have said, a steam engine for himself; and often have I gone to Caldow's foundry for things that he required in its construction. The foundry was at Stakeford, where Messrs Shortridge now have their works. After fitting up that engine, Mr.Charteris hardly ever used it but stuck to the water power. He also put a steam mill into the premises of Mr Beveridge, baker, at the Maxwelltown end of the New Bridge; and I worked at it. It was the first steam mill in Dumfries, and people came from far and near to see it. He went to Glasgow to get a boiler for it also. This was in 1834 or the beginning of 1835.

"Mr Charteris made quite a study of electricity. When his day's work was ended, perhaps about nine or ten o'clock, he would go to his room upstairs and work at the construction of electric machines. People came from long distances to be electrified with his machines, for the cure of rheumatism and various slight ailments. He was one of the founders of the Mechanics' Institute and gave several lectures on electricity in connection with it."

Mr Charteris, we may add, died in 1861, at the age of 75 years.

Sources - N

The Hub, 4 March 1899

The Invention of the Bicycle

To the Editor of The Hub.

Sir, - Kindly allow me to supplement your remarks, editorial and otherwise, in reference to the position held by Kirkpatrick Macmillam. I have written so much MS. on the subject these last ten years that the subject matter is somewhat stale. The claim, however, of Macmillan, to be the first man to solve the problem of balancing and propelling two wheels by mechanical driving with the feet off the ground is indisputable, and recognized by every cycling authority who has taken the trouble to study the evolution of the cycle. Macmillan's name and fame now take their proper place in several text-books, and it is therefore somewhat surprising to find Mr. George Edwards unaware of this. In the issue of The Hub in which reference to the matter is made at some length, the opening sentence contains an obvious clerical blunder in stating that "not much is known about Macmillan" (I make this quotation from memory), whereas it should have read "A great deal is now known about Macmillan". As a matter of fact the

great difficulty I have always had to contend with in correspondence with cycling papers and their respective editors has been their reiterated requests to "boil down" the large mass of evidence I have collected on behalf of Macmillan; so bulky has it become that it would easily make a special edition of The Hub itself.

In the spring of 1892 I completely upset all preconceived theories that the late Gavin Dalzell first applied driving gear to two wheels, as, after two interviews with his son, Mr. J.B. Dalzell, the latter kindly gave me a holograph letter, dated April 16th, 1892, acknowledging that I had clearly proved *priority* in favour of Macmillan. The date of Dalzell's bicycle is 1846-7, as verified by the account of John Leslie, blacksmith, Lesmahagow, against Gavin Dalzell, for putting on ironwork on bicycle, and dated January 27th and February 10th, 1847. It may be conceded, for argument's sake, the woodwork was commenced in 1846. It is believed that Macmillan brought out his invention about 1839-40. He soon became a daring and expert rider, and a great number of old residenters still living in Dumfriesshire remember this man and his wonderful "horse" well. A native of that county,

The Origins of the Bicycle

writing from Toronto, Canada, in 1892, said he knew Macmillan well, and remembered him performing a journey to Glasgow on his bicycle "in the early forties", on a visit to three of his brothers resident there, and that a report of it appeared in a Glasgow paper, and was copied into a Dumfries one. I had heard this story often, and after eight years' inquiry I was successful in tracing it, although at one time I had given up all hope of doing so.

It appears that Macmillan left his home in Dumfriesshire on June 6th 1842, stayed over-night at Old Cumnock, in Ayrshire, and arrived in Glasgow on the following day. His progress on the way caused great wonder and excitement, and a great multitude of people surrounded him in Glasgow. To escape from the crowd he rode his machine on to the footpath, but, unfortunately, knocked down a child, who, however, was more frightened than hurt. For this offence, he was fined 5s. on June 8th, 1842, at the Gorbals South Side (Glasgow) Police Court, and this wonderful historical incident was duly reported in the *Glasgow Herald* of that week and transferred to the columns of the *Dumfries Courier*, June 13th, 1842. Macmillan thus established two records: 1) The first long distance ride of about 180 miles, and 2) the first case of a genuine cyclist being fined for footpath riding.

Quite recently I was introduced to an elderly gentleman who saw Macmillan going through Kilmarnock on his way to Glasgow with his bicycle. Referring to the coach story and Dalzell as mentioned by Mr. Edwards, I have been repeatedly told by old residents in Macmillan's native district that this belongs to Macmillan and not to Dalzell at all. Macmillan's machine may, therefore, be correctly called the first rear-driver and the prototype of the present-day style of bicycle. Many attempts have been made to oust Macmillan from his position, but all have failed, and I have been through three paper wars on the subject. No doubt, like Thomson with the pneumatic tyre, he was before his time; and, although many copies of his machine were made in Dumfriesshire, and also at Old Cumnock and Kilmarnock, in Ayrshire, the sport did not "catch on". When history repeated itself, his disciples were ridiculed just like the dandy horse riders of 1819. It was not until the introduction of the :boneshaker" of the 'sixties that that the public caught the craze of bicycle riding.

Although the rear-driver was first introduced it was the last to be perfected. Thanks, however, to the foresight of Mr. J.K. Starley, of Rover cycle fame, in the 'eighties, the rear driver was again improved and brought to the front. With the exception of a short interregnum caused by the introduction of the geared front driver, it has remained with us since, and will not be easily set aside.

I have gleaned the following personal references to Macmillan, which may prove of interest to your readers. He was born near Courthill, in the parish of Keir, Dumfriesshire, in 1813, and the Christian name of Kirkpatrick was given him by his parents out of respect for, and in memory of, Sir Thomas Kirkpatrick, Sheriff of the County, who had shown a kindly interest in the Macmillan family. Macmillan followed his father's profession of a country blacksmith. He succeeded to his father in business about 1843, and carried on the same till his decease in 1878. He had three brothers and three or four sisters (so far as I can ascertain), and two of the latter still survive. The family were reckoned clever and intelligent, the eldest brother, John, being, at one time, tutor to the late John Bright; and he was afterwards successively Rector of Dumfries Academy, Glasgow High School, and, at his death, of Edinburgh High School. Kirkpatrick, before commencing business on his own account, appears to have spent some years at the smithy on Drumlanrig Estate, belonging to the present Duke of Buccleuch's father, and he was also a short time in a Glasgow foundry. He was a very clever tradesman, and of a determined and ingenious disposition. Having set his mind on any object or subject, he never rested until he accomplished it. In appearance he was tall – fully six feet – and of a muscular and wiry build, and at the time he cycled to Glasgow he looked the very picture of an athlete. He was of a kindly nature – one of the hale-fellow-well-met sort – a lively companion, and a man devoid of any pride. This was shown by his willingness to exhibit his bicycle, and to assist anybody to make one for himself. He took out no patent. He was too busy with his otherwise lucrative country business, although he found time occasionally on a fine day to cycle to and from Dumfries – twenty-eight miles – on market days, when he had no difficulty in keeping up with farmers in their gigs. He was about forty or forty-two when he married, his wife being only half his age, and he used to jocularly observe that he would not live to be double her age again. He died at sixty-five, his wife having predeceased him by many years. Two of his family now survive – a son in Liverpool, and a married daughter in Walsall. A tablet on the wall of the Courthill smithy now records the fact that "Here the first bicycle was made by Kirkpatrick Macmillan about 1840".

On inquiry I find that Macmillan's original machine was taken to Liverpool, about 1859, by one of his nephews, James Macmillan, and there broken up. The only person who appears to have made any commercial capital out of the invention was Mr. Thomas McCall, joiner and wheelwright, Kilmarnock – still alive, and a native of Macmillan's district – who rode, built, and sold many copies of Macmillan's bicycle at £7 each. One of these was to the order of an English medical gentleman, which was in turn re-copied considerably, and, in proof of that, an advertisement appeared in the *English Mechanic*, or *English Magazine* (I write out of town, from memory, but have the facts at home), of 1868, offering the "Killarnock" bicycle – a misprint for the word "Kilmarnock" – at the same price as charged by McCall. By this time the names of Macmillan and Dalzell were so mixed up that in error it was called the "Dalzell" bicycle in the advertisement, which stated that he had beaten the king's coach with it – a story I have already referred to as belonging to Macmillan. Mr. McCall has the old patterns and plans of the bicycle in his possession, and at my request he built another facsimile of it, which we conjointly sent to the Crystal Palace for exhibition in the chronological collection of cycles held there in the summer of 1896; and which we, later on, presented to the Dumfries Observatory of Antiquities, where it can now be seen.

In conclusion, it may be asked what particular object or interest I have had in gathering information about Macmillan, Well, that is easily answered. For love of the sport, and as an old cyclist, I was anxious to prove that to my native county of Dumfries belongs the honour of being the birthplace of the clever genius who produced the missing link in the history of the evolution of the cycle, between that of the "dandy-horse (which the rider propelled by his feet on the road) and the "boneshaker" of the 'sixties, driven by the front wheel. The French nation, some years ago, put up a statue to Michaux, as the inventor of the latter machine, not knowing that such a man as Macmillan had ever lived.

Yours truly, Jas. Johnston, Glasgow Cycling Club.

Sources - O

C.T.C. Gazette, September, 1899

The Early Days of the C.T.C.

[This brief summary account is included here as representative of what a responsible, formal journal thought and was prepared to publish about Macmillan and the early history of the bicycle right at the end of the period of research which has been examined here. It is true that this article cannot really be called a primary source since it uses information gleaned from other sources. Nevertheless, it is close enough in time to the publication of James Johnston's work to represent a well-informed comment on that work. It also publishes five interesting and significant photographs, which were not published in other sources.]

By the Editor

A "full, true and particular account" of the conception, birth, and development into manhood of the C.T.C. would fill a volume…It may therefore be forgiven us if in the limited space at our disposal we content ourselves with touching but cursorily upon the more prominent events in the Club's history. Before doing so, however, we think it not amiss to again place upon record the fact that although the hobby-horse of 1818 was the invention of a foreigner – one Baron von Drais – it is to an Englishman, or rather to a Scotsman, that the honour of devising and constructing *the first practicable bicycle* belongs. When we use the term "bicycle," we *mean the first two-wheeler propelled and steered with the feet off the ground.*

For many a year after cycling became popular it was currently believed that Gavin Dalzell, of Lesmahagow, was the real inventor of the machine, but thanks to the indefatigable labours and painstaking research of Mr. Jas. Johnston, of Glasgow, it has been proved beyond question that Dalzell merely copied the original bicycle,

devised and made by Kirkpatrick Macmillan, blacksmith, of Courthill, Dumfriesshire. Macmillan, who was born in 1813 and died in 1878 (the year in which the C.T.C. was formed), appears to have been a highly ingenious man, for not only is he entitled to the credit of discovering that two wheels placed in line could be balanced and propelled with the feet off the ground, but he in the year 1839 to all practical purposes anticipated the rear-driven bicycle in universal use at the present day. It is true that he did not employ chain driving, and that his machine was level-geared, but the latter deficiency was in a sense met by the use of a driving wheel ten inches larger than the steerer.

Upon the machine thus constructed Macmillan proved to have ridden from Courthill to Glasgow in the year 1842 on a visit to his brothers. He left his home on 6th June, and arrived at Old Cumnock, in Ayrshire, that night. Next day he reached Glasgow, where he had great difficulty in getting along on account of a dense multitude of people. In the excitement of trying to escape from the crowd he rode his bicycle on to the footpath, and unfortunately knocked down a child. For this offence he was fined 5s. next day (8th June, 1842) at the Gorbals South Side Glasgow Police Court, an incident he regretted all his life, and which he did not like mentioned. Fortunately, however, for his after fame the *Glasgow Herald* duly recorded the event in its issue of that week, and the paragraph was copied into the *Dumfries Courier* of 13th June, 1842.

After his Glasgow trip many copies of Macmillan's machine were made in Dumfriesshire and Ayrshire, and one of these was sold for £7 by Thomas McCall, Kilmarnock, a native of Macmillan's district, to an English medical gentleman, who allowed it also to be copied extensively. A photograph of a machine made by McCall from Macmillan's model is hereto appended, together with one of the "smithy" in which

The Origins of the Bicycle

Macmillan evolved and built the original bicycle. [For these illustrations we are indebted both to Mr. Johnston and to his friend, Mr. James Fingland, of Thornhill, a clever amateur photographer.] It will be noted that the historical facts have of late years been suitably recorded upon a table placed upon the wall of Macmillan's house as well as upon his tombstone in the local churchyard.

Although Macmillan evolved a practical bicycle, its use did not become at all general, and it may be regarded as certain that the two-wheeler had fallen into desuetude when in or about the year 1866, it occurred to one, Pierre Lallement, a Frenchman, to fit a pair of cranks to the front wheel of a bicycle…….

Sources - P

The Gallovidian, Winter 1899

The First Bicycle

By James Johnston, Glasgow Cycling Club

No apology is required for the introduction of this subject. The cycle, as an institution, has come to stay, and, judging from present day appearances, the next generation will all ride on wheels. Cycling is at once the King of sports, and more money is spent on it than on any other form of recreation. As a pastime it is beyond doubt the most enjoyable, and, at the same time, the most healthy if indulged in moderately. A brief glance therefore, at the origin of the machine that has produced such a universal sport may now be appreciated. The first bicycle, regarded as a subject for investigation, says a cycling critic, "Is about as fitful, as elusive, and as generally unsatisfactory as the so-called missing link. The first bicycle is discovered, not to say invented, periodically. At different times it has been definitely located in the Egypt of remotest antiquity, in prehistoric China, in mediaeval England, and among other effete civilizations, and its reappearance (in the columns of the various newspapers) is always hailed with a cry of delight. The first bicycle is strictly impartial as regards latitude and longitude, and, if the period be sufficiently remote, is liable to fix upon any quarter of the globe as the scene of one of its numerous incarnations".

For a long time the history of the development of the cycle was hid in obscurity, but it has been cleared up very much of late years. Until 1808 no trace can be found of anything analogous to the modern bicycle. In that year, however, the "hobby-horse" appeared in Paris, so called from the body or connecting bar being made to represent a horse, and the machine had no menas of turning. In 1818 an improved pattern was patented in France by Baron Von Drais, and was called the "Draisena", "Draisinne", or "Dandy horse". This type at once became popular, and in 1819 it was a common sight in Hyde Park, London, hundreds of them being in use by the dandies of the period, although the price was prohibitive. Cruickshank and other artists of the time, however, ridiculed the new sport unmercifully by their caricatures, and, like a flash in the pan, it dies out, as there had been no improvement in the node of progression, and the rider had still to touch the ground

alternately with his feet. Odd specimens of these dandy horses found their way here and there over the country, and one landed in Dumfries, and was the property of a Mr. Charteris, wood turner. It was seen, or a drawing of it secured, by a clever young mechanic, Kirkpatrick Macmillan, blacksmith, of Courthill, Parish of Keir, near Penpont, Dumfriesshire.

> "You've guessed him a Scotchman, shrewd reader, at sight,
> And perhaps altogether, shrewd reader, you're right".

And he made a copy of it, and so did a shop-mate of his, John Findlater. At this time – in the thirties – Macmillan was an employee in the smithy of Drumlanrig estate of the late Duke of Buccleuch, and Findlater, still alive, has very circumstantially related how Macmillan and he used to ride these old machines by pushing them along with their feet on the ground. Macmillan tired of thus crude style of propulsion, and after long and anxious thought he successfully devised a plan to get rid of it. Many others had experimented in this direction, but all their attempts had failed. For this purpose he built a second or improved dandy-horse, and affixed driving gear to it in the shape of cranks and levers. Hitherto all dandy horses had equal-sized wheels, but Macmillan's new type was unique in that the rear or driving-wheel was much the larger of the two, so as to secure increased pace, somewhat analogous to the present day system of gearing up by means of the chain running round different sized cog wheels – (see accompanying photograph of the machine, and the mechanism will be understood at a glance; it has been so often detailed that it is superfluous to do so here).

The word "bicycle" means, of course, properly speaking, *the first two wheeler propelled and steered with the feet off the ground*, and he was undoubtedly the first man to solve this problem and construct a *really practicable bicycle*. His position is recognized by every cycling authority who has taken the trouble to study the evolution of the cycle, and his name and fame now take their proper place in several text books on cycling. As there was another Richmond in the field, all this was not accomplished without a great deal of labour, extending over many years, but success crowned my efforts at last. It is not my intention here to detail all the evidence collected, which is now so bulky that it would easily make a special edition of *The Gallovidian* itself, and the following must suffice. In the spring of 1892, with the kind assistance of many old Dumfriesians, Ayrshire folks, the Dumfries press, etc., I completely upset all the preconceived theories that the late Gavin Dalzell, cooper, Lesmahagow, first applied driving gear to two wheels, as, after two interviews with his son, Mr. J.B. Dalzell, the latter kindly gave me a holograph letter dated 16th April, 1892, acknowledging that I had clearly proved *priority* in favour of Macmillan. The date of Dalzell's bicycle is 1846-7, as verified by the account of John Leslie, blacksmith, Lesmahagow, against Gavin Dalzell for putting on ironwork on bicycle, and dated 27th january and 10th Feb., 1847, although it may be conceded for argument's sake that the woodwork was commenced in 1846. It is believed that Macmillan brought out his invention about 1839-40. He soon became a daring and expert rider, and a great number of old residenters still residing in Dumfriesshire remember the man and his wonderful "horse" well, so called from a prettily carved head he had affixed in front of his machine. A native of that country, writing from Toronto, Canada, in 1892, said he knew Macmillan well, and remembered him performing a journey to Glasgow "in the early forties" on a visit to three of his brothers resident there, and that a report of it appeared in a Glasgow paper, and was copied into a Dumfries one. I had heard this same story frequently, and after eight years inquiry, was successful in tracing it, although at one time I had given up all hope of doing so.

It appears that Macmillan left his home in Dumfriesshire about eight o'clock on the evening of 6th June, 1842 – according to the evidence of one of his sisters – on the memorable Glasgow trip. As he had no lamp he depended on Nature's light.

> "Soon as the evening shades prevail
> The moon takes up the wondrous tale"

And having pedalled the length of Old Cumnock he stayed over night, and proceeded for Glasgow the following day. His progress on the way caused great wonder and excitement, and he was escorted into that city by an immense multitude of people attracted by the strange novelty of the steed and its rider. To escape from the crowd he rode his machine on to the footpath, but, unfortunately, knocked down a child, who was more frightened than hurt. For this offence he was fined 5s on 8th June, 1842, at the Gorbals, South Side (Glasgow), Police Court, and this wonderful historical incident was duly recorded in the *Glasgow Herald* of that week, and transferred to the columns of the *Dumfries Courier* of 13th June, 1842. Macmillan thus established two records: - 1) The first long distance spin of about 130 miles to Glasgow and back home again, and 2) the first case of a genuine cyclist being fined for footpath riding. Two years ago I was introduced to an elderly gentleman in Dumfries who saw Macmillan and his bicycle going through Kilmarnock on his way to Glasgow.

Some of Macmillan's relatives think that his original machine was taken to Liverpool about 1858 by one of his nephews, James Macmillan, and there broken up. Although many copies of his machine were afterwards made in Dumfriesshire, and also at Old Cumnock, yet it appears that the only person who made any commercial capital out of the invention was Mr Thomas McCall, joiner and wheelwright, Kilmarnock – still alive, and a native of Macmillan's district – who rode, built, and sold many copies at £7 each. His first experiment in fitting Macmillan's driving gear was to apply it to John Findlater's old dandy horse, which he purchased from him for 5s. [This is proof positive Charteris's old dandy horse had no driving gear, because Findlater's one, as before observed, was a copy of Charteris's.] Other evidence collected on the point in Dumfries and elsewhere is as strongly corroborative. One of the machines made by McCall was in turn re-copied considerably, and in proof of that an advertisement appeared in the *English Mechanic* of 11th June 1869, offering the "Killarnock" bicycle – an evident misprint for the word "Kilmarnock" – at the same price as charged by McCall.[143] Some years later the Lion Bicycle Co., Coventry, offered Macmillan's type for sale, but in their advertisement it was called the "Dalzell" bicycle, and stated how the latter gentleman had beaten the King's coach with it on one occasion; a traditional incident often repeated to me by old Dumfriesians as taking place with Macmillam, which he enjoyed repeating, and not to Dalzell at all. This can only be explained by the names of the two gentlemen becoming mixed up in the long course of years. Be that as it may, in conversation with McCall, I found he had still the old patterns and plans of the bicycle in his possession, and at my request he most willingly built another *fac simile* of it, which we conjointly sent to the Crystal Palace for exhibition in the chronological collection of cycles held there in the summer of 1896, and which we later on presented to the Dumfries Observatory of Antiquities, where it can now be seen.

Macmillan's bicycle must, therefore, be correctly called the first rear-driver, and although it had not chain driving, yet it clearly anticipated the present day style of chain driver. Many attempts have been made to oust him from his position, but all have failed, and I have been through three paper wars on the subject.[144] No doubt, like Thomson and the pneumatic tyre, he was before his time, and both he and his disciples were subjected to a deal of ridicule, just like the dandy horse riders of 1819 – another instance of history repeating itself. Even the *Glasgow Herald* reporter's reference to him in 1842, when speaking of his machine, said it was "ingeniously constructed", yet further observed "this invention will not supersede the railway".

Although the rear-driver was first introduced, it was the last to be perfected. Thanks, however, to the foresight of Mr. J.K. Starley, of "Rover" Cycle fame, the rear-driver was again improved, and brought to the

The Origins of the Bicycle

front in the eighties. With the exception of a short interregnum, caused by the introduction of the geared front driver, it has remained with us since, and will not be easily set aside. Of course, it must not be lost sight of that until the introduction of the "boneshaker" of the sixties (driven by cranks direct on the axle of front wheel, and from which emerged the big or ordinary bicycle, now almost extinct) the public did not thoroughly take up what many people call it, the craze of bicycle riding.

The following personal references to Macmillan may prove interesting to your readers. He was born near Courthill in the parish of Keir in 1813, and the Christan name of Kirkpatrick was given him by his parents out of respect for, and in memory of the family name of Sir Thomas Kirkpatrick, Sheriff of the County, who had shown a kindly interest in the Macmillan family. Macmillan followed his father's profession of a country blacksmith, and succeeded his father about 1843, and carried on the business until his decease in 1878. He had several brothers and sisters, and some of the latter still survive. The family were reckoned clever and intelligent, the elder brother, John, being at one time tutor to the late Mr John Bright, M.P., and he was afterwards successively rector of Dumfries Academy, Glasgow High School, and, at his death, of Edinburgh High School. Macmillan, before commencing business on his own account, in addition to the time he spent in Drumlanrig estate smithy, was also a short time in a Glasgow foundry. As a trademan he was considered very clever, and of a determined and ingenious disposition; having set his mind on any object or subject he never rested until he accomplished it. In appearance he was tall – fully six feet – and of a muscular and wiry build, and at the time he cycled to Glasgow, when 29 years of age, he looked the very picture of an athlete. He was of a kindly nature – one of the hale-fellow-well-met sort – a lively companion, and a man devoid of any pride. This was shown by his willingness to exhibit his bicycle, and to assist anybody to make one for himself. He took out no patent, being too busy otherwise with his lucrative country business. Occasionally he found time, however, to cycle to and from Dumfries – twenty-eight miles – on market days, when he had no difficulty in keeping up with the farmers in their conveyances. He was about forty-two when he married, his wife being only half his age, and he used to jocularly observe that they would not live until their ages were doubled again. He died at sixty-five, his wife having predeceased him by some years. Two of the family now survive – a son in Liverpool, and a daughter married to a Walsall gentleman. A tablet on the wall of Courthill smithy now records the fact that "Here the first bicycle was made by Kirkpatrick Macmillan about 1840", and his tombstone in Keir old Churchyard also bears a suitable inscription.

In conclusion it may be asked what particular object or interest I have had in gathering information about Macmillan. Simply for love of the sport, and as an old cyclist I was anxious to prove that to my native county of Dumfries belongs the honour of being the birthplace of the invention of the bicycle. The French nation some years ago put up a statue to Michaux as the inventor, not knowing that such a man as Macmillan ever lived. It has been wisely observed "That the man who invented the bicycle deserves the thanks of humanity", and if Kirkpatrick Macmillan did not do so, then I wonder who did?

[We are indebted for the use of blocks in this article to the Cyclists' Touring Club and Mr Fingland, Thornhill.]

Sources - Q

Kilmarnock Standard, 9 April 1904

Death of Mr. Thomas McCall, 1834-1904 – A Bicycle Pioneer

We regret to record the death of Mr. Thomas McCall, cartwright and lorry builder, High Street, which occurred yesterday morning from pneumonia following upon influenza with which he was seized on Saturday last. Deceased, who was 70 years of age, was a native of Penpont and served his apprenticeship in Sanquhar. About fifty years ago he came to Kilmarnock and was employed for seven years at the turning of beechwood pistons for the Kennedy water meter, as originally made by the Company at their works in Townholm. Subsequently he started business for himself in Langlands Street, and after being there for about a year he removed to High Street where he gradually built up an extensive trade, latterly in conjunction with his sons, in commodious premises splendidly equipped with the latest machinery. Deceased had considerable mechanical ability and was notable as having been one of the earliest pioneers of the bicycle manufacture. When a boy at school in his native village, he had seen Mr. Kirkpatrick Macmillan, the inventor of the rear-driven bicycle, riding his machine and later when serving his apprenticeship he constructed one for himself which is believed to have been the second ever made. After coming to Kilmarnock he manufactured for the Glasgow market, bicycles of the Macmillan type, with various improvements of his own. Some 10 years ago a model of the original bicycle made up almost entirely of the materials of the machine first constructed by him, was exhibited at the Crystal Palace, and afterwards gifted to the Dumfries Museum. It has a surprising resemblance to the most up-to-date machine, though formed of wood, with iron tyres, the main difference being that the present bicycle is driven by pedals and chain gear, while the original machine was driven by swinging pedals coupled by connecting rods and cranks on the back wheel. Deceased was of a quiet, retiring disposition and a much respected member of the Christian Brethren. He is survived by three sons who were associated with him in the business. One of

these, Mr. Samuel McCall, has been closely identified with the Rev. Rioch Thom, in the working out of his various inventions, particularly the new "Marvo Electric Railway", in connection with which Mr. McCall's mechanical skill has been of great assistance.

With reference to the origin of the rear-driven bicycle, the following letter from the late Mr. Thomas McCall, published in February 1892, by the *Bicycling News*, will be of interest to many of our readers:

[The entire text of McCall's letter follows, which is included in Appendix G]

Sources - R

Two letters written by James Johnston to E.A.Forward, curator at the Science Museum (now I assume still in their possession; underlining as in originals)

6 Nov. 1911

E.A. Forward Esq.

Dear Sir,

Macmillan

I am obliged for your interesting letter duly to hand in my absence from home and I now hasten to reply.

I suppose you are quite satisfied in your own mind that the machine you refer to which originally came from Scotland is really of the Macmillan type, viz driven by cranks and levers from <u>rear</u> wheel, say 10 in larger than front wheel. If driven by <u>front</u> wheel it is a "Boneshaker" and if it has <u>no driving gear</u> at all then it is a <u>"Dandy Horse"</u> propelled by riders feet striking the ground. You do not give me the name of the gent who gave it to you or that of his father, what part or town of Scotland he came from.

How many copies of Macmillan's may be (in) existence? What a problem! I wish I could tell you. At this distant date I have not come across any except one I saw in the Glasgow Exhibition of 1887 or 1888 (speaking from memory) so that if your Museum contains a copy then you are the proud possessors of an interesting relic.

Just like the action of Macmillan's nephew, anybody who had such a machine broke them up long ago. Copies were made in Dumfriesshire, and also at Old Cumnock after Macmillan's visit there en route to Glasgow. No records or dates of the actual time they were made can I trace. The folks who had them are mostly all dead.

I was in hope at one time of fixing dates from the Books of an engineering shop at Old Cumnock where the copies were built later than 1842, but the Books were all consumed by fire in the shop sometime afterwards.

Thos McCall, Kilmarnock is gone over to the great majority too. He built the model in 1896 "from Drawings and Patterns in his possession", those were his own words to me. I will be in Kilmarnock in a week or two and see his surviving son and inquire if he has any record of the (times? - illegible) when his father made and sold the copies. From a card now affixed to the machine built at my suggestion, McCall mentions that he rode this type so many miles one day in 1858, so that would I think fix about the time that he was taking a strong interest in the matter.

Better wait however till I get to Kilmarnock before fixing any date and I will write you afterwards.

I need scarcely say I would very much like to see your collection of cycles.

Yours truly,

Ja. Johnston

30th Nov 1911

E.A.Forward Esq

Dear Sir

Macmillan

I duly sent you a card acknowledging your last letter.

The measurements you send of the Macmillan specimen in your Museum are very interesting indeed.

I have also in looking thro' Cycling papers come across the copy of "Cycling" you refer to noticing the exhibits

The Origins of the Bicycle

you had at the time (about 2 years ago). Of course they were wrong in assuming that the Machine you had was Macmillan's original one. That was in possession of his nephew in Thornhill many a day, but he broke it up stupidly a long time ago, more's the pity.

I see "Cycling" of 15th inst. (ie. 15 Nov 1911) had an article "The Crude beginnings of the Bicycle" in which they jump at one whoop from the <u>Dandy Horse</u> of 1819 to the <u>Boneshaker</u> of the <u>sixties</u>! A more "crude" attempt on the subject I never read and this notwithstanding the fact that a number of years ago I supplied them - free gratis - with a long article on Macmillan, also his portrait which they gladly published and thanked me. Such is gratitude and latter day journalism - poor Macmillan is ignored altogether!! A new Editor I suppose and new ideas, but thank goodness they cannot disturb Macmillan's claim or position - I have read "Cycling" for years but never again. I would not be bothered writing them on the subject which was thrashed out 19 years ago.

As I said before, Thos McCall died some years ago and with him perished the genuine information - when he actually built these models of Macmillan's machine. His widow is now 75 and has no papers on the subject - neither has his son who carries on his late father's business - everything destroyed years ago.

Well then, how are we to arrive at anything like the time when he built and sold these models. Taking the Boneshaker of the middle sixties (driven by front wheel) as a standpoint, McCall must have been on the job about 1856-7 to begin with at least, so that if you said the early <u>sixties</u> as the probable date of your machine, you would I <u>think be on safe ground</u>. McCall was born in 1833 - married when he was 24 1/2, his wife three years younger, and she can strongly remember

him coming on one of those machines to see her when she was on a visit to some friends a long distance. One day, and when they were busy courting - probably 1856-7.

This is the result of a conversation I had with Mrs. McCall on Friday last.

On reflection, I am now sorry when McCall was making the model or copy of Macmillan's machine (in 1896), lately in Glasgow Exhibition, that when I had several conversations with him that I did not put the question "<u>When</u> did you make these other models which you say you sold at 7 pounds?" My visits to him were between trams and rather hurried if my memory is good. I can remember him distinctly saying that one of these machines was sold to an English Doctor, and he afterwards received information that it in turn was being re-copied and suggesting that he should take action and stop this, to which McCall replied he could not do this as no patent had been taken out.

I was more concerned and interested in the driving gear, which I was anxious to show to the cycling world as successfully used and invented by Macmillan as bother about the particular dates when McCall was making capital out of it.

If there is any point I have missed or I should have referred to, kindly write me again.

Yrs very truly,

Ja Johnston

I write this from home - down the Borders at Galashiels and have hurried up to catch the post 10 pm.

Sources - S

The Gallovidian Annual, 1940

J. Gordon Irving: "He Builded Better Than he Knew: the story of Kirkpatrick Macmillan"

[J. Gordon Irving's account of Macmillan, published in his 1940 article "He builded better than he knew" is speculative and unreliable. But it does contain one valuable source of information, the transcription of an interview with John Macmillan, Kirkpatrick's only surviving son. For the sake of the completeness of the record, relevant sections of this interview are included below.]

I was fifteen years old when my father died in 1878....My father began life as a farm labourer at the farm of Morton Holm, across Scaur Water, then he became a coachman and later a blacksmith. He could

also make wooden pumps, play the harmonium, pull out teeth, and was well known at parties in the district for his grand whistling and fiddling....

My grandmother saw to the education of the oldest members of the family, and since my father was one of the youngest he got only the 'scrapings of the pot'. It was his boast that he received most of his education by attending a night school when he was thirty years of age. What money was made from the smithy went towards the schooling of my father's older brothers...

He made two ploughs different from the ordinary plough, and one of these must have been made some years before his death. At least I don't remember every seeing it, but I was told he showed it at the Dumfries Highland Show....

As a young man my father worked at a smithy near Moniaive. As well as being called 'Pate', he was often known as 'Peter' McMillan. At the Courthill smithy he ministered to both man and beast. There was no veterinery surgeon within miles of Courthill, so that the folk round about, if anything went wrong with their horses, cattle, dogs, or cats, sent immediately for my father. Several times I helped my father in bleeding horses when they were brought to the smithy....My father bled cows as well, and sometimes he attended to horses' teeth. He never went near a horse without speaking to it, more so the dangerous ones. On the kitchen shelf at Courthill stood a large bottle...When my father died it was within an inch of being filled with teeth that he had pulled....

It was really marvellous how quickly he fashioned any article he was making. When he was delivering one blow with the hammer he always seemed to know where he would strike with the next. He detested the tip-tapping of the hammer on the anvil instead of striking the article that was being made. I once saw him make eight pairs of horse-shoes in an hour, just about a

few months before he died. In everything he did he was very quick....

My father was a devout Christian, he was very bitter against drink and tobacco. Sometimes he offered the apprentices two shillings or a half-a-crown if they would stop smoking...."

Of the alleged 1842 ride into Glasgow, John McMillan had the following recollections:

It is said that the magistrate paid his fine of 5s, and that after the trial my father performed in the courtyard before the magistrates and officials, cutting the figure eight in style. My father hardly ever mentioned his cycle trip to Glasgow because, I think, he was ashamed of having fallen into the hands of the law.

Whenever my father appeared in Thornhill on his velocipede, all the boys in the neighbourhood use to run barefooted to the Boat Brae to see him ride down it. This steep incline is about 100 to 150 yards long...There was no brake of any description on my father's machine, so this must have been something of a feat...."

Notes

[1] See: www.bbc.co.uk/history/historic_figures/ macmillan_kirkpatrick.shtml

[2] These include: N.G. Clayton, "The First Bicycle?", *The Boneshaker* #113, Spring 1987; Nicholas Oddy, "Kirkpatrick Macmillan: the inventor of the pedal cycle or the invention of cycle history?", *Proceedings of the 1st International Conference of Cycling History*, Glasgow, 1990; Alastair Dodds, "What did Kirkpatrick Macmillan invent?", *The Boneshaker*, No. 127, Winter 1991 and Alastair Dodds, "Kirkpatrick Macmillan: inventor of the bicycle, fact or hearsay", *Proceedings of the 3rd International Conference of Cycling History*, Neckarsulm, Germany, 1992. Keizo Kobayashi, *Histoire du Vélocipède de Drais à Michaux, 1817-1870* (Bicycle Culture Center, Tokyo, 1993), Chapter 11, pp.333-340, also gives an excellent account of Macmillan and Dalzell.

[3] The spelling of Macmillan's name is usually given as "M'Millan" in the 19th century, and then later as either "McMillan" or "Macmillan". I have standardized here with "Macmillan" except in quoting other sources which spell it differently.

[4] *Scottish American Journal*, 11 Oct 1883.

[5] The word "velocipede" was used universally to describe all types of human-powered vehicles until about 1868, when the word "bicycle" began to be used, and entered into general usage by the early 1870s, though "velocipede" (literally "swift foot") is still frequently found later, particularly in referring to earlier vehicles.

[6] *Scottish American Journal*, 27 Sept. 1883.

[7] See Sources R.

[8] *The Scottish Cyclist*, 27 April 1892.

[9] *Bicycling News*, 23 April 1892.

[10] Earl of Albemarle and G. Lacy Hillier, *Cycling*, 1896 edition, p.59

[11] *The Scottish Cyclist*, 23 Jan. 1889.

[12] *The Scottish Cyclist*, 20 Feb. 1889.

[13] *The Scottish Cyclist*, 27 April 1892.

[14] The *Oxford Dictionary* offers the following definitions. Invent: "3. To find out in the way of original contrivance; to create, produce, or construct by original thought or ingenuity; to devise first, originate (a new method of action, kind of instrument, etc.). The chief current sense". Invention: "1. The action of coming upon or finding; the action of finding out; discovery (whether accidental, or the result of search and effort)". Inventor: "1. One who finds out, a discoverer (whether by chance, or by investigation and effort)".

[15] Optical character recognition, or O.C.R., allows source material which has been digitized to be computer searched for the mention of certain words or groups of words.

[16] See Andrew Ritchie, *King of the Road*

[17] *Bartleet's Bicycle Book* (1931) and C.F.Caunter *Bicycles and Tricycles* (Science Museum, 1972).

[18] *Newnes Practical Mechanics*, Feb. 1952.

[19] *The Scotsman*, 17 Nov. 1962.

[20] J. Gordon Irving, "He built better than he knew - The story of Kirkpatrick Macmillan", *Gallovidian Annual*, 1940; *Devil on Wheels, The story of the world's first pedal cyclist*, 1946.

[21] I am indebted to Alastair Dodds, "What did Kirkpatrick McMillan invent?", *The Boneshaker*, No. 127, Winter 1991, for much of the information in this section, Mr Dodds, of the Royal Museum of Scotland, Edinburgh, also supplied me with copies of documents obtained during his archival work.

[22] The sources for the Macmillan family documentation are Keir Parish Birth, Death and Marriage Registers. Residency, professions and ages are documented by Keir Parish Census Records for 1841, 1851, 1861 and 1871; by Barony Parish (Blythswood), Glasgow Census Records for 1841; and by Edinburgh Census Records for 1851, 1861 and 1871. Street directories for Glasgow and Edinburgh give names, addresses and occupations.

[23] For John McMillan interview, see J. Gordon Irving, "He built better than he knew", *Gallovidian Annual*, 1940.

[24] *Dumfries and Galloway Standard and Advertiser*, 24 Feb.1892

[25] J.Gordon Irving, op.cit.

[26] Alastair Dodds, "What did Kirkpatrick McMillan invent", *The Boneshaker*, No, 127, Winter 1991.

[27] Quoted in J.Gordon Irving, "He built better than he knew", *Gallovidian Annual*, 1940.

[28] *The Hub*, 4 March 1899.

[29] *The Scottish Cyclist*, 17 Feb. 1892.

[30] *Bicycling News*, 5 March 1892.

[31] Information about John Macmillan is from Harry Ashmall, *The High School of Glasgow* (publisher and date unknown).

[32] *Dumfries and Galloway Standard and Advertiser*, 24 Feb.1892

[33] *Dumfries and Galloway Standard and Advertiser*, 8 Oct. 1862

[34] Quoted in J.Gordon Irving, op.cit.

[35] See Chap. 2, "Amateur Mechanics", in Andrew Ritchie, *King of the Road* (London: Wildwood House, 1975), pp.29-51.

[36] The "pavement" here should be understood in the British sense, but what is known in America as the "sidewalk".

[37] The story appeared in a number of different newspapers, suggesting that it was considered an interesting, newsworthy tidbit. The newspapers and dates were as follows: *Glasgow Argus*, 9 June; *Glasgow Herald*, 11 June; *Glasgow Courier*, 11 June; *Dumfries and Galloway Courier*, 13 June (all 1842).

[38] *North British Daily Mail*, 27 August 1884.

[39] *Dumfries and Galloway Standard and Advertiser*, 24 Feb. 1892. She was being interviewed in 1892, I believe, because of the then current spate of articles about the invention of the bicycle being published in various Scottish newspapers.

[40] The Disruption of 1843 was a significant political division within the established Church of Scotland..

[41] *The Scottish Cyclist*, 17 Feb. 1892, see Sources I.

[42] *English Mechanic*, 14 May 1869, p.173.

[43] *English Mechanic*, 11 June 1869, p.271.

[44] *Kilmarnock Standard*, 10 April 1869.

[45] "The Origin of the Rear-driven Bicycle", *Bicycling News*, 6 Feb. 1892.

[46] "Velocipedes and Bicycle Riding", letter from Frederick Shearing, *English Mechanic*, 7 Oct. 1870.

[47] "Bicycle Construction, Fallacies, etc", letter to *English Mechanic* from 'Irish Mechanic', 6 Jan. 1871. The writer continues: "The machine I saw had a driving wheel (as near as I remember) of about 48", and a guiding wheel of 20 or 24". The defects of the machine I should say were these….The loss of power owing to the distance of the foot from the crank of the driving wheel, and the movement of the legs in working the treadles, which was a sort of horizontal drag, the weight of the rider not by any means coming into action as in the modern bicycle."

[48] *Cycling* (Newcastle), August 1879, see Sources C.

[49] *Bicycling News*, 24 Dec. 1880, see Sources C.

[50] Charles Wheaton was a bicycle maker in London from about 1875 to 1881. According to an advertisement in *The Bicycle Journal*, 24 Nov. 1876, "Mr. Wheaton has had eight years' experience as a rider, and tests every machine sold". He also sold other makes from his shop in Long Acre, Covent Garden, London. "Charles Wheaton was shot dead in a lodging house in Camden Town", *The Tricyclist*, 13 March 1885 (I am indebted to Nick Clayton for these references).

[51] See "First Bicycle and Velocipede", *Bicycling News*, 7 Jan. 1881. Dalzell is called "Mr. Edwin Dalzell" in Thomas Brown's account as printed here. The full text is published in Source C.

[52] Charles Spencer, *Bicycles and Tricycles* (1883), reprinted by John Weiss, Oakland, California.

[53] *Scottish American Journal*, 27 Sept. 1883.

[54] This sentence again suggests that the publication of this discussion conducted in the *Scottish American Journal* was preceded by discussion in the British press on the same subject which has yet to be discovered.

[55] *Scottish American Journal*, 11 Oct. 1883 (for full text see Sources D).

[56] *North British Daily Mail*, 21 Aug. 1884.

[57] *North British Daily Mail*, 27 Aug. 1884.

[58] *Scottish National Memorials*, ed. James Paton (Glasgow, 1890).

[59] *The Irish Cyclist and Athlete*, 28 Nov. 1888, see Sources F.

[60] *The Scottish Cyclist*, 20 Feb. 1889.

[61] "The Stanley Show", *Bicycling News*, 2 Feb. 1889.

[62] This photograph, which is now in the Bibliotheque nationale in Paris (Bibl. Nat. Est., If2fol., tome 3, p.2, #6), is the earliest surviving actual photographic evidence of any of the earliest bicycles. The machine may have been reported in a French paper

[63] Editorial, *The Scottish Cyclist*, 23 Jan. 1889.

[64] "The Original Bicycle. The Prototype of the Modern Rear-driving Safety", *The Scottish Cyclist*, 20 Feb. 1889.

[65] *Bicycling News*, 6 April 1889

[66] *The Scottish Cyclist*, 12 Dec. 1888.

[67] *The Scottish Cyclist*, 20 Feb. 1889.

[68] *The Scottish Cyclist*, 23 Jan. and 20 Feb. 1889.

[69] Confirmation of the occasional use of the name 'Peter' for Macmillan is given in Sources R, John Macmillan's memories of his father.

[70] "The Origin of the Rear-driven Bicycle - Gavin Dalzell's claim disputed", *Bicycling News*, 6 Feb. 1892. McCall's assertion that McMillan was also known as 'Peter' or 'Pate' is confirmed by son John McMillan in his much later interview with Gordon Irving (*Gallovidian Annual*, 1940).

[71] See Sources -P, "Death of Mr. Thomas McCall, 1834-1904 – A Bicycle Pioneer", *Kilmarnock Standard*, 9 April 1904.

[72] "The First Rear-driven Bicycle - Gavin Dalzell's claim further disputed", *Bicycling News*, 13 Feb. 1892.

[73] "Mr. James Johnston - Glasgow Cycling Club", *The Scottish Cyclist*, 27 April 1892; "James Johnston, Glasgow T.C.", *Bicycling News*, 28 May 1892.

[74] *The Scottish Cyclist*, 12 Dec. 1888.

[75] *The Scottish Cyclist*, 10 Feb. 1892.

[76] *The Scottish Cyclist*, 10 Feb, 1892.

[77] "More about the origin of the rear-driven bicycle", *Bicycling News*, 20 Feb. 1892.

[78] *The Scottish Cyclist,* 10 Feb. 1892.

[79] *The Scottish Cyclist*, 10 Feb. and 17 Feb. 1892.

[80] All quotes from Mrs. Marchbank and Mrs. Watret are from "The Inventor of the Bicycle - McMillan's claim fully established", *Dumfries and Galloway Standard and Advertiser*, 24 Feb. 1892.

[81] *Glasgow Evening Times*, 6 Feb. and 13 Feb. 1892.

[82] *The Hub*, 4 March 1899, See Sources N.

[83] "The First Bicycle", *Gallovidian*, Winter 1899 and *The Hub*, 4 March 1899.

[84] *The Scottish Cyclist*, 27 April 1892.

[85] J.Gordon Irving, "He builded better than he knew", *Gallovidian Annual*, 1940.

[86] *The Hub*, 4 March 1899.

[87] *Gallovidian Annual*, Winter 1899.

[88] *The Scottish Cyclist*, 17 Feb. 1892.

[89] "The Origin of the Cycle - A talk with an old Dumfriesian about this and other things", *Dumfries and Galloway Standard and Observer*, 2 June 1897.

[90] Bryce Craig, "John Gibson: an Early Nineteenth Century Innovator", *Transactions of Dumfries and Galloway Natural History Society*, Vol. XXIV, 1945/6.

[91] Henry Broughtam, "Address to the Members of the Manchester Mechanics' Institution, July 31 1835", quoted in David Vincent, *Bread, Knowledge and Freedom, A Study of*

The Origins of the Bicycle

Nineteenth-Century Working Class Autobiography (London: Methuen, 1982).

[92] See W.B.de Bear Nicol, "The Dumfries and Maxwelltown Mechanics' Institute, 1825-1900", *Transactions and Journal of the Dumfriesshire and Galloway Natural History and Antiquarian Society*, 1949-50; Shoji Katoh, *A History of Mechanics' Institutions in Great Britain up to the 1850s* (Japanese publisher, in Japanese, 1987).

[93] Timothy Claxton, *Hints to Mechanics on Self Education and Mutual Instruction* (London, 1839).

[94] *The Glasgow Mechanics' Magazine; and Annals of Philosophy*, Vol.1, 1824 (Glasgow).

[95] *Scottish Guardian*, 1 Nov. 1836.

[96] Quoted in "Literacy among the Working Classes in 19th century Scotland", *Scottish Historical Review*, Vol.33, 1954.

[97] *Glasgow Daily Herald*, 1 May 1869.

[98] op.cit., 5 May 1869.

[99] op.cit., 5 May 1869.

[100] op.cit., 12 and 16 July 1869.

[101] Acte de Naissance, Prefecture du Département de la Seine (author's files).

[102] Marriage and birth certificates supplied by Bibliothèques and Archives, City of Saint-Denis (author's files).

[103] *Sacramento Evening Bee*, 2 May 1900, from microfilm in U.C. Berkeley Library, Berkeley, California.

[104] See Frank Cameron, "The Pacific Coast Velocipede," *The Wheelmen*, Nov. 1987.

[105] Certificate of Death, City of Alameda, State of California (author's files).

[106] Lapierre was a witness at the marriage of Antoine Lefebvre and Constance Bainville; copy of marriage certificate supplied by Bibliothèques and Archives, City of Saint-Denis.

[107] The picture was published in the *Oakland Tribune*, 2 June 1933, the *Saint Louis Post-Dispatch* and the *San Francisco News* (no dates).

[108] Certificate of Death, rural district of Hayward, State of California (author's files).

[109] Andrew Ritchie, "Stashed Away in San Jose," *Bike World*, October 1975.

[110] Certificate of marriage of Antoine Lefebvre (see Note 106 above).

[111] Lapierre's sketch of the drive-mechanism shows that, in fact, he remembered the velocipede inaccurately, if we assume that the surviving machine is genuinely from Lefebvre's hand, and an original conception of his. Lefebvre's machine has curved, but fixed, cranks, whereas Lapierre's sketch shows a machine with swinging crank arms. Lefebvre's design is more intricate and complex than Lapierre's simplified memory of it. Graber is correct in identifying this drive-mechanism as perhaps the most sophisticated aspect of the machine in its understanding that an up and down motion of the cranks is superior to the backwards and forwards motion applied by McMillan et al. It is also a better designed machine than the McMillan-style machines because the steered front wheel does not come into disfunctional contact with the pedals.

[112] Letter from Sécretariat of Ville de Saint-Denis to Estelle Cardinet, 14 Oct. 1896 (xerox copy of photostat print at San Jose Museum)

[113] Letter from Mayor of Saint-Denis, including affadavit of Ernest Lapierre, to Estelle Cardinet (xerox copy of photostat print at San Jose Museum)

[114] *Sacramento Evening Bee*, 2 May 1900; the same issue also contains an article entitled "Birth and Development of the Street Fair Idea."

[115] See various articles by and about James Johnston, in *Bicycling News*, 13 Feb., 20 Feb., 5 March and 19 March 1892; *Scottish Cyclist*, 10 Feb., 17 Feb., 9 March, 23 March and 27 April 1892; *Glasgow Evening Times*, 4 Feb., 6 Feb., 13 Feb., 16 Feb., 17 Feb. and 20 Feb. 1892. See also James Johnston, "The First Bicycle," *Gallovidian*, Winter 1899; James Johnston, "The Invention of the Bicycle," *The Hub*, 4 March

[116] See Jean Althuser, *Pierre Michaux and His Sons – The Pioneers of the Bicycle* (translation by Derek Roberts, 1986).

[117] If the San Jose Museum were determined upon further evaluation of the machine, a collaboration between the Museum and French experts would be an extremely useful and logical place to start. All kinds of scientific and materials tests are available: it would seem to be relatively easy for technical experts to analyze the Lefebvre velocipede. Historical research can make use of both written accounts (involving primary documentation - newspapers, first-hand accounts,etc) and analysis of artifacts to construct an interpretation. The presence of both a substantially unaltered machine and a number of interesting documents in the case of the Lefebvre velocipede gives the opportunity for further research and the construction of an accurate historical picture. A convincing historical scenario should be easier to construct in the case of Lefebvre than in the case of Macmillan or Dalzell, where copies or restored and altered originals are involved.

[118] The most recent attempt to make historical sense of the Macmillan documentation is in David Herlihy's *Bicycle: The History* (Yale University Press, 2004), pp. 65-71. Herlihy does not succeed in creating a plausible scenario, and his interpretation of the source material is questionable. He announces his conclusions before he has examined any of the evidence: "these purported machines amount to historical footnotes at best…", "they exerted no influence on development…" Herlihy bends the evidence to make every Macmillan/McCall-style machine post-1869, and thinks that all the velocipedes made pre-1868 were of necessity three- or four-wheelers. The evidence simply does not support such a conclusion. Nevertheless, Herlihy still admits that, "given the sporadic ongoing velocipede experimentation in Scotland and elsewhere between 1820 and 1869, a mechanic here or there might well have experimented with mechanicized two-wheelers before the introduction of the French bicycle."

[119] The story appeared in a number of different newspapers, suggesting that it was considered an interesting, newsworthy tidbit. Newspapers and dates as follows: *Glasgow Argus*, 9 June; *Glasgow Herald*, 11 June; *Glasgow Courier*, 11 June; *Dumfries and Galloway Courier*, 13 June; all 1842. Reports are identical except for very minor wording differences: *Glasgow Argus*, for example, reported "Yesterday, a gentleman, belonging to Dumfries-shire, was placed……."

[120] *Bicycling News*, 7 Jan. 1881. Dalzell is called "Mr. Edwin Dalzell" in Thomas Brown's account as printed in *Bicycling News*.

[121] Almost the entire text of this letter written by Thomas Brown of Lesmahagow, quoted by C. Wheaton in this 1881 *Bicycling News* article, was included by Charles Spencer, an influential early cyclist, in his book. *Bicycles and Tricycles, Past and Present*, published in 1883. Spencer subtitled his book "A complete history of the machines from their infancy to the present time", and it is one of the most significant early histories of the bicycle. Commenting on the Thomas Brown letter, Spencer says: "With these full details, there seems no adequate reason for disputing Mr Brown's facts, and, these being admitted, it seems to be incontestable that Scotland may claim the barren honour of having been the birthplace of the bicycle properly so-called; and if I were called upon to sum up the case judicially, I should say that the two-wheel machine owed its origin to Germany; that the crank action was, first of all, of English – or Scotch – invention, afterwards brought into practical use by the French, and still later, improved and perfected by the English. As to the American claim, I will only say that, if it have any justification at all, the Americans have been very slow, for such a go-ahead people, in allowing the English so far to excel them in the manufacture both of bicycles and tricycles as is notoriously the case." Spencer's book thus helped in disseminating the case for Dalzell as the inventor of the bicycle.

[122] The specificity and precision of this request for information about an insignificant event which happened nearly 40 years before is extraordinary. Did the writer keep a diary which noted it? The tone of the letter suggested that this was perhaps not the first letter of this series, but a search of the *North British Daily Mail* back to the beginning of August 1884 failed to yield any previous discussion of velocipedes.

[123] Had the machine in question been an old-style hobby-horse, it would hardly have been likely to attract the attentions of such "a large crowd".

[124] Once again, the specificity of this writer's memory of the year 1846, and of Macmillan, is remarkable. He might well have disputed the exact year, but accepts with it without hesitation. Slamannan is a few miles south of Falkirk.

[125] With reference to this letter and the second letter from 27th August below, Macmillan's son, John, confirmed that he was often called 'Pate' or 'Peter' (see Sources Q).

[126] Mention here of Strathaven – see the 1871 *English Mechanic* letter discussed in Chapter 4b and Footnote 44.

[127] This letter pointing out that hobby horses were used in Dumfries thirty years before the 1846 event being discussed is hardly surprising. It illustrates the continuity between the old-style hobby horse and the newer style velocipede, with driving-gear. It is true that none of this group of letters from 1884 specifically mentions the use of driving-gear, but other evidence (as pointed out above) indicates that the 1846 machine under discussion was unlikely to have been simply a hobby-horse.

[128] The most important letter of this group strongly supports the suggestion that Macmillan developed his driven velocipede from the earlier hobby-horse. He "made his first wooden horse" and "by and by he made another on an improved scale." It also transmits two other components of the Macmillan story, that he had an accident in Glasgow, and that he raced against other road users – "none of the farmers could beat him."

[129] Once again, the description of Macmillan's machine as a hobby-horse – "It had no treadles, and was propelled forward by just touching the ground with the point of the boot" - does not preclude the more advanced machine, with "driving gear," since there is also strong evidence here of a progression of development in Macmillan's machines.

[130] This letter, looking more ambitiously for "the honour of inventing the velocipede", again casts doubt on whether Macmillan progressed beyond the hobby-horse, "the machine of K. M'Millan had no treadle, and was merely moved by the foot pressing against the ground."

[131] It is interesting that McCall calls him 'Peter' here. Macmillan's son, John, confirmed that he was often called 'Pate' or 'Peter'.

[132] This mention of William Nichol by James Geddes emphasizes that the testimony given can sometimes be extraordinarily accurate in its detail. Nichol is also mentioned later by another source, Andrew Todd, who wrote to *Bicycling News* (26 March 1892) that Nicol, his uncle, "made the woodwork for Macmillan's machine."

[133] Farmer Thomas Haining's memory of the Glasgow incident here should be noted. Macmillan and his "horse" were both "fined and confined in the Glasgow Prison prior to 1846", but only "for causing an obstruction on the streets". Where could Haining have taken this information from other than from popular memory of the event?

[134] A small detail, typical of the destiny of many people's papers! But John Brown's memory that he did not find "any papers in reference to his dandy horse amongst his effects" could also be seen as typical of a craft-made object, probably built without designs or plans.

[135] The specificity and precision of this request for information about an insignificant event which happened nearly 40 years before is extraordinary. Did the writer keep a diary which noted it? The tone of the letter suggested that this was perhaps not the first letter of this series, but a search of the *North British Daily Mail* back to the beginning of August 1884 failed to yield any previous discussion of velocipedes.

[136] An astute observation by the editor of *The Scottish Cyclist*; there is a lack of precision from witnesses about the exact date of the addition of the "driving gear" which is quite comprehensible, and yet the approximate suggested years are firmly fixed in the late 1830s and early 1840s.

[137] "Fashed their thoom", means "bothered their heads".

[138] The failure of J.R. Nisbet, the editor of *Scottish Cyclist*, to publish in full the documents that he had in his possession, and to ensure that they were conserved for posterity, was of course a drastic mistake. The idea that somehow or other "a certain modicum of honour to the memory of Gavin Dalzell" had to be preserved was merely a tactful way of saying that Nisbet did not want to be seen as exposing the invention fraud that Gavin Dalzell's son, J.B. Dalzell had been in the process of perpetrating.

[139] The criticism of Johnston's research, that he was primarily interested in proposing a Scottish "inventor" of the bicycle, should be tempered by the realization – well expressed here – that Johnston's work on Macmillan was in fact directed at enthroning one Scot – Macmillan – at the expense of another – Dalzell! It is not as though Johnston was proposing Macmillan in place of an English or French candidate!! As Editor Nisbet puts it: "To Mr Johnston chiefly belongs the great honour of having collected that evidence, and having demonstrated......Macmillan was before Dalzell".

[140] The logic of these assertions, that somehow Macmillan's design was "obtained" from "the first steamboat experimented with on Dalswinton Loch", or that Dalzell "obtained his idea from the spinning wheel", escapes me.

[141] Nisbet's final comments show him as determined to sit on the fence, and to pacify the feuding parties who had perhaps

been sitting in his office! Even though Macmillan was first, he suggests, Dalzell did not copy from him, but their "conceptions were quite independent of each other" – an assertion not borne out by the evidence of the machines still in existence. And anyway, they were both Scottish "worthy sons". Journalism, of course, is not the same as history!

[142] Johnston's position here appears to want the best of both worlds – Macmillan's is first, but in fact they are "independent conceptions", and Dalzell didn't copy Macmillan!! Why can't Johnston, and Nisbet with him, simply admit that the idea was shared around, but that Macmillan was there first.

[143] Johnston's memory was inaccurate on this point. Both 1869 *English Mechanic* mentions of the McCall machine print the word 'Kilmarnock' correctly, although both print the word 'velocipede' incorrectly as 'velocipe'.

[144] This refers to Johnston's extended 1892 correspondence with *Bicycling News*, *The Scottish Cyclist*, the *Glasgow Evening Times* and the *Dumfries and Galloway Standard*.

Bibliography

The bibliography is divided into four sections:

A. Items which contain primary source material relating to discussion about the origins of the bicycle.

B. Secondary material, mostly other writers comments on and discussion of the early history of the bicycle.

A. Primary source material

Early references:

Glasgow Argus, 9 June 1842, *Glasgow Herald*1, 11 June 1842, *Glasgow Courier*, 11 June 1842, *Dumfries and Galloway Courier*, 13 June 1842.

English Mechanic and Mirror of Science:
- 14 May 1869, "The Kilmarnock velocipede"
- 11 June 1869, "The improved Kilmarnock velocipede"

Chronological sequence of research and comment on the origins of the bicycle published in print, 1881-99:

Bicycling News, 7 Jan. 1881, quoting letter written by Thomas Brown on Dalzell

Charles Spencer, *Bicycles and Tricycles*, 1883

Scottish American Journal
- 27 Sept. 1883, "The Inventor of the Bicycle"
- 14 Oct. 1883, "Inventor of the Bicycle"
- I Nov. 1883, "The Bicycle Invention"
- 22 Nov. 1883, "Inventor of the Bicycle"

North British Daily Mail
- *21 Aug. 1884, "An early Scotch velocipedist"*
- *23 Aug. 1884, "An early Scotch velocipedist"*
- *27 Aug. 1884, "An early Scotch velocipedist"*

The Scottish Cyclist
- *12 Dec. 1888, mention in editorial*
- *23 Jan. 1889, Editorial, "En Passant"*
- *20 Feb. 1889, "The Original Bicycle"*
- *24 April 1889, "The Original Bicycle"*

Bicycling News
- 26 Jan. 1889, Editorial, "The first bicycle"
- 2 Feb. 1889, "The Stanley Show"
- 6 April 1889, George Moore illustration "The first rear-driving bicycle, invented by Gavin Dalzell"
- 6 Feb. 1892, "The origin of the rear-driven bicycle. Gavin Dalzell's claim disputed"
- 13 Feb. 1892, "The first rear-driven bicycle. Gavin Dalzell's claim further disputed"
- 20 Feb. 1892, "More about the origin of the rear-driven bicycle"
- 5 March 1892, "More about the origin of the rear-driven bicycle"
- 19 March 1892, "The first rear-driven bicycle" and "More about the origin of the rear-driven bicycle"
- 26 March 1892, "The first rear-driven bicycle"

This *Bicycling News* documentation overlaps, and intermeshes with:

Evening Times (Glasgow)
- 4 Feb. 1892, "Who invented the bicycle?"
- 6 Feb. 1892, "Who invented the bicycle?"
- 8 Feb. 1892, "Letter"
- 13 Feb. 1892, "The invention of the bicycle"
- 16 Feb. 1892, "Who invented the bicycle?"
- 17 Feb. 1892, "Who invented the bicycle?"
- 20 Feb. 1892, "Who invented the rear-driven bicycle?"
- 22 Feb. 1892, "The inventor of the bicycle"
- 23 Feb. 1892, "The inventor of the bicycle"
- 27 Feb. 1892, "Who invented the bicycle?"

The Scottish Cyclist
- 10 Feb. 1892, "The first rear-driven bicycle. A revival of the question of origin"
- 17 Feb. 1892, "The first gear-driven bicycle"
- 9 March 1892, "The first gear-driven bicycle. Macmillan versus Dalzell"
- 23 March 1892, Editorial, "Macmillan v. Dalzell"
- 27 April 1892, Editorial, "Macmillan v. Dalzell - a satis-factory conclusion" and "With lens and pen. Mr. James Johnston, Glasgow Tricycling Club"

Dumfries and Galloway Standard
- 24 Feb. 1892, "The Inventor of the Bicycle - McMillan's claim fully established"
- 15 June 1895, "More about the first bicycle and its inventor"
- 2 June 1897, "The origin of the cycle. A talk with an old Dumfriesian about this and other things"

Gallovidian (Dumfries)
- Winter 1899, James Johnston, "The First Bicycle"

C.T.C.Gazette
- Sept. 1899, "The early days of the C.T.C."

The Hub
- 4 March 1899, "The invention of the bicycle", letter to the Editor from James Johnston

The Origins of the Bicycle

B) Secondary sources and critical discussion

- Gordon Irving, *The Devil on Wheels - The story of the world's first pedal cyclist* (Dumfries, 1946)

- Gordon Irving, "He builded better than he knew", *Gallovidian Annual*, 1940

- Andrew Ritchie, "Alexandre Lefebvre's Velocipede", *The Boneshaker*, Spring 1987

- 'Petronella', "The Birth of the Bicycle", *CTC Gazette*, Nov. 1938

- N.G.Clayton, "The First Bicycle!", *The Boneshaker*, Spring 1987

- Alastair Dodds, "What did Kirkpatrick Macmillan invent?", *The Boneshaker*, Winter 1991

- Nicholas Oddy, "Kirkpatrick MacMillan, the inventor of the pedal cycle or the invention of cycle history?", *Proceedings of the First International Conference of Cycle History*, Glasgow, 1990

- David Herlihy, "The First Bicycle", *Bicycle Guide*, May 1992

Figs. 36 & 37 A newly discovered photograph at first thought to be of Macmillan was later found to be of a Mr. J.Hastings. [Source: *English Mechanic* 9 Oct. 1868 and National Museums of Scotland]

List of Illustrations

Fig 1 This velocipede now in the collection of the Science Museum in London, in fact made by Thomas McCall in the 1890s and arguably based on an original by Macmillan, is now frequently presented as a Macmillan bicycle. [Source: Science Museum, London]

Fig. 2 This portrait of Macmillan was first reproduced in 1899, captioned "the Inventor of the Bicycle". The whereabouts of the original of this photograph remains unknown. [Source CTC Gazette Sept. 1899]

Fig 3 J. B. Dalzell's recognition of Macmillan's "claim to priority" published in Bicycling News, 23 April 1892.

Fig. 4 The controversial nature of Macmillan's velocipede design remains central to a discussion of the early evolution of the bicycle. [Source: The Boneshaker 145, Winter 1997]

Fig. 5 The jaunty hobby-horse rider of about 1820 depicted in an 1869 publication was active and athletic. [Source: "Velox", Velocipedes, Bicycles and Tricycles, 1869]

Fig. 6 The authenticity of the Macmillan "invention" was firmly incorporated into the official history of the British bicycle industry. [Source: Gordon Irving, The Devil on Wheels, 1946]

Fig. 7 The restored Macmillan family tombestone in Keir churchyard.

Fig. 8 The smithy in Courthill, where it is alleged that Macmillan produced his velocipedes. [Source: CTC Gazette, Sept. 1899]

Fig. 9 Macmillan's sister, in centre, and two of his nieces, with Anne Marchbank on the left. [Source: CTC Gazette, Nov. 1938}

Fig. 10 Mary Marchbank, Macmillan's niece. [Source CTC Gazette, Nov. 1938]

Fig. 11 Published in at least three different newspapers, this Glasgow news item is one of the most important pieces of historical evidence in the Macmillan story. But was it about Macmillan? [Source: Glasgow Herald, 11 June 1842]

Fig. 12 McCall's "Kilmarnock Velocipe" was illustrated in 1869. [Source: The English Mechanic, 14 May 1869]

Fig. 13 A second letter described changes made in the design of the McCall machine. [Source: The English Mechanic, 11 June 1869]

Fig. 14 A copy of McCall's 1869 machine, made in 1896 by McCall himself at James Johnston's request for the Stanley Show, is now in the Dumfries Museum, here inspected by curator Truckell. [Source: Dumfries Museum]

Fig. 15 Dalzell's machine was illustrated in The Scottish Cyclist in 1889 [Source: The Scottish Cyclist, 20 Feb., 1889]

Fig. 16 A letter in the North British Daily Mail, 21 August 1884.

Fig. 17 "A Native of Keir" sent a letter replying to the earlier request for information about the Scottish velocipedist. [Source: North British Daily Mail, 27 August 1884]

Fig 18 Gavin Dalzell's bicycle, severly damaged was exhibited at the International Exhibition in Glasgow in 1888 [Source: James Paton, Scottish National Memorials, 1890]

Fig . 19 With the publication of George Moore's illustration in Bicycling News in 1889, Gavin Dalzell was briefly enthroned as "the inventor" of the bicycle. [Source: Bicycling News, 6 April 1889]

Fig .20 The publication of this illustrated article in Bicycling News in 1892, containing a crucial account from McCall, questioned Dalzell's role and elevated Macmillan's status as a bicycle pioneer. [Source Bicycling News, 6 Feb 1892]

Fig 21 Continuation of Bicycling News article from 6 Feb 1892

Fig. 22 A portrait of Glaswegian James Johnston, called "the discover of Macmillan", was published in 1899. [Source: the CTC Gazette, Sept.1899]

Fig. 23 The Dalzell velocipede now in the collection of the Glasgow Museum of Transport, was photographed at the time of its acquisition. With it is either Dalzell's son, who presented it, or a museum curator. [Source: Glasgow Museum of Transport]

Fig. 24 The Dalzell machine (probably copied from Macmillan), as it now exists. [Source: Glasgow Museum of Transport]

Fig. 25 A fanciful pre-bicycle, allegedly sketched in the 1830s was described as "rude and primitive in constuction" [Source: 'Velox', Velocipedes, Bicycles and Tricycles 1869]

Fig. 26 Two fanciful 'celeripedes' in action, illustrated in 1869, may have been actual one-off creations, variations on the theme of the hobby-horse.[Source: "J. F. B." The Velocipede, Its past, Its Present and Its Future, 1869]

Fig 27 Map of south-west Scotland, to show the geographical relationship between Thornhill, Glasgow and Dumfries

Fig. 28 The Lefebvre velocipede, now in the San Jose Museum, California. [Source: Andrew Ritchie]

Fig. 29 Estelle Cardinet photographed in 1933 with her father's velocipede. [Source: Oakland Tribune]

Fig. 30 Text of Houdebert's letter to Estelle Cardinet, 1896. [Source: San Jose Historical Museum]

Fig. 31 Text of Lapierre affadavit, 1896. [Source: San Jose Historical Museum]

Fig. 32 Sketch by Ernest Lapierre of a Lefebvre velocipede, 1896. [Source San Jose Historical Museum]

Fig. 33 News item concerning the Lefebvre velocipede. [Source: Sacramento Evening Bee, 2 May 1900]

Fig. 34 Bourne's patent of 1869 was perhaps the last attempt to manufacture a treadle-driven rear-driven bicycle.[Source: Andrew Ritchie]

Fig 35 Thomas McCall as a prosperous master-wheelwright in the mid-1890s. It shows him holding a hammer surrounded by his workmen. [Source: Royal Scotish Musems]

Figs. 36 & 37 A newly discovered photograph at first thought to be of Macmillan was later found to be of a Mr. J. Hastings. [Source: English Mechanic 9 Oct. 1868 and National Museums of Scotland]